Facing the Other
The Ethics of Emmanuel Levinas

CURZON JEWISH PHILOSOPHY SERIES
Series editor
Oliver Leaman
Reader in Philosophy, Liverpool John Moores University

It is the aim of this series to publish books and collections of essays in the general area of Jewish philosophy. A broad interpretation will be taken of what Jewish philosophy comprises, and the series will be interested in receiving proposals which involve a philosophical treatment of a Jewish thinker or topic, or which look at some aspect of Jewish cultural life from a philosophical perspective. The only other requirement is that authors will be expected to write clearly and concisely on the issues which they wish to discuss, so that any generally interested reader will be able to understand the book.

Jewish philosophy is currently going through a very exciting period of development, both in its treatment of major historical figures and in is exploration of some of the major issues of the modern world, and the Curzon Jewish Philosophy Series sets out to provide a natural home for many of the relevant texts.

Medieval Jewish Philosophy
An Introduction
Dan Cohn-Sherbok
University of Kent

Facing the Other
The Ethics of Emmanuel Levinas
Edited by Seán Hand
London Guildhall University

Facing the Other
The Ethics of Emmanuel Levinas

edited by
Seán Hand

CURZON

First published in 1996
by Curzon Press
St John's Studios, Church Road, Richmond
Surrey, TW9 2QA

© 1996 Seán Hand

Typeset by LaserScript, Mitcham, Surrey

Printed in Great Britain by
TJ Press (Padstow) Ltd, Padstow, Cornwall

British Library Cataloguing in Publication Data
A catalogue record for this book is available from the British Library

Library of Congress in Publication Data
A catalogue record for this book has been requested

ISBN 0–7007–0415–9 (hbk)

Contents

Preface

'Men have been able to be grateful for the very fact of finding themselves able to thank' (Levinas, 1981: 10). The nature and expression of ethics in Emmanuel Levinas are such that it is with a particularly satisfying logic that I am able to open this collection of essays with a record of my thanks. This book arose out of a one-day colloquium on Emmanuel Levinas held on 18 May 1995 at the Institute of Romance Studies, University of London. I am grateful to everyone who took part on that day, whether by giving a paper or by participating in discussion. My particular thanks go to Professor Annette Lavers for having sollicited and encouraged the colloquium, and to Simona Cain of the Institute for her help in organizing the day. The occasion was marked by the breadth of approach to Levinas's work, and it became quickly obvious that we could not do justice in such a short space of time to the resonances of his writings or the range of theoretical reactions which they have provoked. I was therefore delighted when Oliver Leaman expressed an interest in publishing a collection of essays on Levinas in the series of which he is General Editor, and I am grateful to him for the guidance and commitment which he has shown. Some of the essays here are based on papers given at the colloquium; others were specially commisioned with a view both to stimulating debate and to complementing the existing contributions. In particular, and in keeping with the series in which it is published, the collection seeks to explore and comment on some of the Jewish dimensions of Levinas's work. Recognizing that Levinas often privileges Judaic conceptions in a contrastive way, this has led many of the contributors to elaborate contextualized readings whose conjunctions generate new and

Facing the other

illuminating perspectives on Levinas's meaning. As in Levinas, where the face-to-face introduction of the Other represents the surpassing of self-maintenance and the welcoming enjoyment that constitute the nature of true Being, so the opening up of Levinas's statements by other ethical visions generates here a further level of gratitude for an inspiration that goes beyond a mere dialectic of negation. Such readings, of course, force us to work hard, and Levinas's phenomenology, as explicated for example in *Existence and Existents*, is fully aware of the fatigue (as well as solitude) associated with such a burden. My efforts to bring this collection to publication were assisted greatly by the encouragement of Connie Ostmann, the Head of the Department of Language Studies at London Guildhall University and by the intelligent and speedy work of the Department's Research Assistant, Rima Dapous. Lastly, I am thankful to Dominic Terence Hand, who has introduced me with a timely and intimate force to facing the Other through the reciprocity of paternity and who presently has the protoethical habit of reacting to any overconfident generalization with an enthusiastic 'Er, er, er'.

Seán Hand
London Guildhall University

viii

Notes on Contributors

Dr. Alison Ainley is a Lecturer in Philosophy at Anglia Polytechnic University. She has published essays on Levinas, Irigaray, Kristeva, Nietzsche and Heidegger in various collections and is currently writing a book about Irigaray and feminist philosophy.

Dr. David F. Ford is Regius Professor of Divinity at the University of Cambridge, and Chair of the Centre for Advanced Religious and Theological Studies. He is the author of *Barth and God's Story* (Frankfurt-am-Main, Berne, New York, 1985), with Daniel W. Hardy of *Jubilate: Theology in Praise*, (London, Darton, Longman and Todd, 1984, published in USA as *Praising and Knowing God*, Westminster, 1985), and with Frances M. Young of *Meaning and Truth in 2 Corinthians*, London, SPCK, 1987.) He is also editor of the two-volume *The Modern Theologians: an Introduction to Christian Theology in the Twentieth Century*, Oxford, Blackwell, 1989.

Dr. Steven Gans is a member of the Philadelphia Association, and works in private practice in London. He is the author of articles on Heidegger, Derrida, Lacan, Merleau-Ponty and Levinas, and is currently developing a phenomenological and ethical approach to psychoanalysis.

Dr. Seán Hand is Professor of French Cultural Studies and Director of the Centre for Research in Language and Culture at London Guildhall University. He is the editor of *The Levinas Reader* (Oxford, Blackwell, 1989) and the translator into English of Levinas's *Difficult Freedom*. He is the author of forthcoming books on Michel Leiris and Levinas.

Dr. Michael Holland is Fellow in French at St. Hugh's College Oxford. He is the editor of *The Blanchot Reader* (Oxford, Blackwell, 1995), an editor of the journal *Paragraph* and the author of forthcoming books on Blanchot and Ionesco.

Dr. Benjamin Hutchens is Visiting Fellow at the University of Warwick. He recently completed a D. Phil. thesis on *Levinas and the quest for a coherent post-humanist ethics.*

Dr. Philip Leonard is Lecturer in English at Nottingham Trent University. He is currently writing a book on post-structuralist theory and editing another on negative theology, mysticism and theory.

Mr. Harry Lesser is Senior Lecturer in Philosophy at the University of Manchester. He is the author, with Raymond Plant and Peter Taylor-Gooby, of *Political Philosophy and social welfare: essays on the normative basis of welfare provision* (London, Routledge and Kegan Paul, 1980) and editor, with David Braine, of *Ethics, tecnology and medicine* (Aldershot, Avebury, 1988) and, with Andros Loizou, of *Polis and politics: essays in Greek moral and political philosophy* (Aldershot, Avebury, 1990). He is currently writing an introductory book on Ancient Philosophy and editing another on ageing, autonomy and resources.

Dr. Graham Ward is Dean of Peterhouse, Cambridge. He is the author of *Barth, Derrida and the language of theology* (Cambridge, Cambridge University Press, 1995) and of the forthcoming *Theology and Contemporary Critical Theory* (Macmillan).

Introduction

Emmanuel Levinas is one of the key philosophers in the post-Heideggerian field and an increasingly central presence in contemporary debates about identity and responsibility. His work spans and encapsulates the major philosophical and ethical concerns of the twentieth century, combining the insights of a basic phenomenological training with the demands of a Jewish culture and its basis in the endless exegesis of Talmudic reading. His concerns and subjects are wide: they include the Other, the body, infinity, women, Jewish-Christian relations, Zionism and the impulses and limits of philosophical language itself. This collection explicates Levinas's major contribution to these debates, namely the idea of the primacy of ethics over ontology or epistemology. It investigates how, in the wake of a post-structuralist orthodoxy, scholars and practitioners in such fields as literary theory, cultural studies, feminism and psychoanalysis are turning to Levinas's work to articulate a rediscovered concern with the ethical dimension of their discipline. It recognizes that with such an involvement comes a necessary critical reaction. And it takes as an implicit and recurring concern the often overlooked Jewish dimension to Levinas's work.

Each of the essays in this collection is original, and offers a complete perspective on Levinas from a particular starting-point. Alison Ainley presents the mixed response from feminist thinkers and in particular Irigaray to Levinas's sensitivity to the language and metaphors of virility and sexual definition in philosophy. Such an awareness could be read as a valorization of the place or activity of the feminine (and it is fitting that the reputed primordiality of the feminine in Levinas should be reflected in the fact that this essay opens the collection). But Ainley shows how a thinker such as Irigaray, working from the meanings attached to 'home', 'dwelling' and intimacy in Heidegger and Levinas, registers an unease with the materiality of the female implicit in their characterizations, and with the very real prisons which their writings as forms of dwelling can continue to represent for sexual difference. David Ford tests Levinas's criticisms of theology's dramatic and anethical nature (criticisms which closely resemble his characterizations of Heideggerian idolatry) against the representation of worship, prayer and the Other developed in the writings of the theologican Eberhard Jüngel. Stephen Gans offers a new perspective on the well-known theory that Freud deliberately downplayed the Talmudic dimensions of his practice, by firstly comparing the general distance taken from appropriative thinking, and the specific methodologies employed in conse-quence, in Levinas and Freud, and then by proposing a Levinasian reading of the famous Dora case. Seán Hand's essay seeks to account for some of the tensions and contradictions in Levinas's reactions to aesthetics and the art-image by exploring the contextual meanings which can be attached to his judgements. Michael Holland offers a close reading of Blanchot's disagreement with and rewriting of the grounds of *Totality and Infinity*, highlighting in passing the political and discursive dimensions of this attempt to move via Levinas's presentation of the *there is* beyond the limits of both literature and philosophy. Benjamin Hutchens argues that Levinas's ethical egoity is more fundamentally Spinozist than Hegelian or Heideggerian, focussing on the themes and manifestations of infinition and expression, and especially the relation between the act of expressing and what is expressed, in *Totality and Infinity* and *Otherwise than Being* respectively. Philip Leonard, drawing on the postcolonial formulations of Spivak, probes the seemingly non-theoretical writings on Judaism in such collec-tions as *Difficult Freedom* in order to ascertain to what degree their empirical, codified and hierarchical underpinnings belie a cultural agenda which has its own ignored others. Harry Lesser's essay could be said both to concur and to dissent from that idea, since it relates the hermeneutic of the writings concerned openly with Judaism, and in particular the Talmudic readings, to the tradition of the wise man or *Hakham*, but clarifies how that tradition nurtures an interpretative practice that seeks to be consistent with tradition and with common sense. As a result, the ignored other would become in this scenario the principled exception which must take priority for reasons of absolute responsibility. Graham Ward's essay on messianic eschatology, rather felicitously if apocalyptically coming last in the collection, focusses on the borderline between the end of philosophy and the beginning of theology, concluding provocatively that in Levinas each area provides the conditions for the possibility and understanding of the other, and that both are governed by the structure and economy of the eschatological.

The essays implicitly follow the Levinasian belief that it is in dialogue rather than in solitude that existing is ethical. Thus a complex series of contrastive relations is drawn by the collection as a whole. Levinas is here explicitly situated within the schemes of existence and meaning developed by such thinkers as Spinoza, Hegel, Freud, Heidegger, Jüngel, Blanchot, Irigaray, Derrida and Spivak. And his writings are taken as an exemplary testing of the dialogues and silences between ethics, ontology, philosophy, feminism, theology, psychoanalysis, politics, cultural theory and aesthetics. But the essays also uncover the subtle dialectic taking place in Levinas's work between male and female or masculine and feminine categories, between the European and non-European, Greek and Jew, Jewish and Christian discourses. And in the course of their commentaries, the essays not only expose the extent and the extensions of Levinas's vocabulary but themselves also introduce challenging and limit-testing terms and references into philosophical language which have been inspired by Levinas's work: thus we read of both divinity and daytime TV, of midrash and moonshots, of colonialism and the conatus essendi. The provocation of this sort of language is twofold: it acts in the essays, as it does in Levinas, as an indicator of a vigilant occupation of the margins with regard to the assumptions and expressions of institutionalized philosophy; it reminds us of how the law of Levinas's writing may be that of the Book but the world of his ethics is that of our day-to-day lives.

Notwithstanding my earlier remarks about the first and last essays in the collection, the place of each essay has simply been determined alphabetically. There are two main reasons for this. The essays offer distinct and largely self-contained readings rather than contributions to a chronological and cumulative presentation of Levinas's work. And the collection does not wish to create illusory priorities between the different aspects of Levinas's work by presenting essays on, say, *Totality and Infinity* before others on *Difficult Freedom* or Levinas's Talmudic readings. We feel that this arrangement also has the benefit of encouraging a reading of the essays that takes them in different orders. Thus it is entirely possible to reconstruct a chronologically dictated approach to Levinas's work, by beginning with Ward's reading of *Time and the Other*, proceeding through Hand's review of the postwar essays on aesthetics to Holland's contextualization of *Totality and Infinity*, before reading Ainley and Hutchens who in different ways examine the move from *Totality and Infinity* to *Otherwise than Being*, continuing with Leonard's critique of *Difficult Freedom*, then pursuing Ford's analysis of *Otherwise than Being* and concluding with Lesser and Gans who draw on both the *Quatre lectures talmudiques* and the later *Du sacré au saint*. Equally, just as the essays suggest that a crucial way of reading (for) Levinas is a contrastive one, so a productive approach to these essays is to read them dialogically. From this approach a critical testing of certain thematic concerns emerges quite rapidly. To suggest a few possibilities which in each case throw up a critical *difference* and which build into a sinuous and rhizomatic reading process: Gans and Lesser are in different ways concerned with the theme of counselling; Lesser and

4

Leonard react differently to the question of cultural identity, and the competing claims of rationalism and tradition; Leonard and Holland develop different readings out of the idea of colonization; Leonard and Ainley exploit to different ends the major feminist reactions to Levinas; Ainley and Hand develop different arguments out of the agendas and inspirations behind Levinas's figurations; Hand and Holland offer different readings of Levinas's relation to aesthetics; Holland and Hutchens present different perspectives on the relationship in Levinas between God and expression; Hutchens and Ward offer different reactions to a philosophy of transcendence and the place of violence; Ward and Ford differ significantly in their reading of Levinas's relation to theology.

In each of the above cases, it is tempting to indicate a difference with the typographical V sign. In reading Levinas, though, we become aware of how such a sign might wrongly designate an absolute schism or a wilful instrumental opposition. In suggesting it here, we have instead in mind a more complex relation of connection and separation, akin to the simultaneous rupture and recourse assumed by the father and son at the end of *Totality and Infinity*. The V is perhaps better viewed, therefore, as a hinge that simultaneously divides and joins two planes or levels. Thus it is the co-dependent articulation of these levels which generates a significant operation and defines whether or not the result can be called an opening or a closing. The essays here on Levinas, both in their actual contrasts and in their potential dialogues, generate the same effect as the metaethical positions produced by Levinas: at stake is the closure or opening up of metaphysics by an ethics of reading.

As philosophical speculation succumbs in certain quarters to millenial melodrama and in others to a no less violent sense of autonomy, then, Levinas's dramatization of the conditions for and the excess of philosophy re-presents the future more challengingly. The readings gathered here register as professional and ethical practices, in the curiosity and generosity of their approaches, the obligation followed in Levinas to resist the moment of arrival and accomplishment and to work instead towards the announcement of what is always yet to come.

Chapter 1

The Feminine, Otherness, Dwelling
Feminist Perspectives on Levinas

Alison Ainley
Anglia Polytechnic University

The feminine is described as the of itself other, as the origin of the very concept of alterity.

The pathos of love consists in an insurmountable duality of beings. (Levinas)

In developing an ethical philosophy which attempts to approach relations with others in a very different way, Levinas also opens up the question of sexual difference. From his earliest works where he first formulates the connection between *le féminin*, ethics and otherness, through his discussion of eros, voluptuosity and fecundity in *Totality and Infinity*, to the section on maternity in *Otherwise Than Being*, Levinas explicitly raises the issue of embodiment and sexual difference in the context of philosophy. This approach to difference conjoins with Levinas' thinking about radical otherness and ethics in a way which seems to offer some scope and potential for feminist philosophy.[1] Levinas is an intriguing figure in this regard, partly because of his strikingly different approach to ethics and partly because it is unusual for a philosopher to give such a central place to sexuality and to write so specifically about otherness as feminine. But Levinas' equivocal stance on these questions perhaps gives rise to similarly equivocal responses to his work. Luce Irigaray, philosopher and psychoanalyst, has

7

written remarkable essays on Levinas' work from a feminist perspective,[2] and it is her reading of Levinas I will consider shortly.

Although the connection between ethics and otherness as feminine in Levinas' writing was first noted by Simone de Beauvoir in *The Second Sex* as early as 1949[3] as part of her examination of Woman as Other, her footnote on Levinas is quite dismissive. Given that her project in that book is to explore the damaging conflation of femininity as a quality or property with the female sex, where women are cast as Other in ways which appear to compromise their freedom, it is perhaps not surprising that she is wary of Levinas' account of *le féminin*. For de Beauvoir, Levinas is presenting yet another image of the eternal feminine as man's other, thereby placing women back into the problematic or inappropriate role of the essentially other once again.

But both de Beauvoir and Levinas do recognize that the issue of sexual difference raises questions for traditional philosophical approaches to ethics. Bringing attention to this issue through the history and vocabulary of philosophy ensures that this problem can be re-addressed in a philosophical context. This approach makes it possible to put together the questions raised by phenomenology and existentialism regarding embodiment and lived experience on the one hand, and feminist questions about power and relations between the sexes on the other. After de Beauvoir, feminists have continued to reflect on the philosophical resources available for approaches to questions of sexual difference. Some have extended or expanded de Beauvoir's thoughts about Woman as Other, but have also raised doubts about the particular goals of equality and freedom that de Beauvoir seems to espouse. De Beauvoir's existentialist approach aims to establish reciprocity as a relation of equality which would level out differences and makes women equal to men. But the projects for both sexes are assumed to be the same, to unite them under a universal principle of similarity and make them part of a moral community whose existence is assumed before ethics. The particularity of difference, the very reason ethics calls for respect for others, seems to be effaced by making such differences merely contingent features.

It is these assumptions which Levinas challenges by making ethics 'prior' to ontology and suggesting the face-to-face relation comes 'before' philosophy, in immediacy. The suggestion that it might be possible to think 'otherwise' to the mainstream Western tradition attracts the attention of feminists seeking to raise critical questions about the construction and maintenance of that philosophical tradition.

I will begin, however, with the question of dwelling in Levinas' work, since it introduces the general problem of 'being at home' and what this might mean. The explicitly Heideggerian theme of 'homelessness' as the deracinated condition of modernity seeks to capture a sense of crisis in contemporary relations, and, perhaps, to provoke a search for more appropriate forms of living. The question of dwelling also opens up the contrast of the privatized realm of the home with the public sphere, a prevalent theme in feminist ethics when the public/private split maps on to sexual divisions (although I do not deal with this area of feminist theory here). Dwelling also raises questions about what it might mean for women to feel 'at home' in philosophy, particularly when the discipline has tended to prioritize particular clusters of questions and practices associated with masculinity.

What Levinas has to say about dwelling in *Totality and Infinity* clearly refers back to Heidegger. The possibility of 'dwelling poetically', of building locations in language, in the material world and in philosophical ontology, is, for Heidegger, a re-thinking of an elemental, material basis of existence. It implies a reconsideration of the philosophical history which has housed our metaphysical questioning since the beginnings of Greek philosophy, and an attempt to re-address the destructive technological potential now threatening to annihilate our world utterly. To dwell for Heidegger, then, is obviously much more than the domesticity of home living. In the course of the essay 'Building, Dwelling, Thinking', he points out that the old meaning of building as dwelling – literally staying in the same place – also had connotations of being at peace, to free or to spare as an activity of 'letting be' (1977: 327). This also signified preserving, cherishing, care and cultivation. But building can also be read as the creating of edifices, construction and making, suggesting a merely instrumental relation to a location. Cultivation, care in order to allow growth, has been replaced by domination and control. Heidegger's essay then calls for the recognition of the older version of dwelling which would, in 'sparing the earth, set it free into its own essence' (1977: 318) and allow us to see 'the real plight of dwelling' (1997: 339). This recognition can also be connected to the development of more ethical intersubjective relations, and the possibility of allowing the flourishing of different forms of life. The phenomenological and hermeneutic dimensions to Heidegger's suggestions about dwelling (he points out that it is really by virtue of human horizons that location or space are to be grasped at all [1977: 334]) would suggest that the understanding of space is open for revision and re-interpretation. But whether Heidegger's 'dwelling' is in fact another form of colonization, closure, and repression, subsuming relations with others under more anonymous headings, is the question which preoccupies both Levinas and Irigaray.

Despite the obvious and acknowledged influence of Heidegger upon his work, (Levinas writes: 'It is impossible to be stinting in our admiration for the intellectual vigour of *Sein und Zeit*, particularly in the light of the immense output this extraordinary book of 1927 inspired. Its supreme steadfastness will mark it forever.' [1989b: 487]), Levinas attempts to separate his own phenomenological reading of dwelling from Heidegger's, in three main ways. Levinas sees Heidegger's attempt to return to the elemental through a re-thinking of 'dwelling' as a will to return to 'a peasant rootedness', 'a pagan existence' entailing 'a rule of power more inhuman than technology' (1987: 52). The question of being, understood from this perspective, is not merely about the 'letting be' of Being, but the brutal imposition of an impersonal ontology, which Levinas links with Heidegger's Nazi connections. Levinas also suggests that in making death or mortality the horizon of Being, Heidegger foregrounds negation at the expense of the dimension of lived existence, and prioritizes the individual's relation with his own death at the expense of relations with others (Levinas prioritizes 'enjoyment', and being with others). Finally, because Levinas employs a sensualized, erotic phenomenology, he is able to accuse Heidegger of making Being neutral, asexual or de-sexualised.[4] As Irigaray will suggest, not all of the criticisms Levinas makes are exactly fair, although she does make use of the last criticism for her own feminist reading of Heidegger. She writes:

> Being (*être*) is used to refer to a disposition which leads me to approach any being (*étant*) in a certain way. In this sense, the philosophy of Heidegger cannot be seen simply as an 'ethics of the "fruits of the earth"' (*nourritures terrestres*), nor of the enjoyment (*jouissance*) of objects, such as the other in sexual love. (cf. *Totalité et infini*: 45–6, *Totality and Infinity*: 62–4). The philosophy of Heidegger is more ethical than the expression conveys, than his philosophy itself says explicitly. To consider the other within the horizon of being should mean to respect the other. It is true that the definition of Being in terms of mortal destiny rather than in terms of living existence raises questions about the nature of respect. And in addition, this philosophy is more or less silent on man's sexual dimension (*la dimension de l'homme comme sexué*), an irreducible human dimension (1991: 114).

In *Totality and Infinity* Levinas explicitly links the notion of 'the welcome of the home', and dwelling with *le féminin*, as one means of elucidating the 'immanent transcendence' of his thought, and as an attempt to redress the neutrality of Heideggerian dwelling (1969: 154). For Levinas, otherness and ethical care are already present in the structures of 'interiority' and 'habitation', and already imply a feminine dimension, a dimension which disrupts 'the virility of the force of Being'. The 'intimate familiarity' (1969: 154) of the feminine is a realm where dwelling is in enjoyment, the proximate contact with an other neither based upon disembodied consciousness nor on physical mastery. The feminine, as the

11

instantiation of interiority and habitation, is 'a dimension' through which it will be possible to 'await the revelation of transcendence' (1969: 150). As a *dimension*, rather than an essential definition of a sex, the feminine presents another way of approaching questions of subjectivity and ethics.[5]

This equivocal realm is later characterized in terms of a relation of love (*éros*), an ambiguous and erotic encounter which establishes both vulnerability and the responsibility owed to an other. The caress, the mode of touch which brings two into close contact, does not suggest a prior structure into which the particular instance will fit, but a 'fundamental disorder', an immediacy of discovery which engages with the material and carnal existence of an other without exhausting its meaning.

> The caress consists in seizing upon nothing, in soliciting what ceaselessly escapes its form toward a future never future enough, in soliciting what slips away as though it were not yet . . . It is not an intentionality of disclosure but of search . . . what the caress seeks is not situated in a perspective and in the light of the graspable. (1969: 257)

For Irigaray, this mode of relation accords with her own attempts to think the ethical implications of sexually different beings in close proximity, where difference is preserved even as an exchange takes place, and where the flourishing of new potential is born out of the creativity of discovery. It is Levinas' description of a relation where possession is suspended and the fixity of subject/object transformed that intrigues Irigaray, and influences her reading of ethics in a phenomenological mode. The possibility of 'rebirth', mutual enrichment, and a freeing of the dangerous constrictions of stereotypical sexual roles suggests, for Irigaray, ethical potential for relations with others which opens up the radical difference of alterity. It is 'the fecundity of a love whose most elementary gesture, or deed, remains the caress' (1993: 186). In seeking 'an ethics of the passions' (1981: 12) Irigaray seems to share Levinas' view that ethics might arise in the material and carnal encounter, in the 'ambiguity of love' (1969: 254).

Levinas suggests that the equation of otherness and the feminine can be taken up as an existing equation – but the context in which he places this equation also has potentially subversive implications, not only for philosophical themes but also for method. Rather than domesticating the feminine, the preservation of difference as absolutely other is a prelude to ethical relations which do not seek to reduce, capture or flatten out the specificity of the other. One of the reasons Levinas characterizes otherness in this way, as we have seen, is to reproach Heidegger for what seems to have been forgotten; the question of sexuality in relation to ontology. This question might be re-phrased as it was put to Derrida in an interview (1982: 66): 'Is sexuality merely a regional question within ontology, or would sexuality challenge the very possibility of a general ontology?' Because Levinas identifies ontology with totality, or Being as such, sexuality (or sexual difference) is one way to disrupt the totalizing closure of metaphysics and open it up for ethics, or to ensure that the other retains the otherness of difference. As Derrida comments in an essay on Levinas, '*Totality and Infinity* pushes the respect for disymmetry so far that it seems impossible, essentially impossible that it could have been written by a woman . . . Is not this principled impossibility . . . unique in the history of metaphysics?' (1981: 320, fn. 92). This mode of writing is a way of approaching philosophical questions which refuses to assume neutrality or objectivity and seems prepared to recognize the embodied nature of thought, to try to think 'otherwise' to existing patterns of thought.

However, Levinas' evocation of *le féminin* has to face the charge that it is merely instrumental, in so far as it is used as a reminder of the materiality of lived existence, but ultimately seems to be in service to a larger conception of ethical goodness: the path of metaphysical transcendence. Despite Levinas' insistence that this path is opened through experience and through ethical relations with others, the feminine seems to 'furnish' the face-to-face relation. Irigaray takes issue with Levinas on this point in her essay 'Questions to Emmanuel

Levinas', a clarification and counterpoint to the earlier essay 'The Fecundity of the Caress'. She had already warned of the danger that:

> The beloved woman would be mute or reduced to speaking in the spaces between the male lover's discourse. She would be relegated to his shadow as double . . . She is brought into a world that is not her own so that the male lover may enjoy himself and gain strength for his voyage toward an autistic transcendence. (1993: 208)

In 'Questions to Emmanuel Levinas' she reiterates this charge, suggesting that although Levinas 'opens the feminine in philosophy' yet he still seems to 'write out' the feminine, so that there is no place for women in what Levinas proposes – as she puts it: 'the caress, that "fundamental disorder", does not touch the other' (1991: 110). She adds:

> To caress, for Levinas, consists, therefore, not in approaching the other in its most vital dimension, the touch, but in the reduction of that vital dimension of the other's body to the elaboration of a future for himself . . . This description of the caress is a good example of the way in which the temporality of the male subject . . . makes use of the support of the feminine in the intentionality of pleasure for its own becoming. (1991: 110)

She goes on to argue that we have not yet reached an age in which onto-theological issues can simply be reintroduced with impunity – therefore she suggests that although Heidegger may have 'shelved' the question of the relation between philosophy and theology, Levinas mixes them together (or rather, 'intentionally fails to distinguish the foundations') (1991: 114). The divine, which is the incomplete, unfinished promise to come, glimpsed through the other, is really a promise held out for the male lover, the male philosopher, and represents another closure of the potentials initially opened up by Levinas. For her, the commitment to ethics as relations with others demands 'ethical fidelity to incarnation. To destroy it is to risk

14

the suppression of alterity, both God's and the other's. Thereby dissolving any possibility of access to transcendence' (1993: 217).

Why does she raise these objections, when Levinas had seemed to be an ally in her critique of Heidegger, and of the neutrality of philosophy? In Irigaray's work, the ground upon which dangerous and destructive repetitions are built is continually identified with the materiality of the female body, the symbolic instantiation of *le féminin* and the maternal. *Matière première* or prime matter ('mother-matter') (1985: 77), is figured as Mother Earth or Mother Nature, the realm of the sensible or the flesh, by analogy, symbol or association. This ground has been objectified, devalued, suppressed or excluded, she suggests. To revalue what has been excluded is, she writes, 'the burning issue of our age . . . a revolution in thought and ethics is needed if the work of sexual difference is to take place' (1993: 6).

Her specific slant is to look at the crisis of the modern age as primarily a crisis of sexual relations, an inability to negotiate and comprehend sexuality in a way other than by the terms of 'masculine logic'. By 'jamming the theoretical machinery' it might be possible to allow 'a disruptive excess on the feminine side' (1985: 78), the emergence of an articulation of the female sex or *le féminin* in its/her own right, and thus 'true' sexual difference. If this successful negotiation could be realised, it might lead to more 'fertile' relations between the sexes, mutual enrichment and an opportunity for the sexes to be more 'at home' with themselves and with each other.

Thus according to Irigaray, although Levinas initiates a consideration of the feminine in the context of philosophy, in evoking the Good beyond Being he effaces sexual difference in favour of transcendence. The relation of eros, the suffering of maternity, ultimately serve to teach the (male) philosopher/lover the way towards a mode of being in righteous responsibility, in thrall to an other (whether divine or corporeal), but the feminine is left in 'the abyss', abandoned to profanity so 'he may rebound into the transcendent' (1993: 183). As she writes: 'If some God obliterates respect for the other as other, this God stands as the guarantor of a deadly infinity' (1993: 205). The woman is left with no relation to herself, or any possible relation to the divine.

If the feminine remains the silent and equivocal other, connoting profanity, infancy, animality and yet the mystery of absolute otherness, it is unclear how women philosophers and readers of Levinas are to situate *themselves* in relation to this feminine. Do women take up an opposing stance to the feminine, making themselves other to otherness, or identify with the feminine other? In either case, it is unclear that the presence of the feminine and the relation of women to ethics and otherness has been 'thought through as such' (1993: 209). It is Irigaray's aim to keep this possibility alive.

Ultimately, she suggests Levinas is as guilty as any other metaphysician of covering over, obscuring or denying *le féminin*. 'For him, the feminine does not stand for an other to be respected in her human freedom and human identity. The feminine other is left without her own specific face. On this point, his philosophy falls radically short of ethics' (1991: 113).

Similarly, the ethical implications in Heidegger's work of 'respect for the other' are not borne out, she suggests, because the elemental is once again symbolically feminine/maternal, a 'forgotten, unthought and hated' ground (1983: 35). Once again, the furnishing role of growth and life, equated with the feminine, is omitted and suppressed by the theoretical house of language built upon it for the masculine. Even though nature and the earth are the basis of dwelling, the 'debt owed to the feminine' is never acknowledged, and so for Irigaray Heidegger perpetuates the immobilizing, exploitative tendencies of metaphysics.

And yet, in many ways Irigaray is quite 'at home' with both Heidegger and Levinas. The phenomenological and hermeneutic roots common to all three mean that she shares some of their perspectives on philosophical content and method. All three suggest that philosophy is characterized by compulsive and repetitive patterns of thought which have failed to provide an adequate statement of the problem(s), let alone an adequate solution. Identifying philosophy as 'the master discourse, . . .

the one which lays down the law to the others, including even the discourse held on the subject of these others; the discourse on discourses . . .' (1985: 149) is the first stage in Irigaray's analysis, which suggests at once the centrality and yet distorting effects of philosophical thought.

Like Heidegger and Levinas too, for Irigaray the issue of language in philosophy and of philosophy leads to the deployment of an oblique and sinuous style of writing.

> [P]hilosophical mastery . . . cannot simply be approached head on, nor simply within the realm of the philosophical itself. Thus it was necessary to deploy other languages – without forgetting their own debt to philosophical language . . . so that something of the feminine at the limit of the philosophical could be heard. (1985: 150)

Through the revealing/concealing 'truth' of these 'other languages'; primordial, sensual experience incarnate, the caress, and poetic thought, the spaces of airy song, of body and earth, and of some possibility of the divine, might be opened up in new ways. Thus her criticisms do not lead to the abandonment of the philosophical project altogether, but constitute attempts to enrich its vocabulary and self understanding.

But Irigaray considers these questions, has to consider the questions of sexual difference and the feminine, from the point of view of one who is not 'at home' in philosophy. If the feminine is providing a dwelling for man, woman lacks a home for herself and is in effect 'homeless'. She lacks not only the interiority of self-possession, but also the means to 'come and go', and the language of a being of her own. Irigaray's project is to build a position from which women might speak in their own right. 'The house of language which for men goes so far as to supply his dwelling in a body . . . woman is used to construct it, but, then, it is not available to her' (1993: 15).

Homelessness is only one aspect of the problem: another is imprisonment. Irigaray suggests the feminine can become locked into the forms of representation used by the philosopher and restrictively defined as such. In exchange for what the philosopher has 'borrowed' from the feminine in order to construct his spatiality;

> . . . he buys her a house, even shuts her up in it, places limits on her that are the opposite of the unlimited site in which he unwittingly contains her. He contains or envelops her with walls . . . visibly limiting and sheltering, but at the risk of being prison-like or murderous. (1993: 11)

Either way, the result is a denial of a 'proper place' for women/ the feminine, whether by immobilization or exclusion.

Irigaray characterizes philosophical method as follows: 'a project, conscious or not, of turning away, of deviation and of reduction in the artifice of sameness, of otherness. In other words, speaking at the greatest level of generality so far as philosophical methods are concerned; of the feminine' (1985: 150). Thus, in order to address this philosophical problem philosophically, it is necessary for her to find an oblique approach. The 'path of mimicry' is, she suggests, one way to 'get back into the philosopher's house'; to play the role of the philosopher's wife, and so take on accepted symbolic 'roles' within philosophy, whether this is 'like Plato's *chora*' (the black hole of chaos that is also the fertile replenishing womb) or 'the mirror of the subject' (the reflection of the narcissistic self), the other or nature and earth, or even 'the feminine' as philosophical trope. But as she suggests, if women are to find their own way of dwelling in language they cannot simply continue to occupy the role of complementary term, secondary other. There is little solace is being the philosopher's wife as such, merely a handmaiden to the more serious business of the day, unless such a role can be subverted and transformed. Without the recognition of the mimicry inherent in this role, the 'elsewhere kept in reserve' (1985: 76) the subversive masquerade is once again recuperated. Irigaray's thought remains nomadic, keeping a vigilant critical distance, while her detailed and attentive readings of philosophical texts continue to regenerate philosophical resources for the future.

NOTES

1 See bibliography for details of the texts where Levinas discusses the feminine and sexual difference; principally Section IV of 'Time and the Other', Section II. D 'Interiority and Economy' and Section IV Beyond the Face in *Totality and Infinity, Otherwise Than Being*, the essay 'Judaism and the Feminine Element' and the Talmudic reading 'And God created Woman'. Discussions of Levinas from a feminist perspective include Chanter (1995), essays in R.Bernasconi and D.Wood(eds) (1988) and Grosz (1989). Derrida (1991) also writes about sexual difference in Levinas' work.
2 Irigaray's essays on Levinas are 'Fecundity of the Caress' (1993), 'Questions to Emmanuel Levinas' (1991).
3 De Beauvoir writes that 'it is striking that he (Levinas) takes a man's point of view, disregarding the reciprocity of subject and object. When he writes that woman is mystery, he implies that she is mystery for man.' (1984: 16).
4 Levinas also pre-empts Irigaray's criticisms of Heidegger when he writes: 'Being directs its building and cultivating, in the midst of a familiar landscape, on a maternal earth. Anonymous, neuter, it directs it, ethically indifferent, as heroic freedom, foreign to all guilt with regard to the other.' (1987: 53).
5 Levinas also suggests this when he writes in 'Judaism and the Feminine Element': 'So that the inevitable uprooting of thought, which dominates the world, be reconciled with peace and quiet by returning home, into the geometry of infinite and cold space must enter the strange failure of sweetness. Its name is woman . . . this appearance of place in space, does not result, as in Heidegger, from a builder's labour, from an architecture which shapes the countryside, but from the interiority of the Home – the reverse of which would be 'any place' without the essential moderation of feminine existence living there, which is the feminine itself' (1993: 33).

BIBLIOGRAPHY

Beauvoir, Simone de (1984) *The Second Sex*, Harmondsworth: Penguin; trans. of *Le deuxième sexe*, Paris: Gallimard, 1949.
Bernasconi, Robert and Wood, David (eds) (1988) *The Provocation of Levinas: Re-thinking the Other*, London: Routledge.
Chanter, Tina (1995) *Ethics of Eros: Irigaray's Re-writing of the Philosophers*, London: Routledge.
Derrida, Jacques (1981) 'Violence and Metaphysics; an essay on the

thought of Emmanuel Levinas', in *Writing and Difference*, London: Routledge and Kegan Paul: 77–153.

—— (1982) 'Choreographies', interview with Christie V. McDonald, *Diacritics* 12: 66–76. Also published in C. McDonald (ed.) (1988) *The Ear of the Other: Otobiography, Transference, Translation*, Lincoln: University of Nebraska Press.

—— (1991) 'At this very moment in this work here I am', in R. Bernasconi and S. Critchley (eds) *Re–Reading Levinas*, Bloomington: Indiana University Press: 11–46.

Grosz, Elizabeth (1989) *Sexual Subversions: Three French Feminists*, Sydney and London: Allen Unwin.

Heidegger, Martin (1977) *Basic Writings*, ed. D. Farrell Krell, San Fransisco: Harper Collins.

Irigaray, Luce (1983) *L'oubli de l'air chez Martin Heidegger*, Paris: Minuit.

—— (1985) *This Sex Which is Not One*, New York: Cornell University Press.

—— (1991) 'Questions to Emmanuel Levinas: On the Divinity of Love', in R. Bernasconi and S. Critchley (eds) *Re–Reading Levinas*, Bloomington, Ill.: Indiana University Press: 109–118.

—— (1993) 'The Fecundity of the Caress: A Reading of Levinas, *Totality and Infinity*, "Phenomenology of Eros"', in *The Ethics of Sexual Difference*, London: Athlone: 185–217.

Levinas Emmanuel (1969) *Totality and Infinity: An Essay on Exteriority*, Pittsburgh: Duquesne University Press.

—— (1981) *Otherwise Than Being or Beyond Essence*, The Hague: Martinus Nijhoff.

—— (1987) *Collected Philosophical Papers*, Dordrecht: Martinus Nijhoff.

—— (1989a) 'Time and the Other' (extract), in S. Hand (ed.) *The Levinas Reader*, Oxford: Blackwell: 37–58.

—— (1989b) 'As If Consenting to Horror', *Critical Inquiry* 15 (2): 485–8.

—— (1990) 'And God Created Woman', in *Nine Talmudic Readings*, Bloomington, Ill.: Indiana University Press: 161–177.

—— (1993) 'Judaism and the Feminine Element', in *Difficult Liberty: Essays on Judaism*, London: Athlone: 30–38.

Whitford, Margaret (1991) *Luce Irigaray; Philosophy in the Feminine*, London: Routledge.

Chapter 2

On Substitution

David F. Ford
University of Cambridge

> But communication would be impossible if it should have to begin in the ego, a free subject, to whom every other would be only a limitation that invites war, domination, precaution and information. To communicate is indeed to open oneself, but the openness is not complete if it is on the watch for recognition. It is complete not in opening to the spectacle of or the recognition of the other, but in becoming a responsibility for him. The overemphasis of openness is responsibility for the other to the point of substitution, where the for-the-other proper to disclosure, to monstration to the other, turns into the for-the-other proper to responsibility. This is the thesis of the present work. (Levinas 1981: 119)

> No one can substitute himself for me, who substitutes myself for all. (Ibid.: 126)

Substitution is perhaps the most important focal term in Levinas's last major work, *Otherwise Than Being or Beyond Essence* (1981). It can be seen, with closely related ideas such as being a hostage, expiation for the other, responsibility for the freedom of the other, responsibility for the persecutor, and the gratuity of sacrifice, as his culminating expression of radical responsibility. It is extremely provocative in many respects. I want to explore one area of fruitful provocation, taking the chapter entitled Substitution (Chapter IV) as my text from Levinas and bringing it into dialogue with a few other texts.

Levinas's terminology is frequently innovative in relation to philosophical discourse. One recurring feature is the use of words which have strong religious associations. Examples from the chapter on substitution include: God, incarnation, election, hypostasis, soul, inspiration, creation, expiation, sacrifice, kerygma, vocation, redemption; and others which often resonate religiously in context, such as: death, fulness, passivity, absolute, debt, exile, infinite, obedience, freedom, guilt, pardon, gratuity. The usage is often doubly provocative. On the one hand, contemporary Western academic philosophy's habitual exclusion of the religious from serious consideration is challenged by having to wrestle with unfamiliar vocabulary. On the other hand, Levinas repeatedly distances himself from many of the usual associations of the words. The distancing is most vehement with regard to theology. This is a discourse which he habitually dismisses. He employs many of its[1] richest words but forbids his usage being identified with that of theology's and urges readers to resist the temptation to develop his discussions theologically. The usual explicit or implicit reference of theology for Levinas seems to be Christian theology, though insofar as Jewish and other thinkers have adopted comparable approaches to religious subjects they too of course come under his ban.

My concern is to explore the meaning of substitution in Levinas and in one Christian theologian. Substitution is immensely important for both. Is theology inevitably an opponent or even a persecutor of Levinas's thought on this topic? Or vice versa? Or is there a significant witness of each to the other? The discussion will begin with some of Levinas's remarks on theology and its key terms. The main theologian who will be read alongside Levinas is Eberhard Jüngel. He too gives a central place to substitution and the culmination of the essay will be an engagement with both of them on this topic.[2]

DISMISSING THEOLOGY

I have discussed in an article elsewhere (Ford 1994: 23–59[3]) with reference to Levinas's various works how he regards theology. His negative view is summarized as follows:

> Theology, he says, thematizes or objectifies what it should not; it is mythological, or suggests that there is a divine drama in progress in which people are participants, often unwittingly; it suggests that it is possible to participate directly in or have cognitive or emotional access to the life of God; it finds intrinsic links between human nature and the divine; it tends to confuse creation with causality or to conceptualise creation in ontological terms; it makes ontology absolute, with God as the supreme being and therefore inevitably totalitarian; it argues analogically from the world to God; it signifies God in terms of presence, action, efficacity in the world; above all, its alliance with ontology conspires against doing justice to an ethics which resists the assimilation of the other person to oneself and one's overview, and which finds in the face to face[4] an unsurpassable imperative directness and immediacy. (ibid.: 27f.)

One problem with Levinas's assessment is that it stereotypes theology without engaging in any discussion with particular theologians. He ignores the actual voices of these 'others' in relation to his philosophy. This can be seen as justifiable in various ways (ibid.: 29f.). But it should not prevent the engagement taking place, and in that article I began a dialogue between Levinas and Jüngel which I will now take further. I argued that Jüngel (despite his own stereotyping of Levinas in certain respects) sufficiently escapes Levinas's strictures to make it worthwhile having a detailed discussion.

There are several key points[5] at which Jüngel does not fit Levinas's stereotype and develops a theology which has significant resonances with Levinas's philosophy. Jüngel is concerned about the unobjectifiable mode of address, the event of 'coming' in language, and this has much in common with Levinas's ideas of proximity and approach. Jüngel's rejection of natural theology, his learning from modern atheist critiques of theism and his notion of a 'non-necessary' and 'more than necessary' God give him many common causes with Levinas in relation to theological and philosophical approaches to God and religious language. Jüngel, like Levinas, has radical notions of the absence and otherness of God. He rethinks the meaning of analogy in a way which both enables a defence against Levinas's rejection of analogy in relation to God and also challenges Levinas's extreme scepticism about the language of correspondence.

Chapter IV in *Otherwise Than Being* includes several of Levinas's key objections to theology in relation to substitution. I will now examine some of those points and see how Jüngel might respond to them, in order to help set up a worthwhile dialogue on the central matter of substitution. There are three main texts.

The first is at the beginning of sub-section 4, specifically entitled 'Substitution'. Levinas says:

In this exposition of the in itself of the persecuted subjectivity, have we been faithful enough to the anarchy of passivity? In speaking of the recurrence of the ego to the self, have we been sufficiently free from the postulates of ontological thought, where the eternal presence to oneself subtends even its absences in the form of a quest, where eternal being, whose possibles are also powers, always takes up whatever it undergoes, and whatever be its submission, always arises anew as the principle of what happens to it? It is perhaps here, in this reference to a depth of anarchical passivity, that the thought that names creation differs from ontological thought. It is not here a question of justifying the theological context of ontological thought, for the word creation designates a signification older than the context woven about this name. In this context, this said, is already effaced the absolute diachrony of creation, refractory to assembling into a present and a representation. But in creation, what is called to being answers to a call that could not have reached it since, brought out of nothingness, it obeyed before hearing the order. Thus in the concept of creation *ex nihilo*, if it is not a pure nonsense, there is the concept of a passivity that does not revert into an assumption. The self as a creature is conceived in a passivity more passive still than the passivity of matter, that is, prior to the virtual coinciding of a term with itself. The oneself has to be conceived outside of all substantial coinciding of self with self. (1981: 113f.)

Here Levinas is questioning himself about his faithfulness to elements in his thought which are vital if it is to sustain its witness to what is 'otherwise than being'. He contorts language in order to articulate a subjectivity which is so radically passive that it is not possible to conceive of a time when it was not under an absolute obligation. It is a self 'obsessed' by something distinct from all that can be represented under the category of 'being'. Levinas reaches for terminology that can express the drastic discontinuity between this 'election' to responsibility and 'being'. The discontinuity is so radical that it is wrong to subsume both sides of it under the discourse that most Western philosophy takes as unsurpassable, that of ontology. He suggests his agreement with the judgement that ontological thought has a 'theological context' (sometimes labelled 'ontotheology'). But the idea of creation *ex nihilo* is detached from that context in order to signify a discontinuity ('anarchy' and 'diachrony' are also concepts that try to suggest this discontinuity in relation to notions of beginning, sovereignty and time) that allows for an absolute passivity, what the previous section had called 'the infinite passion of responsibility' (ibid.: 113).

The main claim about theology here is that its 'said', its thematising and representation, efface 'the absolute diachrony of creation'. My question is whether this blanket verdict is just in relation to Jüngel. Might Jüngel's wrestling with similar issues at least leave the matter sufficiently open so that his whole theological enterprise is not dismissed? It would not be surprising if, given the resonances between Levinas and Jüngel mentioned above, there were not more to be said between the two at this point.

The obvious major topic in Jüngel which relates to the array of points made by Levinas in the passage under discussion is that of justification by faith. There are deep and irreconcilable differences between the two on this, yet Jüngel's concerns often parallel those of Levinas. Overall, Jüngel's theological project might be seen to be as obsessed by justification (and the for him inseparable event of the crucifixion of Jesus) as Levinas's is by responsibility. Jüngel too, in pursuing his obsession, sees the need to criticize radically many Western philosophical and theological traditions. More specifically in relation to this passage in *Otherwise Than Being*, Jüngel's treatment of justification draws together fundamental themes of his theology. Justice, righteousness, peace, goodness and ethics are intrinsic to the concern with justification. Substitution is an essential category for describing this.[6] Creation by God is understood primarily through the event of justification (Jüngel 1983: 218), and creation *ex nihilo* is a critical concept in expressing radical difference and discontinuity between God and humanity (ibid.: 199–225).[7] Though he does it very differently[8] Jüngel wants to relativize being and non-being with reference to justification (ibid.: *passim*). He also gives a major role to the category of interruption and recognizes his own kinship with Levinas in this (Jüngel 1995: 89ff.) And the radical passivity of Levinas has an analogy in Jüngel's notion of faith as 'pure passivity' (Jüngel 1983: 340) which is the subjective counterpart of the 'new creation' of justification. This forbids Jüngel too to have any 'substantial coinciding of self with self', and like Levinas he works this out partly in critical opposition to modern notions of the 'self-securing ego' (ibid.: 169ff.). 'The ego is always defined by a word that lays claim to it' (ibid.: 171); 'God alone comes in the word alone' (ibid.: 177, quoting Ebeling).[9]

There remains the fundamental question about the representation of these matters in language. This is best discussed in relation to the next text from the chapter on substitution to be examined.

> Phenomenology can follow out the reverting of thematization into anarchy in the description of the approach. Then ethical language succeeds in expressing the paradox in which phenomenology finds itself abruptly thrown. For ethics, beyond politics, is found at the level of this reverting. Starting with the approach, the description finds the neighbour bearing the trace of a withdrawal that orders it as a face. This trace is significant for behaviour, and one would be wrong to forget its anarchic insinuation by confusing it with an indication, with the monstration of the signified in the signifier. For that is the itinerary by which theological and edifying thought too quickly deduces the truths of faith. Then obsession is subordinated to a principle that states a theme, which annuls the very anarchy of its movement. (Footnote [p.197]: The theological language destroys the religious situation of transcendence. The infinite 'presents' itself anarchically, but thematization loses the anarchy which alone can accredit it. Language about God rings false or becomes a myth, that is, can never be taken literally.) The trace in which a face is ordered is not reducible to a sign: a sign and its relationship with the signified are synchronic in a theme. The approach is not the thematization of any relationship, but is this very relationship which resists thematization as anarchic. To thematize this relationship is already to lose it, to leave the absolute passivity of the self . . . the absolute passivity of being a creature, of substitution. (Levinas 1981: 121)

This should be taken together with footnote 19:

> All the descriptions of the face in the final three studies of the second edition of our book *En découvrant l'existence avec Husserl et Heidegger* which describe the very ambiguity or enigma of anarchy – the illeity of infinity in the face as the

trace of the withdrawal which the infinite qua infinite effects
before coming, and which addresses the other to my
responsibility – remain descriptions of the non-thematizable,
the anarchical, and, consequently, do not lead to any
theological thesis. Language can nonetheless speak of it, if
only by an abuse of language, and it thus confirms the fact
that it is impossible for the anarchical to be constituted as a
sovereignty – which implies the unconditionality of anarchy.
But the hold of language on the anarchical is not a mastery,
for otherwise anarchy would be subordinate to the *arche* of
consciousness. This hold is the struggle and pain of
expression. Whence comes discourse and the necessity of
the *arche* of sovereignty and of the State . . . It is clear also
that in our way of interpreting signifyingness, the practical
order (and the religious which is inseparable from the
practical) is defined by the anarchical. Theology would be
possible only as the contestation of the purely religious, and
confirms it only by its failures or its struggles. (Levinas 1981:
195ff., note to p.117)

Here Levinas is wrestling with the 'pain of expression' in order
to try to keep some hold on the anarchic passivity of
substitution. As throughout *Otherwise Than Being* there is a
complex interplay of 'saying', 'unsaying' and 'resaying'. The
rejection of theology is again vehemently affirmed, the crowning
accusation against it being that its language 'destroys the
religious situation of transcendence' (détruit la situation
religieuse de la transcendence). How conclusive is that
devastating indictment? I will respond to it with five comments,
the last leading into the final text on theology.

Firstly, when one looks for substance in the accusation one is
disappointed. It is followed by the statement that 'language
about God rings false or becomes a myth, that is, can never be
taken literally'. Can that really mean the dismissal of centuries
of wrestling with theological language, including a great deal
that has taken account of philosophers from whom Levinas
himself has learnt? With regard to Jüngel, for whom the wrestle

with theological language and with philosophers such as Heidegger and Levinas himself has been a pervasive feature of his thought, the indictment itself rings false and should not be allowed to preclude further discussion.[10]

Secondly, Levinas is concerned about theology too quickly deducing the truths of faith by forgetting the anarchic discontinuity between the infinite and the trace of its withdrawal in the face of the neighbour. The danger is that it will be treated as an 'indication' or 'monstration' in a direct way, and by being thematized have its religious significance destroyed. There are theologies which might justly be accused of such deductions, but any which has grappled with, for example, the thought of Kierkegaard, is likely to be alert to the danger. Jüngel's discussion of Kierkegaard's *Philosophical Fragments* (Jüngel 1995: 20–34) shows him coming to conclusions about 'truth' and 'faith' (and about the relation of philosophy to theology) which, however far they are from Levinas's own positions on these issues, yet cannot justly be said to fall under this condemnation.

Thirdly, the wrong overhasty movement which Levinas ascribes to theology can be seen as 'starting with the approach'. I have already mentioned the consonance between Levinas's notion of the approach with Jüngel's notion of advent (cf.Ford 1994). In Jüngel's own discussion of Levinas he finds that 'in many particular points of analysis and definitions, our own reflections are very close to those of Levinas. This is particularly the case in the distinction between (on the one hand) apophantic statements which assert *something* and are always oriented towards worldly being, and (in contrast) the event of a more primal saying.' (Jüngel 1995: 97) Jüngel then goes on to make what I consider a misinterpretation of Levinas comparable to Levinas's unjustifiable blanket condemnation of theology (Ford 1994: 33–35), with the result that each misses the advantage of further engagement with the rejected other.

Fourthly, perhaps the most important statement of all is in footnote 19. Here Levinas faces the obvious objection that nevertheless he himself does engage in discourse which could be called thematising, representation, and language about God. 'Language can nonetheless (cependant) speak of it, if only by an abuse (fût-ce par abus) of language . . .'. That *cependant* is the concession that inevitably involves Levinas in what many theologians do. Whether he calls it theology is not the main point, but those who read much theology will often recognize there comparable 'struggle and pain of expression'. What he goes on to say gives the heart of the matter. It is a double concern: that the anarchical not be understood to be 'constituted as a sovereignty' (l'impossibilité pour l'anarchique de se constituer en souveraineté); and that the 'hold of language on the anarchical' not be seen as a 'mastery' (l'emprise du langage sur l'anarchique n'est pas une maîtrise). Thematizing language gathers all under the dominating overview of consciousness; the abuse of language is required in order to allow language to subvert its own mastering 'emprise' and in so doing to signify an anarchy that is not dominating. Here we are beyond polemics against a stereotyped theology and have engaged with the key ethical and religious matter: how can substitution be witnessed to through a language that does not betray it? It is his extraordinarily thorough and rich attempt to witness in this way that makes Levinas such a profound and 'very disturbing'[11] challenge to any Christian theology of substitution. Jüngel is attempting to witness to substitution in just as radical a way as Levinas. If Levinas is not allowed to disqualify Jüngel's testimony on the basis of generalisations about theology, there might be a worthwhile engagement between the two very different testimonies.

Fifthly, there is Levinas's definition of the religious in terms of 'the practical order' and his view that 'theology would be possible only as the contestation of the purely religious, and confirms it only by its failures or its struggles'. This identification of the religious and the practical leads directly to the final text concerning theology, with which Chapter IV of *Otherwise Than Being* concludes:

If one had the right to retain one trait from a philosophical system and neglect all the details of its architecture (even though there are no details in architecture, according to Valéry's profound dictum, which is eminently valid for philosophical construction, where the details alone prevent collapse), we would think here of Kantism, which finds a meaning to the human without measuring it by ontology and outside of the question 'What is there here . . .?' that one would like to take to be preliminary, outside of the immortality and death that ontologies run up against. The fact that immortality and theology could not determine the categorical imperative signifies the novelty of the Coperni-can revolution: a sense that is not measured by being or not being; but being on the contrary is determined on the basis of sense. (Levinas 1981: 129)

This could open a long debate on the nature of religion and the common tendency, intensified since Kant, to see pure religion as practical or moral. It is sufficient for my purposes now to draw attention to the need to have the debate. Jüngel does this, and his *God as the Mystery of the World* has an engagement with Kant as a thread running through it.[12] However one judges his position, it at least is a thorough problematizing of Kant's understanding of God and of theology. Jüngel's constructive response to Levinas's final sentence might be to offer his understanding of revelation as the 'sense' on the basis of which being is understood.

At the end of this section on Levinas's dismissal of theology and Jüngel's failure to fit Levinas's notion of theology, more has been gained than just clearing away an obstacle to bringing them into dialogue. The question of communication is not extrinsic to substitution. My opening quotation from Levinas shows how for him opening oneself to the other is the meaning of communication, and for that to be complete there needs to be 'responsibility for the other to the point of substitution'. One never arrives there if one tries 'to begin in the ego, a free subject'. Likewise for Jüngel there is no beginning with the free subject but with the self claimed from outside. Jüngel too has an understanding of substitution which is inextricable from his conception of language; but for him this is at its most complete in justification by faith communicated through 'the word of the cross'. My second opening quotation points to how deep the difference is between these ideas of substitution, and I will now explore how each might be questioned by the other.

QUESTIONS TO JÜNGEL

No one can substitute himself for me who substitutes myself for all. (Personne ne peut se substituer à moi qui me substitue à tous.) (Levinas 1981: 126)

The word *I* means *here I am*, answering for everything and for everyone. (*Je* signifie *me voici*, répondant de tout et de tous.) (ibid.: 114)

Those statements stand in extreme tension with Jüngel's contesting of the definition which says that 'I am human, because and to the extent I am there for other people (Ich bin menschlich, weil und insofern ich für andere Menschen da bin.)'. He proposes instead that 'the humanity of the human ego consists of my allowing someone else to be there for me. Only on the basis of that can I be there for someone else. The main theological point is that *I am human in that I let someone else be there for me* (Ich bin menschlich, indem ich einen anderen für mich da sein lasse). That can also be called trust, and with regard to the "someone else" who as God has promised himself to us, we must call this *trust in God*. This is precisely what is meant when we speak of *faith*' (Jüngel 1983: 180).

It would be possible to ameliorate the tension if Jüngel did not affirm one person, Jesus Christ, as the incarnation of God and therefore as the particular one who is there for all others. As it is, the extremism of Levinas seeing 'me' substituting for all confronts Jüngel's extremism of seeing 'Jesus Christ' substituting for all. The fundamental 'witness' of each seems to be irreconcilably opposed to the other. To discuss that with any sort of adequacy is far too large a task for this short essay. But I do want to try to question each of them on this central issue.

Might Levinas's ethical passion challenge Jüngel's position on substitution even in terms of what Jüngel himself would want to do justice to? There are five areas where this seems to me to be so: on the ontology of substitution; on the relation of indicative to imperative; on death in relation to goodness; on God in relation to substitution; and on the relation of substitution to theological language.

First, on the ontology of substitution, it would be possible to argue that the way he defines ontology in relation to God and also conceives God in terms of love, justice, goodness and so on, together mean that we are always to understand his concept of substitution in a thoroughgoingly ethical sense (as Levinas might conceive ethics). But it is also arguable that his notion of ontology could benefit from continual confrontation with Levinas's absolutising of the ethical. The pervasiveness of the language of 'event' and 'story' brings the danger that Levinas sees of a reification which thematizes substitution and occludes the ethical. Jüngel can say that:

> it is decisive for the self-understanding of Christian theology whether the story of Jesus Christ is conceived only ethically, as an example of *right human behaviour, only as exemplum*, or beyond and behind that, as a *history which effectively changes the being of humanity*, as a *sacrament*. (Jüngel 1995: 169[13])

In context that is not as un-Levinassian as it might sound, since the target is exemplarism and there is no downplaying of ethics in Levinas's sense, but the way the effectiveness of Jesus's death is conceived raises one of the recurring accusations against 'objectivist' understandings of atonement in Christian theology. Surely this is a conception that overrules human responsibility? Part of the meaning of Levinas's 'no one can substitute himself for me' is to rule out such vicarious events and the scandal of irresponsibility that they seem to imply. Objectivist conceptions seem sub-moral and also imperialist, including me in a drama that may seem deeply repugnant.

But Levinas's approach to the objective might do better justice to the ethics that Jüngel affirms elsewhere. Levinas's striving for a language that can signify what is 'otherwise than being' might, in relation to theories of atonement in Christian theology, go behind the unsatisfactory alternatives of 'subjective' and 'objective'. Levinas in his chapter on substitution has a helpful footnote on alternatives to 'objectivism' in which he says:

> Quitting the objective order is possible in the direction of a responsibility beyond freedom as well as toward the freedom without responsibility of play. The ego is at the crossroads. But to quit the objective order, to go in oneself towards the privatissime of sacrifice and death, to enter upon the subjective ground, is not something that happens by caprice, but is possible only under the weight of all the responsibilities. (Levinas 1981: 197, note to p.120)

This relates to what Levinas is trying to articulate through such concepts as anarchy, diachrony, obsession and substitution. For Jüngel, a language that might escape the suspicions of objectivism, sub-morality and imperialism mentioned above would be a considerable gain. It would not by any means resolve his tension with Levinas in their clash of extremisms but it would help remove inessential differences and also refine Jüngel's theology.

Secondly, there is the relation of indicative to imperative in Jüngel. The priority of the indicative over the imperative comes from his conviction that there is good news of an event to which the appropriate response is thanks and joy. The initiative of God is conceived as something already done and the passivity of faith hears, receiving its being 'continually anew as a gift' (Jüngel 1995: 237f.). The ungrateful, he says, 'live under the dictatorship of the imperative' and 'lack the oasis of the indicative in which they are nothing more than themselves'. 'That relaxes'! says Jüngel – a tone that could not be more different than that of Levinas on substitution and persecution. A full discussion of this would need to take in Jüngel's appropriation of the Lutheran way of understanding law and gospel. But at the very least Levinas's rethinking of the imperative might stimulate Jüngel to question how shot through with the imperative is the Christian indicative, above all in the 'do this' of the Last Supper and the obedience of Gethsemane. To rethink the Christian story with such Levinassian concepts as election, vocation, kenosis,[14] responsibility for others, expiation and persecution might not only refocus Jüngel's concept of the imperative but also the notion of what it is to 'correspond' to all this in faith.[15]

Thirdly, Jüngel makes death and nothingness key concepts in his theology. It is a complex matter as to just how sin and goodness are related to death. This would be another large discussion. It would press still further the issues raised about ontology and ethics. Levinas's many references to death in the chapter on substitution (Levinas 1981: 108f., 115, 123, 126, 128f.) could be read as an ethical critique of Heidegger's 'being towards death' (cf. de Boer 1992: 289), refusing the centrality of death in relation to substitution. 'Contrary to the ontology of death this self opens an order in which death can be not recognized.' (Levinas 1981: 115) He can even say that the assignation from the Good to me is 'a relation that survives the "death of God"' (ibid.: 123). Jüngel, on the other hand, is more like a Christian response to Heidegger which responds to his concept of death with an understanding of the death of Christ and of God. Levinas could stimulate some radical questions, not only about the extent to which Jüngel allows his understanding of the crucifixion of Jesus to be dominated by a general notion of death as relationlessness, but also about the significance of incarnation and bodiliness.

Perhaps the most fascinating possibility opened up by Levinas is his particularizing of death:

> The approach, inasmuch as it is a sacrifice, confers a sense on death. In it the absolute singularity of the responsible

one encompasses the generality or generalization of death.
(En elle la singularité absolue du responsable englobe la
généralité ou la généralisation de la mort.) (ibid.: 129)

Jüngel's *God as the Mystery of the World* could be seen as
encompassing the generality of death in the absolute singularity
of the death of Christ, with loving sacrifice intrinsic to that.[16]
But the questions above about his conceptions of ontology, the
indicative and death mean that Levinas here too has an ethical
sharpening to contribute. The totality of a generalized death is
by Levinas given the sense of each face (Levinas's notion of
'approach' is linked to that of 'the face') which appeals to me to
be responsible, and this at the very least is a valuable
supplement to Jüngel's 'death' conceived in terms of event,
relationlessness and nothingness.

Fourthly, Jüngel places great emphasis on God alone being
the one who can fully substitute for others. He says that
substitution (Stellvertretung) is 'a category which presupposes
the identity of God with Jesus' (Jüngel 1983: 367). Another
approach he takes is to express sympathy with Heinrich Vogel's
critique of Dietrich Bonhoeffer's ethical idea of substitution
(Jüngel 1995: 153ff.). Bonhoeffer has a position with many
similarities to that of Levinas, linking a radical notion of human
responsibility with substitution. Vogel refuses a general
anthropological framework of substitution within which Jesus
Christ's would make sense, and instead sees the concept of
substitution as 'the essence of the uniqueness of Jesus Christ'.
Levinas is removed as far as possible from such a position while
still maintaining both substitution and a reference to God. It is
this contrast that helps focus on critical questions to Jüngel. If
he has a non-competitive concept of divine and human freedom,
why not a similar concept of substitution? Is Vogel's alternative
between general anthropological framework and christological
uniqueness appropriate? Even if it is, is substitution the right
concept through which to identify that sort of uniqueness?
Jüngel draws on Bonhoeffer for his theology of the worldly non-
necessity of God (1983: 57ff.), but might there not be an

intrinsic connection between that and Bonhoeffer's ethic of human substitutionary responsibility?[17]

Fifthly, to return to language: how not betray with our words the non-mastery of substitution and of the way language has a hold on it? This recapitulates the first two questions to Jüngel: the need for Levinas-like vigilance over an assertive ontological language that might occlude the ethical, and also over the rule of an indicative that is less hospitable to the imperative and interrogative. Levinas's linguistic practice stands as a rigorous ascesis which is especially adept at alerting his readers to our near-irresistible temptation to settle for thought and expression which give us more clarity, control and security than are just, which allows us to 'coincide with ourselves' in self-possession (cf. Levinas 1981: 99), and which reduces our exposure to (and obsession by) the appeal in the face of the other person. His habit of using theological terms in an ethical sense can be especially helpful in the self-examination of theologians.

QUESTIONS TO LEVINAS

At the opening of his chapter on substitution Levinas remarks that the quest for certainty, sovereignty and self-possession mentioned above is really 'no adventure' and rules out anything that might be a 'complete surprise' (ibid.: 99). It is as if nothing that might happen in 'a history of constituted and free egos' (ibid.: 116) can truly interrupt this totality. Substitution itself is not an act (ibid.). Levinas drastically relativizes the contingencies of history, including death,[18] in distinction from the substitutionary self. Jüngel takes one historical substitutionary self and relates everything else to that. He allows for complete surprise in history. In relation to historical contingencies, Levinas's position by contrast can seem something like a stoicism of responsibility: a refusal to be fundamentally surprised by any event, an expectation that most of what will happen will be bad, and a steady maintenance of radical responsibility even for one's persecutors. Here Jüngel's categories of the new and of interruption probe Levinas, who

Facing the other

would probably have to go by way of his Talmudic expositions (and perhaps the eschatology discerned by Graham Ward in his essay in this volume) in order to give his response.

But it is clear what the 'complete surprise' is for the chapter on substitution: it is substitution itself, the astonishing obsessed self with its surplus of responsibility. I substitute myself for all! Jüngel's obvious question might be: can I sustain that? Can anyone? (To which his own answer is: Yes, there is one.) But Levinas is not interested in the possibilities of historical vindication: 'Failing already presupposes a freedom and the imperialism of a political or ecclesiastical ego, that is, a history of constituted and free egos. The self as an expiation is prior to activity and passivity.' (ibid.) This self is 'otherwise' than being and history; it is also utterly 'incarnate', 'being-in-one's-skin, having-the-other-in-one's-skin' (ibid. p.115). There is here a paradox, a scandal, which is analogous to the incarnation of God according to Jüngel. It can be criticized from both sides: it can look preposterously idealistic, not in touch with the 'real world', or it can look realistic enough, but only as an exceptional case and certainly not relevant to everyone or the deepest truth about everyone. Or the combination of the two sides can seem implausible or impossible. In responding to such questioning Levinas is in the same situation as Jüngel: there can be no broader justificatory framework, no more fundamental criterion than what is being affirmed. The apparent impossibility of these extremist statements is related to them making a claim to be that than which nothing is more ultimate. There is no overview of my relation with the other or of the 'diachrony' and 'anarchy' that are at its heart: there is a witness to it in speech that tries, painfully, not to betray it.

So a comparison with Jüngel reveals common issues which could, if there were space, be taken much further. But there is one central similarity and difference. Both emphasize radical asymmetry, non-reciprocity at the core of substitution. For Jüngel this is to do with the free initiative and prevenience of God and the embodiment of that in Jesus Christ. For Levinas it is to do with 'me', with my unique election, and the asymmetry

38

in relations between me and others (especially ibid.: 126f.). I am responsible for all, but I cannot generalize this or 'require substitution and sacrifice' (ibid.: 126) from others. There is to be no comparison of myself with others: I am uniquely chosen, 'overwhelmed by the other in proximity' (ibid.). Levinas has always resisted a conception of self which gives any parity to reciprocity and familiarity, as if the radicality of responsibility would be compromised by it.[19] Jüngel's more mutual self (centred on love[20]) also allows for me to have an identity constituted by someone else substituting himself for me. It asks what the implications for 'me' are of the substitution of another for me and whether this must, in understanding my self, be diachronously separated from my substitution for the other. The ramifications spread through the formation of the self and into notions of community, culture, politics (cf. Gibbs 1992 Chapters 8,10).

Jüngel's conception also gives a straightforward priority to gratitude and joy in relation to what has been done for me. Levinas can call responsibility for another a 'gratuity' (Levinas 1981: 125[21]) and further on in *Otherwise Than Being* he embraces gratitude (ibid.: 149), grace and thanks to God (ibid.: 158[22]) within his understanding of approach and proximity. But 'God is not involved as an alleged interlocutor' (ibid). Jüngel, however, can conceive a joy as extreme as Levinas's responsibility (cf. Ford 1994: 48ff.). Can one responsibly have both? For Levinas this is by no means just an issue with the Christian Jüngel but also within Judaism. The question it puts to him is perhaps the largest of all, if one grants his main concern for substitutionary responsibility. Levinas's thought can be seen as one of the most perceptive exposures of idolatries in late modernity,[23] including those in the thematizings of theology. But its constriction is suggested by its limited willingness to do justice to the positive counterpart which, perhaps, is required all the more by such a devastating 'hermeneutic of suspicion': the praise, thanks, confession and intercession that are, for example, complexly represented by the Psalms. Can idolatries be safely rejected if one does not run the risks of true worship? It is perhaps not only his specific, controversial allegiances within Jewish tradition which condition this but also such philosophical influences as Kant's ethical marginalizing of worship.

The next question to Levinas from Jüngel is related to this. Karl Barth was startled by his own conclusion that invocation of God, especially in petition, is the ground of Christian ethics (Jüngel 1995: 154ff.). For Jüngel, as for Barth, God's embracing command is to call on God. Jüngel's ethic is therefore basically one of commanded prayer. Levinas's concept of prayer in line with his idea of substitution is that of 'Prayer without Demand' (Hand 1989: Chapter 14; cf. Levinas 1994: 127ff.), and it is here that Levinas's giving exclusively ethical content to theological language is most extreme. He will not even call God 'You': only 'He' ('Il') is permitted, and only then on the most severe conditions. It might be therefore that Levinas's privileging of the imperative is not best compared with use of the indicative or of the interrogative but of petition in prayer. And this might, in a world pervaded by evil, be said to 'expose' Jüngel in a way even more easy to ridicule than Levinas's witness to substitution for all. Levinas has learnt well why God's activity in the world, or a God invoked 'behind the scenes' (Levinas 1981: 185), is not to be countenanced. Jüngel has sat in some of the same lessons, yet challenges the veto on God as 'an alleged interlocutor'.

Finally, Gibbs says that Levinas's 'other' is 'strangely undetermined, is almost formal, in its concreteness. This face is anyone we meet, is any other, but it is archetypically a poor person, one who is hungry' (Gibbs 1992: 183). His idea of uniqueness is primarily that of my responsibility in substitution. Yet Gibbs notes that occasionally Levinas also 'grants a parallel uniqueness to the other', as in an essay in *Entre Nous* (Levinas 1991: 214): 'The relation goes to the unassimilable, incomparable, other; to the irreducible other; to the unique other. Only the unique is absolutely other. But the uniqueness of the unique (l'unicité de l'unique), that is the uniqueness of the beloved.' Previously Gibbs remarked about Levinas's own teacher: 'Levinas's account of Shusani's influence is so extreme that one might well ascribe to him the source of Levinas's goal of translation, and even of the lived experience of the face.' (Gibbs 1992: 170) The hungry other; the particular beloved; the particular teacher: these perhaps help to conceive why it is that there can be such strong resonances with a thinker whose differences (theologian, Christian, German, ontologist and much else) are glaring but who is obsessed with a uniqueness traced in one particular face.

NOTES

1 I do not mean by this to suggest that the words can be claimed as somehow the possession of theology – many of them are biblical and have entered into other forms of discourse as well. These include the Talmud and rabbinic discussions, which Levinas does not see as 'theological' but as primarily concerned with the religious in an ethical sense.

2 Robert Gibbs (1992) has discussed similar questions in relation to Levinas and theology, and has developed his own concept of 'correlation' to relate Levinas to Rosenzweig and others. In Chapter 9 on substitution he offers a most helpful commentary on parts of Levinas's Chapter IV (1981) and also relates him to the Catholic thinker Gabriel Marcel. My essay is much more limited in scope than Gibbs' book and is indebted to it.

3 That is a companion piece to the present paper and should ideally be read alongside it.

4 It might have been wiser to say '. . . in the face to face *the trace of* an unsurpassable . . .'.

5 For an expanded discussion see Ford 1994: 30ff.

6 See especially his essays 'The Mystery of Substitution' and 'The Sacrifice of Jesus Christ as Sacrament and Example' (Jüngel 1995: 145–90).

7 John Webster suggests that this differentiation is pivotal for Jüngel's whole theology (Webster 1986: 4).

8 It is confusing that, as described in Ford 1994: 36, Levinas is negative about 'ontology' but positive about 'metaphysics', whereas Jüngel's usage is the reverse.

9 Jüngel seems to me to go a good way towards meeting the criteria suggested by Gibbs for a theology that can be 'correlated' with Levinas's thought (Gibbs 1992: 210f.).

10 I have raised a number of points in Ford 1994: 51–57.

11 Jüngel's words about Levinas (Jüngel 1995: 97).

12 The most relevant references are Jüngel 1983: 20; 129ff; 196; 263ff. 363.

13 Cf. p. 176: '. . . before Jesus Christ comes to be considered an *exemplum* for our behaviour, he must be affirmed as the sacramentum that changes our being.' Cf. also the condensed summary of Jüngel's understanding of substitution in 1983: 367 on 'the event of divine love', 'the turning-point of the world' and the creation of 'a new relationship with God'.

14 Kenosis is an important concept in *Otherwise Than Being*, though not in Chapter IV. In 'Judaism and Kenosis' (Levinas 1994) Levinas explores kenosis in explicit contrast to a Christian concept of incarnation.

15 Another fruitful exploration would be of the interrogative in both thinkers – Levinas's more pervasively suspicious, sceptical and self-questioning approach might nuance further Jüngel's indicative.

16 See e.g. Jüngel 1983: 364, but note the negative appraisal of the 'demand' of the law on the following pages.

17 Bonhoeffer is arguing for full human responsibility in the world without any 'God of the gaps'. How does Jüngel argue for the unique, divine character of the substitution of Jesus in such a world? He needs to relate thoroughly his use of Bonhoeffer on God to the ethical substance of Bonhoeffer's theology.

18 Cf. Theo de Boer's remarks on the significance of Levinas seeing death as an enemy attacking unexpectedly (de Boer 1992: 289f.).

19 Cf. his comment on Buber in 1969: 155. For a perceptive analysis of the debate between Buber and Levinas on the latter's concept of asymmetry see Gibbs 1992: 188ff. Gibbs presents both Hermann Cohen and Franz Rosenzweig as more satisfactorily balanced in this respect than either Buber or Levinas.

20 But see too the critique of Jüngel's concept of love in Ford 1994: 55f.

21 He distinguishes this gratuity sharply from one which involved 'pure pardon'.

22 The section in which this occurs is especially significant for the issues mentioned at the end of the previous paragraph above.

23 It is not Levinas's habit to use the language of idolatry in his philosophy, but it does appear occasionally (for example in the course of two important discussions in *Otherwise Than Being*, 44, 150; cf. also the note on p. 199 which perhaps most clearly confirms the thrust of my interpretation) and is understandably more prominent in his explicitly Jewish writings. See for example his description of Judaism in 'A Religion for Adults' (Levinas 1990: 11–23). My interpretation of aspects of his thought in terms

On Substitution

of the exposure of idolatries is a theological one which yet claims
to be in line with what Levinas says. For a perceptive theological
discussion of *Totality and Infinity* in relation to Kierkegaard which
sees idolatry as a key concept see Westphal 1992.

BIBLIOGRAPHY

de Boer, T. (1992) 'Feindschaft, Freundschaft und Leiblichkeit bei
Levinas', in P. van Tongeren et al. (eds) *Eros and Eris. Contribution
to a Hermeneutical Phenomenology*, Dordrecht, Boston, London:
Kluwer Academic Publishers.

Ford, D. F. (1994) 'Hosting a Dialogue: Jüngel and Levinas on God,
Self and Language', in *The Possibilities of Theology. Studies in the
Theology of Eberhard Jüngel in his Sixtieth Year*, ed. John Webster,
Edinburgh: T&T Clark.

Gibbs, R. (1992) *Correlations in Rosenzweig and Levinas*, Princeton:
Princeton University Press.

Hand, S. (ed.) (1989) *The Levinas Reader*, Oxford: Blackwell.

Jüngel, E. (1983) *God as the Mystery of the World. On the Foundation
of the Theology of the Crucified One in the Dispute between Theism
and Atheism*, Edinburgh: T&T Clark; trans. of the third revised
German edition. My German quotations are from the first edition,
*Gott als Geheimnis der Welt. Zur Begründung der Theologie des
Gekreuzigten im Streit zwischen Theismus und Atheismus*, Tübin-
gen: J.C.B. Mohr (Paul Siebeck) 1977.

—— (1995) *Theological Essays II*, ed. J. B. Webster, Edinburgh: T&T
Clark.

Levinas, E. (1969) *Totality and Infinity. An Essay on Exteriority*,
Pittsburgh: Duquesne University Press.

—— (1981) *Otherwise than Being or Beyond Essence*, The Hague,
Boston, London: Martinus Nijhoff.

—— (1990) *Difficult Freedom. Essays on Judaism*, Baltimore: The
Johns Hopkins University.

—— (1991) *Entre Nous: Essais sur le penser-à-l'autre*, Paris: Bernard
Grasset.

—— (1994b) 'Judaism and Kenosis' in *In the Time of the Nations*,
London: Athlone Press.

Webster, J. (1986) *Eberhard Jüngel. An Introduction to his Theology*,
Cambridge: Cambridge University Press.

Westphal, M. (1992) 'Levinas, Kierkegaard and the Theological Task',
in *Modern Theology* 8, 3 (July): 241–261.

Chapter 3

Levinas and Freud
Talmudic Inflections in Ethics and Psychoanalysis

Steven Gans
Philadelphia Association

INTRODUCTION

I argue that the Levinasian Talmudic hermeneutic opens the possibility of making audible the muted Talmudic basis of Freud's psychoanalytic practice and shows the way toward the development of an ethical psychoanalysis.

1st question: Why did Freud keep quiet about the Talmudic influence on his work:

Answer: Let's suppose that Freud found himself in a comparable position to Descartes. Having developed a method that effects a paradigm shift in world view (Descartes overturns theocentricism, Freud egocentricism, Descartes founds the discourse of modernity, Freud problematizes the modern contract) – to whom and how does such a revolutionary thinker/practitioner address him/herself? Taking my clue from Leo Strauss as for example from his *Persecution and the Art of Writing*, I argue that Freud employs an age-old strategy to dissemble what he is saying, a sort of double writing or double talk. This means he addresses the public and the 'powers that be' in an esoterically disguised manner, appealing to the principles of the old paradigm and institutions even as he subverts these very principles and institutions for 'those who have ears to hear' (Freud 1977: 114). This has the advantage of avoiding persecution (if you can get away with it) as for instance when Descartes recommends his *Meditations* to the theological faculty in Paris (they however saw through the subterfuge). This double writing enabled Freud to set up an alternative procedure of authorization and legitimation which mimicked and rivalled the modern medical and psychiatric institution and their claim to power/knowledge. Also anti-Semitism can not be discounted as a factor in explaining why Freud did not flaunt the Talmudic source which underpins his staging of analysis.

Backtracking for a moment a word about Bruno Latour's brilliant analysis of the modern constitution which legislates the divide between the natural and social world. In his *We Have Never Been Modern* Latour lays out the operations and procedures which demonstrate that modernity is constituted by the conjoint creation and separation of man from things. The community of scientists on the one hand and politicians on the other stake out their claim for exclusive license to speak and legislate in regard to these respective territories. To retain their power/knowledge stronghold each of these communities develops a professional exclusive language. Each develops a code of practice which effects this double separation. Each community insists on the purification and non contamination of their field by the other – science by politics/politics by science. Freud is clear that psychoanalysis is going to be a hybrid disciple, thus outlawed according to the modern norm. Its explicit mission is to track the interpenetration of the social and bioneurological, in other words to problematize the mind/brain dichotomy. This will produce a field of 'research' that can only be considered a monstrosity by either side of the orthodox modern divide.

At stake was the potential survival of Freud and his work – so he set about to create an alternative power/knowledge/language community of 'analysts' who would conquer the as yet new uncolonised territory of the unconscious psyche. They would establish this field through the creation of an international institution of psychoanalysis, the I.P.A. I argue that exoteric psychoanalysis is a cover story which enabled Freud to get on with his research in a relatively sheltered fashion. It developed an economy which allowed Freud and his followers to adopt and transform Talmudic hermeneutics into a powerful mode of ethical therapeutic practice.

In the following four sections I sketch the lines of argument I propose to develop (at a later date) to support a Levinasian reading of Freud.

In Section 1 *The Same Is Not The Other* I show that Freud and Levinas break free of the gravitational pull of appropriative thinking that dominates the West from Parmenides to Heidegger.

Section 2) Levinas's Talmudic hermeneutic introduces the precepts of this methodology through a discussion of the first three lessons in Levinas' *Talmudic Studies.*

Section 3) Reading Freud's Dora through Heidegger looks at a recent attempt to read Freud through the lens of Heidegger.

Finally in Section 4) I offer a reinterpretation of the Dora case from a Levinasian perspective to indicate how ethical psychoanalysis works.

THE SAME IS NOT THE OTHER

It is bizarre that the central issue of our time, (perhaps of any time), the ability to distinguish between evil and good, requires such a deep and convoluted meditation. This is evident in the debate regarding the primacy of ethics over ontology. Is there a diabolical element latent in Heidegger's thinking Being project? Does this become patent in the infamous *Geschick* as in Heidegger's response to the call of destiny asserting itself in the spirit of National-socialism? How is Levinas's 'we will do' then 'we will hear' i.e. his exhortation to accept responsibility for the other's responsibility prior to any knowing radically different from Heidegger's faith in the call of conscience? How is it that so basic an issue as our ability to distinguish good from evil involves following subtle and abstruse conversations with and about the philosophic tradition as well as the Talmudic tradition and the tradition of psychoanalysis? No wonder that the question of the Same versus the Other, the debate between Heidegger and Levinas has put off all but the most tenacious and persevering. Obviously I am here only able to touch on some of the considerations regarding the question of the Same and Other. At stake is the question of the status of philosophic discourse as such insofar as it remains bound to Parmedian presuppositions. This investment gives rise to the classic philosophic gesture which separates story, biography, history and context from theory or systematic thought; the supposed truth contained in philosophic argument and texts. Philosophy originated in the attempt to break away from the tyranny of the priests who based their authority on myth. Have we come full circle toward a post philosophic age where we are no longer able to preclude the question of the life and biography of the philosophic practitioner from an appraisal of his/her work? Is this return to story, to history, even to myth regress or rather the realisation that *logos* can never be separated from ordinary living.

Parmenides in his didactic poem and Heidegger in his commentary on it spell out the framework that has separated and enclosed the inside of philosophy from the outside – from its inception to this day. The goddess Truth, in other words the truth of truth, tells the philosopher, 'not evil fate but rule and order (logos) has sent you on the way of well enclosed unconcealment aletheia) outside the (trodden) path of most mortals for whom appearances are dissociated or not based on truth or unconcealment – in short, who are deluded' (Heidegger 1975: 88).

Heidegger, in his 'Moira' piece proclaims and reproduces Parmenides' truth which he asserts is the fundamental template for all Western thinking – It's the Same – awareness and presence (1975: 88); in other words, truth is unconcealment. *Moira* or destiny gives (beschickt) truth, i.e. the way in which what is comes to be. Indeed, Heidegger's hermeneutic circle, the circle of appropriation between Dasein and Sein later amplified as the story of the history of Being plays out the centripetal movement of thought thinking itself. The Same insists on incorporation of the Other into itself. Derrida in an early piece on Levinas falls into line with the classical Parmenidian assumption structure (1978: 126). He argues that the infinitely Other can be what it is only if it is other, that is, other *than*. Other than must be other than myself. Henceforth, it is no longer absolved of a relation to an ego. Therefore, it is no longer infinitely, absolutely other. He continues 'play of the Same' – it would mean that the expression 'infinitely other' or 'absolutely other' can not be stated and thought simultaneously; that the other cannot be absolutely exterior to the same without ceasing to be other; the same is not a totality closed in upon itself. In a footnote to the phrase 'absolutely exterior' Derrida adds the qualification:

> or at least cannot be, or be anything: and it is indeed the authority of Being which Levinas profoundly questions. That his discourse must still submit to the contested agency is a necessity whose rule we must attempt to inscribe systematically in the text. (1978: 126).

Derrida will have occasion to reconsider the gist of his remark in latter texts e.g. in 'Is there a Philosophical Language?' (1995: 216–227). Derrida continues his Levinas critique 'How could there be a "play of the same" if alterity itself was not already *in* the same, with a meaning of inclusion doubtless betrayed by the word in?' (1978: 126). Derrida admits that Levinas would refuse to subordinate his Other to the conceptual *eteron* (i.e. the other as opposed to the one), but he asks how can the 'other' be thought or said without reference? If the Levinasian ethics and Talmudic lessons are indeed generated from a source otherwise than from within the Western thought/Being tradition as is Freud's esoteric psychoanalytic practice, how can we make sense of these practices that are Other rather than self centred? They cannot be assimilated to the Same or conceptual thought – we can understand this through an analogy with music. Music played in a minor key can not be transposed into the major scale without losing its plaintive tonality.

If the philosophical tradition from Parmenides to Heidegger is unified around the notion of the Same, including the Platonic dialogues which stage maieutic dialogues (Socrates draws out truths that were always already known i.e. recollections of the Same) then Western thought culminates in Hegel's absolute systematic solipsism. I argue that Freud and Levinas in their psychoanalytic and ethical practices, founded on Talmudic hermeneutics, are the first to venture on a post philosophic path that takes responsibility to and for the other person as its point of departure and touchstone. I turn to a brief orientation to Levinas' ethical landscape as sketched out in the first three lessons of his Talmudic studies to set out the parameters of Talmudic hermeneutics. I show how these texts elucidate the problematics of relatedness and of bringing out the good in the other, how they work according to a language of the heart as opposed to the philosophic language of the head. This will lay the ground for a Levinasian ethical re-reading of the Dora case after summarizing a recent Heideggerian reading of the case.

LEVINAS'S TALMUDIC HERMENEUTIC

In a way it is an impossibility and a betrayal to write about Levinas' ethical practice or Freud's psychoanalytic practice, although both Levinas and Freud made the attempt, albeit in esoteric fashion. This is the case because both practices are strictly speaking performed in and only in the moment of the relation with an other. The singularity of these moments of relatedness means that the work of ethics and psychoanalysis is not based on principles or concepts nor can they be generalized into systematic thought, into a theory or philosophy. Each moment of ethical practice is context specific and concerns far more the way in which or manner of my relatedness to the other than the actual content of anything said or thought. Nevertheless, there are precepts or guidelines that can be gleaned from a reading of Levinas' Talmudic lessons which point the way toward an ethical response to the other. It is precisely these very precepts (I will argue in Section 4) that govern Freudian practice and his recommendations for future psychoanalytic practitioners.

To give a handle on the difference between the Western philosophical, academic approach which I characterize as egological as opposed to ethical relatedness let me draw an analogy to what I term the tourist mentality in comparison with ethical relating. The tourist wants to look at, preferably through a camera or camcorder. This is a metaphorical caricature of what Levinas calls the temptation of temptation, – putting knowledge first. As he explains:

> we do not want to undertake anything without knowing everything, and nothing can become known to us unless we have gone and seen for ourselves, regardless of the misadventures of the exploration. We want to live dangerously, but in security, in the world of truths. Seen in this manner, the temptation of temptation is, as we have already said, philosophy itself. (1990: 34)

This I call the way of the tourist.

In short, we Western intellectuals want to know before we do. The inversion of this all pervasive attitude, to do and then hear or to commit ourselves, to affirm and surrender to our obligation and responsibility to the other before we know what we are doing is the first ethical precept.

In contrast to Heidegger for whom the essence of truth is freedom (1977: 125) Levinas subverts the cult of autonomy (self-assertion) which underpins the modern contract and proposes that there is no genuine experience that is not committed and limited by our responsibility to the other and the demands of justice.

In the first three lessons of his Talmudic studies Levinas brings out and in a way embodies in his reading how the precept of surrender or obligation informs each of the pillars of ethical practice: 1. in forgiveness in 'Toward the Other', 2. in uprightness in the 'Temptation of Temptation' and 3. in rejection of hypocrisy in 'Promised Land or Permitted Land'.

The way in which Levinas reads the text, indeed bleeds the text, tracing and extracting the secret scent of each passage linked to the next in the Talmudic extract under consideration and then how he extrapolates the multidimensional significance embedded in the ethical biblical landscape, how he points both backwards and forwards to past and contemporary ethical issues calling the reader to face up to their own responsibilities is masterful to a degree that can only be appreciated by careful reading of these lessons. Freud's presentation of the Dora case is again masterful in the extraordinary way he illuminates the ordinary and must be appreciated in a similar careful fashion. Nevertheless, I review the highlights of each of these Talmudic readings in order to prepare the way to see how the ethical precepts that inform Levinas's exegesis are also at the heart of Freud's psychoanalytic practice.

For example, in 'Toward the Other', the topic taken up is forgiveness and we will see in Sec 4 that the pivotal issue for Freud in his interpretation of Dora's 'hysteria' is the question of forgiveness.

In this lesson Levinas recounts how he struggled with the story of Rev Hanina's refusal to forgive his pupil Raba for not going back to the beginning of his commentary on a text when he came in late although Raba had started again three times already.

Levinas has remarked as initiation into the protocol of his hermeneutic that he resists conceptualization which fixes ideas. The apparent hair-splitting of the sages in their arguments he explains always allude to contexts which allow these instances to reveal the import of the meaning of the issue under consideration. In the above example we are introduced to the meaning of affront and to the question of the degree to which an affront is forgivable. Also elucidated are the conditions of forgiveness and the limits at which an offence becomes unforgivable. The key to the question of forgiveness turns on the precondition of forgiveness which is that the offender becomes conscious of the wrong he/she has done. Demanding this consciousness is our responsibility for the others' responsibility and responsibility is for Levinas the essence of language and relatedness. The original function of speech consists not in designating an object in order to communicate with the other in a language game with no consequences but rather is first of all an assuming toward someone of a responsibility on behalf of someone else (Levinas 1990: 21).

Levinas relates the story of Rav Hanna's refusal to forgive to the question of forgiving Heidegger. He writes – 'one can forgive many Germans, but there are some Germans it is difficult to forgive. It is difficult to forgive Heidegger' (1990: 25). If Hanina could not forgive the just and humane Rab because he was also the brilliant Rab, it is even less possible to forgive Heidegger.

The crux of the story turns on the unawareness even unconsciousness of Rab/Heidegger in regard to his offence; 'aggression is lack of action *par excellence*', or worse if Rab or Heidegger was aware and aware of the great destiny before them as 'prophetically revealed to Hanina in a dream' – how much more is it difficult or impossible to forgive.

The second lesson the 'Temptation of Temptation' has as its theme uprightness (Temimut). The Talmud comments on a passage from Exodus – the biblical site of the Covenant. Yet Levinas stresses that his commentary will not be parochial in presupposing a special Jewish pre-eminence in relation to God. Rather, whatever the meaning of divinity is will be revealed in terms of ordinary living and how humans treat one another. The essential teaching of this lesson is that we must give an unconditional yes to every other as if we were receiving the Torah. To be upright is to be responsible in advance for the other, beyond what we have or haven't ourselves done. To be responsible is to substitute ourselves for the others, to put the other first. Every other is the face of the divine turned toward us:

> The Torah is given in the light of a face. The epiphany of the other person is *ipso facto* my responsibility toward him – seeing the other is already an obligation toward him. A direct optics -without the mediation of any idea – can only be accomplished as ethics. Integral knowledge or Revelation, (the receiving of the Torah) is ethical behavior. (Levinas 1990: 47)

This moment of unconditional yes, of receiving the other as sacred is I will argue the esoteric underpinning of the psychoanalytic process, what is therapeutic about it, what makes it work. David Bakhan in his book *Freud and the Jewish Mystical Tradition* had already speculated that Freud named his first full fledged 'case history' Dora as a code name for Torah. He in effect is saying that he accepts the obligation to attend to the other with the same degree of attention and reverence extended to the Torah.

The profound simplicity of the act of acceptance and obligation preserves the other from the danger of being transformed into a mere supporting character in my own scenario. Appropriative thought subordinates the other to my own point of view. The other loses their otherness through the violence of this calculative thinking and becomes assimilated to my perspective, my idea of the total. I no longer relate to the other as neighbour, as coming first but rather see only my narcissistic image reflected back to me.

Levinas' discourse on receiving the Torah or the other is a founding moment prior to knowledge and rationality, prior to the opposition of coercion or choice. This is because the meaning of language, of speaking presupposes an obligation to the other, to hear them and attend. to them, the gift of the Law is a freedom for responsibility as opposed to the thrownness of so called existential free choice. It is what makes choice possible in the way that rules of a game enable the game to be played: without them there is no game. The upright man challenges the game of Power, the powerful who arrogantly claim that their way is the way it is. For Levinas 'being in itself' is nothing but violence and the Law based on fragile human conscience says no to this violence and insists on justice. The meaning of Torah or death is the commitment to justice and a recognition of the desolation and death, the desert that lays waste to all that is of worth when the law and the other are refused i.e. murdered. Is the injunction to uprightness, to the practice of obligation and responsibility to the other a mere Utopian dream – a mere speculative ideal? Levinas takes up this question in his third Talmudic lesson to which I now turn.

In the lesson titled 'Promised Land or Permitted Land', Levinas retells the story of the rebellion of the supposedly righteous who were sent on a scouting mission to report back on conditions in Canaan, the land promised to the children of Israel. His exegesis on the Talmudic commentaries on this text in Deuteronomy gives a cogent account of the meaning of this promise. The story turns on the question of the hypocrisy of the 'righteous' explorers. No sooner do they leave their tribe than they adopt tourist mind so that on return they try to dissuade their people from entering Israel – 'it is a land that devours its inhabitants' they claim and furthermore 'it is already settled by men who are far too powerful'.

Levinas extracts a multiplicity of meanings from this over determined incident. The gist of his finely tuned reading is to remind us of what the rebels forgot – that Moses was not an imperialist. His intention embodied in the Torah was to transform the earthly community inhabited by 'giants' based on the worship of sun, moon and earth, in other words oriented around the Heideggerian celebration of building, dwelling and being into a community of universal justice. 'We will not possess the land as it is usually possessed, we will found a just community in this land' (1990: 66). So Levinas argues, the date of exile is fixed before the conquest – in that 'only those who are always ready to accept the consequences of their actions and to accept exile where they are no longer worthy of a homeland have a right to enter their homeland'. This is the meaning of devouring its inhabitants – it devours them when they are not just. Only the commitment to justice entitles those who accept this condition entrance to the 'promised land'.

READING FREUD'S DORA THROUGH HEIDEGGER

In a recent exposition of the principles of Freudian psychoanalytic practice, *The Truth About Freud's Technique: The Encounter with the Real*, M. Guy Thompson transposes the Heideggarian ontological notion of truth as (alethia) unconcealment on to the Freudian field of experience. Freud's aim

Thompson suggests was 'to get to those truths his patients concealed from themselves as well as from others' (1994: 94). Although Thompson's reading brings us closer to the esoteric Freud, the Freud of practice than most of the writing of orthodox Freudians or his scientific, revisionist historical or feminist critics I argue that a Heideggarian Freud is still bound to the modern paradigm of power/knowledge and self centeredness, in short to appropriative thinking. After reviewing Thompson's Heideggarian reading of the Dora case I re read the case between the lines, in a series of counterpoints to Thompson (sec 4) to make explicit the implicit Talmudic ethical basis that informs Freud's psychoanalytic practice. I show how Freud reintroduces an ancient and at the same time post-modern paradigm of responsible relatedness that is other centered and aims at bringing out the good in the other, in other words that Freud was already practising a version of a Levinasian ethics and that ethical psychoanalysis is the way forward for psychoanalysis.

The Dora story has all the elements of modern soap if it were not written up by Freud in such a subtle, sophisticated, radical and explosive fashion, too fiendish and duplicitous by far for daytime TV. Dora, a young lady of eighteen, is brought to Freud by her father for treatment of 'hysterical' symptoms, a nervous cough and breathlessness. Her suicide threat and fainting spell triggered his request for her treatment. Freud introduces Dora to his psychoanalytic 'technique' – he invites her to say what comes to mind. As Thompson argues, it was not his theories but his 'interrogative manner' that guided Freud and enabled him to learn about human suffering (1994: 94). Thompson sees his process as one of helping Dora 'discover the truth' about her situation (1994: 94). We learn that Dora's situation is hellish; her father is using her as a bribe to buy off his friend Mr K so that he can carry on his affair with Mrs K. When Dora complains to her father of Mr K's propositioning her he takes Mr K's side in denying this ever happened, undermining her perception of reality. Moreover Mrs K, her erstwhile friend, also betrays her by providing her father information on her overactive sexual interest, an appetite whetted by Mrs K herself. It is Thompson's view that Freud believed that Dora will get relief from her hysterical symptoms by revealing her secret desires and intimacies and how her secret lovers, in her case three – her father, Mr K and Mrs K conspired to betray her.

Thompson explains that the 'truths' which Dora's neurosis and symptoms concealed were obtained by Freud not so much 'in' her account of her story but through it, that is by what she omitted and tried to keep hidden, and only revealed by means of Freud's skill at observation and interpretation, especially of her dreams, which helped her to bring these forgotten repressed truths to light (1994: 95).

Clearly it is not in the patient's apparent self interest to reveal secrets which they fear to reveal even to themselves, especially if these secrets become symptoms serve as weapons of revenge. Why give up symptoms and surrender to reality? An additional paradox inherent in the analytic situation comes to light in the Dora case. How can the analyst get trust from a patient when the analyst is inevitably in the transference cast into the role of significant other, in Dora's case a betraying lover. Dora takes her revenge on Freud by abandoning treatment so as not to give him the satisfaction of a cure. Freud could be seen on his part as colluding with Dora's betrayal scenario by betraying confidentiality and publishing the intimate details of her case (counter transference). Thompson concludes his discussion of Dora's analysis, arguing that it is the most exemplary illustration of Freud's analytic technique he ever composed (1994: 107). This is because the efficacy of psychoanalysis can't be demonstrated, as in science, by the outcome of this or that case. Its value can only be determined by first principles. That is what 'rules' are (technique). They are not meant to instruct but to guide. Analysis is rooted in *truth*, thus its 'first principles' are concerned with the means by which truth has its say. Hence, whether the result of analysis is premature termination or permanent remission of symptoms, the truth about Dora's symptoms were revealed as well as her inability to assimilate the truth into her life and to forgive her father and Mr and Mrs K, and Freud – (by extension). For this reason her life in terms of establishing intimate relations with others would prove a failure as it seems to have done as based on a report of Felix Deutsch who saw Ida Bauer (Dora) thirty years after her analysis with Freud. She hadn't changed a bit. Thompson concludes 'Freud believed that uncovering truths was the principal aim of analytic treatment' (1994: 111). Neurotics 'suffer from secrets' (1994: 127) – the difference between neurotic forms of deviousness and the covert acts of deception that characterized Dora's family is in the way the neurotic becomes dishonest with himself. This is not simply an ethical problem, but neither is it strictly speaking a psychological one. For Thompson the crux, essence of neurosis, its knot is that we no longer know who we are, what we want or where we stand with others since we have denied truth and thus cut off our relations to reality.

In counterpoint I argue that 'the problem' which Freud exoterically called neurosis and Thompson after Heidegger, Sartre and Laing calls self deception is in fact ethical in a Levinasian sense.

A LEVINASIAN READING OF FREUD'S DORA

There are numerous remarks by Freud especially in the preface to the Dora case that confirm our hypothesis that Freud is practising the art of double writing; on the one hand offering a popular or public writing that appeals to the scientific and modern assumptions of his age and on the other encrypting an esoteric subtext which draws upon and applies a form of Talmudic hermeneutic in the actual practice of psychoanalysis, which amounts to a method of interpretive ethical practice.

First of all Freud argues contra those who would accuse him of betraying confidentiality in writing up the Dora case in the first place that it is his responsibility to do so. It is in the interest of the many other patients who are suffering or will some day suffer from similar disorders that Freud owes a detailed account of the psychoanalyst's approach to the relief of suffering.

And it is on primarily ethical grounds in the Levinasian sense of putting the other first that Freud no longer uses hypnotism to eliminate symptoms as in the early experimental cathartic method since hypnotism obliterates the potential for establishing a between of responsible relatedness which is the precondition for bringing out the good in the other, the way toward lasting relief from the sufferings of neurotic solipsism (Thompson 1994: 129). Freud continues that his new psychoanalytic method starts by putting the patient first – letting the patient 'choose the subject of the day's work'. It is on the basis of the surface of whatever comes to the other's attention at each moment that he is called upon to attend to, to affirm, accept, listen to, register, remember and in due course interpret when this becomes possible. Freud continues, 'on this plan everything that has to do with the clearing up of a particular symptom emerges piecemeal, woven into various contexts, and distributed over widely separated periods of time' (1977: 41). What does such a procedure resemble if not the Talmudic hermeneutic, the way in which the sages of the Talmud bleed the texts by juxtaposing those texts which have similar ethical significance next to each other to bring out the inner essential significance in its multidimensionality from each of the instances of the events that are cited. This is precisely what Freud attempts in regard to unpacking the multiple levels of interconnected meanings linked by interconnected chains of association to symptoms, dreams and everyday life events. For example Dora's symptom of choking links multiple instances past and present when she is choked up with anger – at her father, Mr K and Mrs K. This choking is also a choking on the sexually charged overtones inherent in her reactions of disgust linked in an indelible seriality of negative moments of overreactions toward those for whom she may have felt erotic stirrings or loving feelings. Freud's reading of Dora's first dream and her association to it is a classic example of a multidimensional hermeneutic which brings forth the overdetermined significance of each of the dream elements – e.g. the house on fire, her father, the bed, the jewel-case, being awakened, escaping the room in the context of her desire and her ambivalence. Re-enacting the prototypical gestures embodied in the dream moments and her posture in them and tying this up with her associations to life events that these moments 'brought to mind' enabled Freud to unravel the threads of the twisted knots of her love and hate for others into which Dora was tied and which her symptoms reflected.

Finally Freud tells us that he has not as a rule reproduced the process of interpretation, to which the patient's associations and communication had to be subjected, but only the results of that process (1977: 41). This means that we have to conjecture the way in which Freud performs psychoanalysis. I argue that he approaches his patients in this case Dora in a Levinasian ethical manner. This means that he initiates and orchestrates the analytic ritual through his responsible obligation, through his surrender and unconditional acceptance of Dora. Freud does not adopt a maieutic method in order to bring Dora out of her self toward a kind of self realisation as in self actualizing approaches to therapy. Rather he showers her with a loving attention so that she might free herself from the spell of self absorption and come to respond to him, to an other and through him to others in a fuller and more fulfilling way despite her anger and inability to forgive. The Talmudic precepts of accepting and doing before knowing, forgiveness, uprightness and responsibility putting the other first, are at the heart of Freud's daily practice with Dora. Each and every moment of his analysis is an invitation to her to accept his welcome. Each interpretation is a provocation to be touched and touch the other, to meet the other face to face in proximity and intimacy.

The Dora case as Freud presents it is a testament to the skill of his therapeutic intervention for it shows to what degree this closed and angry abused young lady was for the time of therapy able to tell her story and in its telling find temporary relief from the suffering of her isolation. She learned that it was possible to turn toward rather than away from her fellow man. In the end Freud's analysis of Dora proved abortive since he failed to turn her permanently around toward an ethical and responsible way of being with others. She could not forgive perhaps because the significant others in her life, her father, Mr and Mrs K never owned up and admitted the degree of their betrayal and offence to her. Ethical psychoanalysis can only rehearse ethical and responsible relatedness it cannot institute justice in everyday life and life lived ethically is after all the best therapy.

Conclusion: I have tried to present a glimpse of the way in which Freudian psychoanalysis is founded on the same Talmudic sources as Levinasian ethics and have proposed that psychoanalysis is therapeutic to the degree to which it is practised as the art of responsible relatedness.

BIBLIOGRAPHY

Derrida, J. (1978) *Writing and Difference*, London: Routledge and Kegan Paul.
—— (1995) *Points –: Interviews 1974–1994*, ed. E. Weber, Stanford, Calif.: Stanford University Press.
Freud, S. (1977) *Case Histories I*, Harmondsworth: Pelican Freud Library.
Heidegger, M. (1975) *Early Greek Thinking*, San Francisco: Harper and Row.
Levinas, E. (1990) *Nine Talmudic Readings*, Bloomington, Ill.: Indiana University Press.
Thompson, G. (1994) *The Truth about Freud's Technique: the Encounter with the Real*, New York: New York University Press.

Chapter 4

Shadowing Ethics
Levinas's View of Art and Aesthetics

Seán Hand
London Guildhall University

Great art, conceived unapologetically in European canonic
terms, occupies a crucial place in Levinas's philosophy. We are
as likely to encounter the texts of Dostoyevsky or Shakespeare,
Agnon or Grossman, as those of Plato or Kant, in Levinas's
philosophical examples and analogies. Nor are the artistic
characters or dilemmas a mere *illustration* of philosophical
concepts or principles; on the contrary, for Levinas they are the
necessary dramatization of ethical being which has become
elsewhere fatally compromised and reduced in the philosophical
process of the comprehension of Being. They operate then as the
ethical shadow within ontological language, as an aesthetic of
the face-to-face relation otherwise threatened with suppression
in the work of the metaphysician.

This surpassing of a merely illustrative status reaches perhaps
its apogée in the very nature of Levinas's two most ambitious
philosophical works, the 1961 *Totality and Infinity* and the
1974 *Otherwise than Being or Beyond Essence*. Here concern
with form and language respectively test the limits of
philosophical reduction. Levinas's approach in the former text
prompted Derrida to comment, in a footnote to *Violence and
Metaphysics*, that Levinas's writing *qua* writing is one 'in which
stylistic gestures (especially in *Totality and Infinity*) can less
than ever be distinguished from intention', and that it 'forbids

the prosaic disembodiment into conceptual frameworks that is the first violence of all commentary'. Later, Derrida comments of the thematic development in the work that it 'is neither purely descriptive nor purely deductive. It proceeds with the infinite insistence of waves on a beach: return and repetition, always, of the same wave against the same shore, in which, however, as each return recapitulates itself, it also infinitely renews and enriches itself. Because of all these challenges to the commentator and the critic, *Totality and Infinity* is a work of art and not a treatise' (Derrida 1978: 312). *Otherwise than Being* can be said to go even further. Recognizing that *Totality and Infinity* was still responding to the self/other duality and the intellectual structure of intentionality, *Otherwise than Being* begins with the situation of saying, which involves direct sensuous contact. It moves, if you like, from a philosophical language of voluptuosity to a voluptuous language of philosophy, employing a deliberately excessive language of the body which acts both as a 'denuding of denuding' and as a scandalously artistic dethematization of the philosophical said.

Given this artistic or aesthetic undoing of ontological totalization in the service of the reintroduction of ethical non-finitude into philosophy, it is all the more astonishing that when one turns to look Levinas's actual comments on art or aesthetics, they appear on first reading to be governed by a negative approach, a determination to react disapprovingly to an existence that is expressed or justified in an artistic or aesthetic manner. This is not due, moreover, to a mere separation of interests, for the critical attitude exists in the key works we have just mentioned. Though Levinas's philosophical logic came to test the limits of the philosophical image, then, the most far-reaching text of this tendency, *Otherwise than Being*, still employs negative judgements of the art-image. In exposing the amphibology of Being and being, for example, Levinas declares there that '[a]rt is the pre-eminent exhibition [*ostension*] in which the said is reduced to a pure theme, to absolute exposition, even to shamelessness capable of holding all looks for which it is exclusively destined. The said is reduced to the Beautiful, which supports Western ontology' (Levinas 1981: 40). The true complexity of this typical judgement lies in its self-contradictory nature. Here, the particular use of the peculiar term *ostension*, with its obvious allusion to the monstrance of the Catholic mass, allows Levinas to associate the art-image not only with the beguiling subjugation of the masses conducted by the artistic arm of the totalized society, but also with those religions which, in their idolatry or mystical spectacle, preserve a paganism and even (sexual) amoralism. Such a complex of associations recurs stubbornly throughout his work, as in, for example, the essays in *Difficult Freedom*, and is employed most powerfully whenever Levinas seeks to suggest the nature of totalitarian society, especially Nazism, or, increasingly, to expose the implications of Heideggerianism.[1] But already in this one example we can see how Levinas's censure of the art-image depends upon all those qualities associated with the image itself. For he has himself thematized and fetishized what he points to as thematization and fetishization. What might otherwise be presented in all its discursive or visual open-endedness has itself been exclusively offered up as an image to our fixated if disapproving gaze. It is not excessive to react by saying that Levinas's own gesture, which is designed to support a sapping of Western ontology, falls short of ethics into easy moralism, and should be censured by us all the more for the way in which it proceeds by way of the poetically generated abeyance of vigilance which it allows itself to criticize. It is certainly ironic that, in the same context of the critique of apophanisis, Levinas goes on to comment that art produces nothing but itself ('In painting, red reddens and green greens') and that 'it does so in isolation: every work of art is in this sense exotic, without a world, essence in dissemination' (Levinas 1981: 40–1). For we could well argue that Levinas himself has produced a self-fulfilling moralism dependant upon a dangerously exotic and ostentatious image of the beautiful in art and, by implication, in the shamelessness of Catholicism at its most baroque. His own essentializing in itself discourages consideration of the exposure, or 'call for exegesis' (Levinas 1981: 41), of thematization, commodification, reification or alienation by the committed exposition of the art-image, or of the representation and enactment of self-dereliction and the sacrificial *ekstasis* of becoming the other by the elevation of the host, pronunciation of the epiclesis and transubstantiation.

We can see from our one example, none the less, that Derrida is absolutely right to suggest that it is through artistic or aesthetic practice, such as repetition and resonance, that Levinas tries to work philosophical language and conceptualization to the point where it can escape the closure of ontological finality and open up to ethical infinitude. Given the paradoxical situation that Levinas exploits to very considerable effect in his work what he appears to regard so negatively in art, we obviously need to look specifically at Levinas's writings on the subject of art and aesthetics.[2] In doing this, I feel it will be useful to look also, albeit briefly, at the aesthetic theories of certain other critics, such as Sartre, Benjamin and Adorno, when they are concerned with the same subject matter, in a limited attempt to elucidate the seeming contradictions of Levinas's position.

The obvious place from which to begin is the essay entitled 'Reality and its Shadow' (Levinas 1989: 130–43). This post-war application of ethical responsibility to the field of aesthetics was published in Sartre's *Les Temps Modernes* in 1948, that is, in the issue after that which saw the publication of 'Black Orpheus', Sartre's essay-long introduction to the poetry of Negritude, and in the year after Sartre's *What is Literature?*.[3] Its premise is therefore the existentialist desire to regard art or an aesthetic pursuit as being the manifestation of a general, indeed revolutionary, transformation of society. Such a gratification would lead, in Sartre's words at the end of 'Black Orpheus', to the unique emergence from the same source of 'the most authentic revolutionary project and the purest poetry' (Sartre 1948a: 606). Levinas's essay opens with the postulation that art seems essential (or the apprehension of essence), whereas criticism seems parasitic. The artwork is complete, whereas criticism is necessarily incomplete. But it is just such a difference which leads Levinas to denounce art. For the completion of the artwork in his view arises from and confirms its essential disengagement from social or material causes (here the 'œuvre dégagée' already contradicts 'l'art engagé'), a disengagement that is not a surpassing of the world (into a Platonic realm) but a falling short. The former would be part of understanding and communication, the latter encourages or permits only evasion, enter-tainment, captivation. Above all, Levinas suggests that art not only thwarts by its nature a discursive or social attempt to understand and to communicate with ideas, but actively promotes a pact with obscurity: 'Does not the function of art lie in not understanding? Does not obscurity provide it with its very element and a completion sui generis, foreign to dialectics and the life of ideas? Will we then say that the artist knows and expresses the very obscurity of the real?' (Levinas 1989: 131). This formulation reorients a Sartrean designation of non-committed art in the rather Gothic direction of a magical and diabolical practice that resists enlightened reason. For Levinas, the essential problem centres on the replacement of a concept with an image, of intellection with passivity. 'Image' here indicates the aesthetic opposite of intellectual grasping. 'An image does not engender a *conception*, as do scientific cognition and truth [. . .]. An image marks a hold over us rather than our initiative, a fundamental passivity' (Levinas 1989: 132). As such, it is related in Levinas's language to rhythm, magic, incantation, possession, a doping of the senses. This voiding of self, the opposite of the emergence of 'conscience', abandons the freedom and density of being-in-the-world for the self-exteriority that places the subject 'among things as a thing, as part of the spectacle' (Levinas, 1989: 133). Levinas also obviously dislikes the paganistic and fascistic overtones of this ecstasy which encourages collective participation rather than individual power, and captivation rather than conceptualiza-tion. Reality, then, is disincarnated by the image or the inducement to immerse oneself in a rythmic relation. This is a further, oblique, rejoinder to Sartre whose *L'Imagination* in Levinas's view presented intentionality travelling with apparent transparency through the image to the object. The image's opacity casts the shadow of a disincarnating double over reality. The existence with concepts that is being-in-the-world is seduced by art and aesthetics, then, the former 'substituting an image for being', the latter stunning intellection with sensation (Levinas 1989: 134). The result for Levinas is the degradation of the absolute or the Platonic world, the reduction of being and disclosure into reality and its resemblance:

> Resemblance is not a participation of a being in an idea [. . .]; it is the very structure of the sensible as such. The sensible is being insofar as it resembles itself, insofar as, outside of its triumphal work of being, it casts a shadow, emits that obscure and elusive essence, that phantom essence which cannot be identified with the essence revealed in truth. There is not first an image – a neutralized vision of the object – which then differs from a sign or symbol because of its resemblance with the original; the neutralization of position in an image is exactly this resemblance. (Levinas 1989: 137).

At this point Levinas gives the example of 'all of Giraudoux's work' which 'effects a casting of reality into images, with a consistency which has not been fully appreciated, despite all Giraudoux's glory' (Levinas 1989: 137). There are at least two reasons why Levinas should give such a singular example of idolatry in art. In the first place, the reference is yet another coded disagreement with Sartre. The latter's review, in *Situations I*,[4] of Giraudoux's Aristotelian 'substantial forms' (Sartre 1947: 84) had recognized how one is possessed by a form in Giraudoux, how his fictional world is 'controlled by the laws of magic or rather alchemy' (Sartre 1947: 90), how character and essence, human potential and nature's determinism are obscurely combined (Sartre 1947: 94). In Sartre's view, such fixed archetypes and concepts represented a false or limited freedom sustained by the illusory reward of happiness on this earth (Sartre 1947: 96). Levinas would be similarly critical of any such 'pagan eudaemonism' and lack of temporal becoming.

But Sartre went on to characterize this art as being precisely the product and the representation of a set 'ethic', the bourgeois idea that 'each man is responsable for universal harmony' (Sartre 1947: 95), this derisory 'humanism' (Sartre 1947: 96) being interiorized by each individual as a moral 'revelation' (Sartre, 1947: 97), when in fact it is nothing but 'the illusion produced by false recognition' (Sartre 1947: 98) and a bourgeois and capitalist evasion. It is obvious that Levinas wishes to undo Sartre's conflation of art as alchemy or mysticism with humanist ethics, and of the idea of evasion with moral responsibility. Levinas therefore uses all the terms employed by Sartre in his essay on Giraudoux, but redeploys them in order to be more absolute, in both his support of the revelation of responsibility that for Levinas is the opposite of fate, and in his criticism of the essentially unethical, even diabolical, nature of art as magic. As he puts it bluntly in his conclusion: 'art, essentially disengaged, constitutes, in a world of initiative and responsibility, a dimension of evasion' (Levinas 1989: 141). The second reason why Levinas focusses on the example of Giraudoux, though, brings him closer to Sartre again, since both are concerned with a specific socio-political context. Giraudoux's work, well-known for its fascination with German culture, had been positively reviewed by the fascist journal *Je Suis Partout* and praised by the fascist writer Brasillach.[5] The writer himself, having been a propaganda minister in the Daladier government, had sought a position in the Vichy régime and had continued to dine with German officers during the Occupation. Above all, he had written typically witty and entertaining pieces, such as *L'Apollon de Bellac* and *La Folle de Chaillot*, during that time. In recalling Giraudoux at this point, therefore, Levinas is attacking the doubly unethical position of artistic enjoyment (which seeks to grasp nothing) in a time of war and its aftermath, when responsible and vigilant demythologizing most urgently needs to take place. This leads him to a strong sense of quasi-Sartrean language as he denounces the myth-inspired suspension of present and future tasks to be found in Giraudoux's plays:

'There is something wicked and egoist and cowardly [*lâche*] in artistic enjoyment [*jouissance*]. There are times when one can be ashamed of it, as of feasting during a plague [*peste*]' (Levinas 1989: 142). When this happens, 'the poet exiles himself from the city', for he has offered an 'appeasement' (Levinas 1989: 141). This reference to the ethical grasping of a particular time rather than the aesthetic appeasement of a plague also predicts a specific Heideggerian context, but it indicates in general here that Levinas views the artistic image as the reduction of life's dimensions to those of an instant, 'congealing the power of freedom into impotence' (Levinas 1989: 139), petrifying humanity and transforming time into the rhythm of fate. All these terms do sound highly Sartrean – except that Levinas calls this frozen interval of the image a 'situation', and then adds his own religious perspective: 'The proscription of images is truly the supreme command of monotheism, a doctrine that over-comes fate, that creation and revelation in reverse.' (Levinas 1989: 141) For Levinas, then, art cannot be committed, by virtue of being art. Criticism, on the other hand, can detach art from its irresponsibility, by envisaging its technique. Such vigilant exegesis helps to separate myth from real being and is, pointedly, 'the true fatherland of the mind' (Levinas 1989: 142).

The pre-emptive introduction to the piece notoriously inserted by the committee of *Les Temps modernes* confines itself to stating that Sartre had already noted the magical or fascinating nature of the image (in *L'Imaginaire*) and the fact that painting and poetry operate beneath the level of a concept (in *Situations II*), that Sartre is therefore both more optimistic than Levinas (since Sartre believes art can liberate itself) and pessimistic (since he believes that philosophical action or expression is not immune to this disengagement or 'mini hell of literary eternity' – this last phrase being taken from 'M. Blanchot'). This otherwise reasonable rejoinder leaves aside altogether the theological angle, while it registers in silence a tense irritation that arises perhaps from the recognition that Levinas has offered a reinvestment of the most negative features of the existential world-view (ethics, the *ratification* of freedom rather than its inhibition) which has seemed somehow to end up being *more* politically demanding! The most significant charge, though, which the preface does seek to make is that, for all Levinas's recasting of Sartrean language, he has not really discussed the *philosophical* image. Given our own particular form of enquiry here, we can add how this evasion shows up in the series of *non-philosophical* images which Levinas is happy to use precisely in order to castigate the world they represent. Thus we read that the most lucid writer can become 'bewitched', fall into 'a world of shadows', and become 'bloodless and awkward' [*exsangue et maladroit*]. He 'speaks in enigmas, by allusions, by suggestion, in equivocations', he wavers, he lacks 'the force to rouse realities' (Levinas 1989: 142). When Levinas contrasts this with a concept of concept as 'the muscle of the mind', we observe clearly the gendering of Levinas's ethical landscape. Whether influenced philosophically by Sartre's or Heidegger's virile presentation of authenticity, or socially by the thirties' intellectual concern with France's apparent 'devirilization', or more intimately by traditional sexual roles, Levinas paints critical vigilance and the land of the mind as being implicitly male, the source of the lucid writer's downfall as a bewitching and dissembling temptress, and the character of the fallen critic as stereotypically feminized. Once again, as in the essentialization of certain religious practices (where sexual personification was equally present), we can see that Levinas relies on an artistic or aesthetic dimension which can be denounced as idolatrous or shameful in order to create the necessary shadow for the foregrounding of an ethical rigour.

The general view of the art-image as propounded in 'Reality and its Shadow' is disseminated throughout a series of specific readings during this period. A typical example, and one which allows us to introduce other critical visions as context, is the 1947 'The Other in Proust' (Levinas 1989: 161–5). Levinas begins with a double dismissal: he discredits a number of past images of the writer by associating them with the violent, reductive or paganistic antithesis of ethical exigency all of which could be characterized as diabolical or simply evil. Thus Proust the recreator of time, who was 'a wizard of inexpressible rhythm' is associated with 'those readers who, around 1933, became attracted to the literature of action, heroism and the soil, and so began to forget him' (Levinas 1989: 161. Levinas also recalls at this point Sartre's 'harsh judgement' of the mechanical and superficial nature of Proust's supposedly profound psychological insights). Proust the sociologist, meanwhile, who seemingly analyzed 'what was frozen in history [and] more concrete than reality itself' was perhaps trapped ambiguously by the very object that stood as his theme, and thus sealed within 'the rhythm', 'spells', 'incantation' and 'charm' through which he thought to diagnose the 'magical' appearance of reality (Levinas 1989: 161–2). This ambiguity is itself ambiguously described as Proust's 'amorality', for the lack of final definition of a state or act in Proust, the way in which 'acts are shadowed by unpredictable "counter-acts", and things by "counter-things"' (Levinas 1989: 162), confers a dizzying sense of freedom on the creative process, but also opens up 'the infinity of what [appearances] exclude' (ibid.). The glittering magic that seemingly begins 'where ethics leave off' (Levinas 1989: 162) is thus ultimately outstripped by the way in which, as reality is seen to exceed its definition, 'the self takes possession of self' in a moment that realizes alterity. It is this realization that saves the Proustian task for Levinas. The move from image to concept necessary to maintain ethical vigilance occurs when the self in Proust is 'doubled by another self' (Levinas 1989: 163). *This* is the mystery in Proust, a 'strangeness of self to self' or 'dialogue in the self with the other' constituting the real 'event' and the real 'grasping'. This is a different social reality, not one of mores but of 'the fundamental strangeness that mocks knowledge' (Levinas 1989: 163). Through the 'nothingness of Albertine' there is discovered total alterity. Once again in contestation of the existential being-unto-death, Levinas states: 'Mere death is the death of the Other, contrary to the view of contemporary philosophy which remains attached to the self's solitary death.' (Levinas 1989: 164) And it is exactly this death which for

Levinas overcomes incommunicable solitude, for it nurtures love. What he means is that authentic being is here no longer to be associated with the drive for unity, for knowledge, for the abolition of the Other's proximity. Nor can it be associated with 'the pathos of socialism' (Levinas 1989: 164) whose concepts of universal brotherhood and common enemy are also predicated on the abolition of otherness. Instead, it is the impossibility of grasping or possessing whatever is Albertine which Proust's 'poetry' powerfully and hopefully communicates. The ethics of Proust's apparent aestheticism, then, is that his work situates reality 'in a relation with something which for ever remains other, with the Other as absence and mystery, in rediscovering this relation in the very intimacy of the "I"' (Levinas 1989: 165).

A fascinating contrast is provided at this point by Benjamin's 1929 essay on 'The image in Proust' (Benjamin, W. 1973: 197–211). Both writers display an ambivalence towards the aesthetics of modernity subtended by *Bilderverbot*, and their readings, though differing, begin with shared concerns and expressions. For Benjamin, the image *of* Proust produced by the work is an 'unconstruable synthesis' (Benjamin 1973: 197) of mysticism, art and scholarship, just as its structure and syntax overflow and transcend. Its exemplary status is dependent on a surpassing achievement in both senses. Similarly its remembered event (as opposed to an experienced one) is infinite, as is its vigilant process of striving to recollect what in each day, like Penelope's work, is forgotten or undone. Yet all of this for Benjamin is determined by a 'frenzied quest for happiness', a 'paralyzing, explosive will' (Benjamin 1973: 199) which leaves him everywhere 'frenetically studying resemblances', desperately finding similarities (Benjamin, 1973: 200). He is 'homesick' for the world behind resemblance, eternally curious for the image. Hence the vegetative existence of his characters, intertwined in fate, and his obsession with curiosity and flattery, twin social manifestations of a need to *copy*. This in turn predicts the essential loneliness of the subject in Proust: he is directive, not touching, with a syntax therefore based on the rhythm not of an encounter with the Other but of his fear of suffocation and death (Benjamin 1973: 209). As a result, 'his sentences are the entire muscular activity of the intelligible body' (Benjamin 1973: 210).

The double structure of nostalgia and messianism, intimate inhabitation and tangential estrangement, which informs Benjamin's reading here, and which is represented elsewhere by Baudelaire's *flâneur* or Klee's *Angelus Novus*, echoes the duality of act and shadowy counter-act which maintains Levinas's ethics of ethics. Benjamin stresses the infinity at the heart of Proust's text, since 'a remembered event is infinite' (Benjamin 1973: 198) and the text's unity is constructed out of the pure act of recollection. At the same time, given Benjamin's desire to see in the structure of a constellation the authentic politico-aesthetic response to totalization, he points to the 'explosive' power of Proust's critique of society, in which superficial images are 'smashed to pieces'. According to Benjamin, Proust uses the aesthetics of belonging (comedy, mimicry, curiosity) to expose the aesthetics of belonging (sexual, familial and professional). Thus his 'analysis of snobbery' is 'far more important than his apotheosis of art', since 'the attitude of the snob is nothing but the consistent, organized, steely view of life from the chemically pure standpoint of the consumer' (Benjamin 1973: 205). In other words, as snobbery is the bourgeois aesthetic of totality, Proust's textual analysis of it becomes not just a political production (though Benjamin argues it also acted as a veil for the mystery of economic reality) but equally an ethical shattering of totality, and hence of resemblance. The resistance to totalization in Benjamin that takes the form of a constellatory refashioning of subject-object relations and of a prophetic focussing on the 'chips of Messianic time' (Benjamin 1973: 252–5) with which the present is flecked, thus seems remarkably sympathetic to Levinas's concerns.

Ironically, however, it is precisely because of Benjamin's aesthetic resistance to totality that, to a Levinasian reading, he remains tragically captivated. The same structure of nostalgia and messianism which leads Benjamin to view the text's unity as impossible encourages a fixation on the ultimately pointless structure of parataxis, the magical multivalence of the image, the passive corporeality of the *mémoire involontaire*, the asthmatic domination of syntax. A reaction in keeping with Levinas's uncompromising approach to the place and problem of aesthetics might conclude that the power of malady, that is the symbiosis and complicity between the body of the writer and the body of the work, is the weakness within Benjamin's vision which he here presents as the strength behind Proust's creation. It is a weakness of realization which – in contrast to Levinas's schematism – shows up as an ambivalent lingering over the personae or part-objects that confirm the withering of the aura in an age of alienation[6]: the occultish and fetishistic clouding of dialectical vision; the consoling cultivation of free-floating or miniaturist meaning. My breath, my pen, my bath: this aesthetic salvation is as psychogenic to Benjamin as it is to Proust. As a result, this knowing and inextricable involvement with commodification produces for Benjamin a spell-binding self-estrangement which tragically is recognized as obliterating a real relation with the Other (Benjamin 1973: 224) and to which one can react only with a weak political protest (Benjamin 1973: 235) that is inflected ambiguously by the *jouissance* of mourning and its tendency to silence (Benjamin 1979: 121).

Many of these complex compromises evoke in turn the aesthetics of Adorno, for whom the concept of constellation was equally important in an age of totalization. Adorno's view of true art – surveyed from the point of the crisis in modernism – is that of a formal expression which can only exist at odds with itself. As a body of work it can validate its metaphysical significance only by way of suffering. The underlying structure of this view, which is that of a lost unity dependant on its agonies of non-identity, has led critics to present Adorno as a protodeconstructionist[7] (for all his unacceptably theological reference to truth); his negative dialectics more properly, however, bring him close to the attempts at non-totalizing conceptualization in Benjamin and Levinas. Thus, for example,

Adorno's well-known remark near the beginning of *Aesthetic Theory* that 'art may be the only remaining medium of truth in an age of incomprehensible terror and suffering. As the real world grows dark, the irrationality of art is becoming rational, especially at a time when art is radically tenebrous itself' (Adorno 1984: 27), strikes a strong chord with Levinas's warning against the celebration of irrationalism, even if Adorno is specifically recommending an art that resolutely pursues its knowledge of self-contradiction and hence must give expression to what cannot be rationalized. (Adorno's example for the worth of this expression is, after all, the suffering that took place under Hitler which in postwar Germany has remained largely 'mute and inconsequential' [Adorno 1984: 27]; from this point of view, Levinas's *Otherwise than Being* is designed to be just such an expression.[8]) The aporia of the authentic art-work as read by Adorno could be called the ethics of irony; as such its entry into the dangerous world of delusion, commodification, *Entkunstung*, in the hope of preserving the true subversion of rational (even patrician) ends, resembles to a degree Levinas's admittance into his ethics of the rhetorical, visual and conceptual lures of an art or metaphysics that totalizes experience. But there are also major differences. Adorno paradoxically champions the autonomy of modernism as the one means of remaining resistant to reification (Adorno 1984: 321); for Levinas, as we have seen, such *dégagement* is dangerously consoling. The promissory nature of art for Adorno inevitably involves it in a dialectic with obscurity and negativity (Adorno 1984: 197); for Levinas, this is to don the tunic of Nessus (Levinas 1989: 120), to poison the desire for revelation with what cannot represent it (Levinas 1989: 132). For Adorno 'the spirit of art works attaches to their shape but also points beyond it' (Adorno 1984: 136); for Levinas, the dialectic of spiritualization in art falls inevitably into the dark night of primitivism and chaos.

Adorno's specific reading of Proust depends on these inherent tensions and dangerous compromises. The beginning of *A la recherche du temps perdu* is viewed as a furtive attempt to outwit illusion and posit immanence of forms (Adorno 1984: 150). In so doing, 'by forsaking all magic, Proust actualizes it' (Adorno 1984: 196). As a simultaneous instance and metaphysic of art, it is artfully drawn to the image of first nature, such as a hawthorn hedge, that resists its own rationalizations (Adorno 1984: 93); while being one of the latest examples of the modernist abstraction of heterogeneity (Adorno 1984: 214). It celebrates the ultimate truth of incommunicable intensity, as with Bergotte (Adorno 1984: 268); and of course not only expressed this idea, but learned its own autonomous truth through imitation of previous writers (Adorno 1984: 399). It transformed our vision and hence the very reality of objects (Adorno 1984: 418); and undercut the omniscience and hence reality of its objective presence (Adorno 1984: 465). These tensions between mimesis and form, sensuousness and sense, reconciliation and resistance, contrive to produce for Adorno the authentic antagonistic totality or alienated reality of the art-work. From Levinas's perspective, though, they carry the unacceptable danger of complicity in the totalization of history on the one hand (an effect of their eurocentrism and Spenglerist pessimism), and of the obfuscation of history on the other (an effect of their spiritualization of desubstantialization and implosion). As Levinas wrote of the suspended time of a statue in 'Reality and its Shadow', 'the power of freedom congeals to impotence' (Levinas 1989: 139). Comparing Levinas with Adorno thus peculiarly foregrounds the political priorities of the former's aesthetic theories, this being a belated and indirect rejoinder to *Les Temps Modernes*'s complaint that Levinas had not attended to the task of making real contact with the world to be faced by philosophical as well as by artistic expression. It makes Levinas seem a committed modernist in relation to Adorno's deconstruction.

A politically inflected comparison of this kind reaches a new pitch, however, once we introduce Heidegger's view of aesthetics, and his appeal to the poetic in his evocation of authentic being, into our evaluation of Levinas's aesthetic determinations. It is through this comparison in particular that

Levinas's strictures acquire an obvious logic and a tight frame of reference. Levinas's ethical refusal to endorse or permit the poetic expression of destiny, and the use of a malleable and uncritical or critically silent art to validate this interpretation and justification of history, can be shown to be a quite specific reading of Heidegger. A full explication of this goes beyond the limits of this essay, but a number of pointers can be offered. In his *Nietzsche* study, Heidegger transforms Kant's Doctrine of Beauty, claiming that the disinterested nature of aesthetic delight is propounded there in a merely 'preparatory and path-breaking way' (and that Nietzsche misinterprets Kant) (Heidegger 1981: 110), as a methodological prelude on the way to the disclosure that celebrates the essential relation of the human subject to the perceived object. Hence, 'in order to find something beautiful', Heidegger says, 'we must let what encounters us, purely as it is in itself, come before us in its own stature and worth' (Heidegger 1981: 109). Aesthetics depends then on passivity or disclosure and on *Befindlichkeit*, man's state of feeling, great art being so because it reflects an absolute need for the absolute, and therefore an authentic mode of Being. The most famous art-image associated with this aesthetic vision is given in 'The Origin of the Work of Art' where in the shoes painted by Van Gogh there supposedly 'vibrates the silent call of the earth, its quiet gift of the ripening grain'. These shoes, which become 'equipment', a tool to hand, belong 'to the *earth*'. Art, then, discloses belonging, bringing temporal and sacral *conscience* to an aesthetics of the 'home-land' (Heidegger 1975: 32). It is in this sense of the ambiguous, even duplicitous relation of *conscience* to homeland that we can trace the evolution of Heidegger's readings of Hölderlin, at least via three pieces running from 1936 to 1951 which betray a circularity related to the moment of their production. In the first of these, 'Hölderlin and the essence of poetry', language is isolated as the precondition for history, the event [*Ereignis*] that prevails over the highest possibility of human beings and the *Augenblick* or originating time of thought (Heidegger 1944: 39–41). This preeminently linguistic sense of place is transformed by the later addition of a 1943 preface whose title is derived from a Hölderlin poem, 'Heimkunft: An die Verwandten', where the poet's intermediary position between Volk and Gods is now presented more dialogically, collectively and forcefully as a sacral act designed to reintroduce the 'holy names' into a bonding language, such that all poems are now 'poems of homecoming' (*Heimkunft*) and 'a return to the vicinity of the origin'. This homecoming and origin are specifically German, and are obviously futural now not merely in an existential sense but also in an aggressively nationalistic way: 'this homecoming is the future of the historical being of the German people' (Heidegger 1944: 21–8). Finally, in post-war work such as the 1951 'Poetically Man Dwells', there is an attempt to re-emphasize how homeland is the metaphysical sense of nearness to being, and perhaps to play down the historical specifications given to it opportunistically during the intervening period. Thus a subtle shift in, and use of, *Zwiesprache* places emphasis once more on the transumption of homelessness provided by *language*. So 'it is language that speaks' (Heidegger 1975: 216) and humans speak in reply to language's appeal. The 'dwelling of mortals' is therefore 'poetic' (Heidegger 1975: 217), and it is in poetry that 'there takes place what all measuring is in the ground of its being' (Heidegger 1975: 221). The emergence of a deliberately vague yet resonant appeal to a nationalism, wherein language and landscape provide the context for the establishment of a real blood bond, is replaced once more by the abstract metaphysics of a 'poetic saying of images [which] gather the brightness and sound of the heavenly appearances into one with the darkness and silence of what is alien' (Heidegger 1975: 226). Yet the evolution of these aesthetic justifications has exposed the violence towards the Other already inherent in this visceral sense and poetic expression of metaphysical being. As early as 1935, after all, in the (in)famous remark made in the first section of *An Introduction to Metaphysics*, delivered originally in the summer of 1935, we can observe how the language of metaphysics supposedly overturned in *Being and Time* was rehabilitated in the service of an emotive evocation of a new German politics:

> [I]t is the most metaphysical of nations. We are certain of this vocation, but our people will only be able to wrest a destiny from it if *within itself* it creates a resonance, a possibility of resonance for this vocation, and takes a creative view of its tradition. All this implies that this nation, as a historical nation, must move itself and thereby the history of the West beyond the centre of their future "happening" and into the primordial realm of the powers of being. If the great decision regarding Europe is not to bring annihilation, that decision must be made in terms of new spiritual energies unfolding historically from out of the centre. (Heidegger 1959: 38–9).

We can see in these brief indications that Levinas's philosophical language and his containment of the unethical art-image both spring from a specific concern to contest the presentation and use of 'art [as] disclosure of the being of the essent' (Heidegger 1959: 132), that is, the aesthetic celebration of a violent or triumphalist belonging. The textual result of the subjugation of ethics to the aesthetics of belonging in Heidegger obviously dictates both Levinas's specific references in 'Reality and its Shadow' to 'evil powers', 'appeasement', 'evasion', 'idols', 'myth [taking] the place of mystery' and 'that fate refractory to the will of the pagan gods, stronger than the rational necessity of natural laws' (Levinas 1989: 138), and his more general denunciation of the hypnosis or rapture induced by the art-image. It also makes logical the co-existence of this stern view with the simultaneous elaboration in his own philosophy of an audacious art-language which is developed with the specific and difficult aim of installing ethics as first philosophy while yet resisting the Heideggerian move of sacralizing a return to the 'new beginning' of a 'historical-spiritual existence', a move instigated and blurred by celebrating in an aesthetic manner those 'spiritual energies' through which 'the beginning must be begun again, more radically, with all the strangeness, darkness, insecurity that attend a true beginning' (Heidegger 1959: 39).

Given the narrow amount of room for negotiation which Levinas has left himself with this double resistance, it becomes particularly interesting to look finally at the kind of art Levinas is prepared to praise, and the terms of such approval. Two contemporary visual artists spring immediately to mind. The first is Jean Atlan (1913–62), a student of philosophy born in Constantine, Algeria, imprisoned by the Nazis, and influenced by the Bible, the Talmud, Berber folklore and the landscapes of North Africa.[9] The second is Sasha Sosno (1937–), born in Marseilles of Latvian/Estonian provenance, and associated with the so-called École de Nice.[10] It needs to be stated baldly that both of these artists are Jewish, and that Levinas undeniably appreciates the particular resonances which this sets up in their work. Beyond this, though, it is interesting to speculate on the degree to which this privilege has allowed these art-works to force a softening of Levinas's philosophical reaction to the art-image's relation to nature and destiny. In a 1986 article, Levinas acknowledges the fundamental rhythmical dimension of Atlan's work, its interplay of figurative and non-figurative elements, of colour and form.[11] In Levinas's words, through the brush Atlan tries to seize 'the diachrony of rhythm or the beat of temporality' that resists synthesis and reduction. This rhythm can apparently be praised here since in Atlan it exemplifies the authentic tension operating between despair and hope, one experienced as 'a struggle that is as dramatic as the unveiling of the True and the imperative exigency of the Good' (Levinas 1991: 509). Yet Levinas still feels obliged to conclude with a reminder of questions once put more forcefully: 'And yet it is not proscribed to wonder whether the analysis of the consciousness of rhythm beating beneath the spread-out painted surface and the analysis of this mysterious life is in any position to suggest to philosophical reflexion the idea of an access to being that goes to things themselves.' Levinas resolves this doubt by viewing the supposed non-concupiscent eroticism of Atlan's non-formal painting as akin to a revelation of 'the interiority of being'. As such, it exposes an identity 'more profound than that of the knowledge unveiled in truth' (Levinas 1991: 510). The tenderness and compassion which he feels are retained and celebrated in this exposure remind him of the Bible. This is literally Levinas's final word in the article.

This resolution of artistic ambiguity as the representation of faith's difficult freedom[12] does nothing, of course, to invalidate a number of different interpretations of the same canvasses. Jean Cassou's view of the same art, for example, stresses precisely those features which Levinas elsewhere most criticizes: rhythm, magic, fascination, a sacred form complete unto itself.[13] Cassou *praises* the fact that Atlan's works offer their own *ostension* as an imperious and incontestable display of sacred presence: 'Atlan's works are masterpieces, masterpieces which are precisely *configured* and which impose a regal presence [*évidence*]. They could not be other than what they are, and this existence is incontestable; their presence has a magical and fascinating effect' (Cassou, 1963). In a phrase ironically reminiscent of Heidegger's appeal to historical-spiritual existence, Cassou views Atlan's work as fundamentally composed of 'black rhythms [which] spread out across the canvas, sacralizing it and in this way making each one into a complete ballet and an image' (Cassou 1963). Moreover, Atlan himself endorsed this 'poetic dwelling' in the same year – 1948 – as the publication of 'Reality and its Shadow': 'in the same spirit in which Mallarmé advised the poet to yield 'the initiative to words', the 'non-figurative' painter will be the person who agrees to yield the initiative to form, colours and lights, without beginning from any preestablished subject'.[14] Atlan in fact goes out of his way to praise the animist and magical dimensions of this coincidence of form and affect. He continues: 'this is why I admire perhaps above all else the art of the Dogons, that of the Precolumbians and the ancient Assyrians'. And, speaking again of his own work, he concludes: 'if these forms which in appearance "mean" nothing, but which must nevertheless be charged with latent, if not manifest, content, manage to come alive, I shall have succeeded. It is this that constitutes the "magical" virtue that is often bestowed on the artistic enterprise'. Indeed, in a further ironic coincidence of dates, the spiritual inhabitation of the landscape evoked in Heidegger's *Introduction to Metaphysics*, published in Germany in 1953, finds an echo in other remarks made by Atlan in interviews conducted the same year. Atlan's description of the vocation of painting closely resembles that of Heidegger's poetic being, in that it is 'an adventure in which man grapples with formidable forces that are both inside and outside him, destiny, nature'.[15] In encountering this fundamental force, and submitting to it without any preconceived idea, the painter partakes of a 'common source', a rhythm which betokens 'something that transcends us totally'. Art is thus 'the necessity of establishing communication with these profound forces and of making others participate'.[16] Such an explicit approval of totemic expression, apocalyptic joy and primitivism[17] contrasts with Levinas's desire to interpret the diachronic rhythm of Atlan's work as a struggle with the angel. Here Levinas's insistence that Atlan's work represent the ethics of the image uncomfortably resembles the wilful 'not understanding' of which, in Levinas's eyes, the image itself is guilty. Moreover, Atlan's terms of reference seem so systematically to contradict those of the ethical unveiling which Levinas has placed on his canvasses as to suggest a forced harnessing of the art-image to a philosophy of spiritual energy. As a politico-aesthetic action, this is uneasily close to Heidegger's contrived poetic apology for a nationalist metaphysics; as a philosophico-aesthetic move, it seems to effect precisely that prosaic disembodiment into conceptual frameworks that Derrida had viewed, in contrast to Levinas's ethical vigilance, as the first violence of all commentary.

At first glance, the work of Sosno, in its sculptural concerns, its massive dimensions, and its marmoreal rigidity, provides a complete contrast to the intimate play and generous warmth of Atlan's paintings. After an early period in which Sosno produced black-and-white photographs, including self-portraits, where the contemporary subject was partially obliterated or effaced by superimposed blocks, arrows, lines and surfaces, he turned to stone and metal in order to fabricate, typically, a block of material wherein a classical head or body is partially visible. The work's force derives not only from its massive dimensions and solidity but also from the frozen moment of the human form, a form which may be viewed as deriving or evolving as well as emerging or escaping from the material. As a result, one could interpret this art as a powerful protest against dehumanization and commodification, including on a representational and institutional level, or, in complete contrast, as intimately, even fetishistically, involved with such reification.

Levinas's 1990 interview with Françoise Armengaud, entitled *De l'oblitération*, chooses to emphasize the ethical potentiality of Sosno's work. Softening his own image somewhat by claiming that he is suspicious of art's ability to produce critical quiescence but that he is not seeking to redeem it or to denounce its idolatry (Levinas, 1990b: 8), he specifies that the art-image can positively encourage a dis-inter-est or disengagement that generates a relation with the Other as more important than myself (Levinas, 1990b: 10). In this spirit, the evident obliterations in Sosno's art can be viewed as a denunciation of facile beauty, and a foregrounding of human oppression and exhaustion (*les usures de l'être*) (Levinas 1990b: 12) or of the existential self-obliterations of inauthentic existence (Levinas 1990b: 14). He credits the geometry of Sosno's sculptural forms for its ability to concretize the essentially unfinished nature of human life (Levinas, 1990b: 18) and hence the 'scandal' of the violence that threatens or destroys it. The violence of artistic obliteration inflicted by Sosno is therefore carried out as a compassionate expose of the violence of real obliteration. This is 'the opposite of the magical operations of art' and as such is the 'ethical moment' of art (Levinas 1990b: 22). Obliteration here invites, indeed forces, reaction and comment, breaks the spell of bewitchment and enthrallment inherent in Heidegger's and Valéry's view of art, and promotes sociality and being-for-the-other (Levinas 1990b: 28).

Once again, Levinas is highly selective in his choices and interpretations. He reads Sosno as an illustration of Nabokov's non-political reading of Gogol (Levinas 1990b: 16–8). He dismisses Sosno's partially obliterated photographic self-portrait for its thoughtless, abstract and narcissistic enjoyment of geometry (Levinas 1990b: 20) though the same geometry is then viewed as crucial to the sculpture's ability to suggest tragic mortality. He is wary of references to Kabbalism or the Zohar in order to enlighten the theme of secrecy in Sosno but links his own approval of the work's ethical appeal to 'the true religion' (Levinas 1990b: 26). These specific refusals betoken his wilful disregard for alternative theorizations. While Sosno himself recognizes an ethical dimension and a relation to the Other in his work (Valdman 1991: 176) and associates obliteration with an existential awakening of the spectator (Valdman 1991: 177), he also carefully emphasizes the physical nature of his work (its involvement with volume and mass) and its institutional context (its equal involvement with abstract painting, classical art and architecture). He also significantly refers to his activity as 'a game of hide-and-seek' (Valdman 1991: 176) and the spectator as a 'magician' (Valdman 1991: 177). Some of these approaches are developed by Michel Thévoz in his highly psychoanalytic reading of Sosno's presentation of the body. For Thévoz, the obsessive obliterations betoken a fetishistic involvement with the primal scene and its revelation of castration (Thévoz 1992: 13). The work's *fort-da* of presence and absence is evidence of a constitutive human want-to-be of which art is the transcendence (Thévoz 1992: 28). Ironically, Thévoz makes the Levinasian point that verbal language is so dominated by ontology that Sosno's 'negative hallucinations' are best presented by the plastic arts, and then in the most parodic fashion possible, that is, by opting for the most massive forms, the most classical materials and the most monumental dimensions (Thévoz 1992: 29). Sosno is therefore knowingly *abusing* the cultural stereotype of enlightened art (again, ironically, Thévoz cites Valéry at this point), *confronting* humanism with the techno-fascism and commodification now inhabiting its images, constructing a postscript to *Civilization and its Discontents* (Thévoz 1992: 32–3). His virtualization of the body and

monumental presentation of the body's traditional support
therefore represents a general parergonal strategy that is both
highly political and self-fulfilling, for in playing one ontological
register off against another it functions like an indecision-
making process (*un dispositif d'indécision*) (Thévoz 1992: 36).
This is the opposite of Levinas's concern, though it does sound
like the effect of Benjamin or Adorno at their most involved.
Sosno's work is less the ethics of ethics than the sculpture of
sculpture.

Levinas's silent obliteration of this and other alternative
readings is no doubt one more manifestation of his determined
resistance to both totalizing systems and somatic submission.
These apparently opposite attitudes come together for Levinas
in their common silencing of the Other by self-sufficiency. The
complex and sometimes contradictory positions to which
Levinas's denunciation of this silencing can lead, and which
we could abstract as the violence implied in the disymmetry of
justice, do not, of course, invalidate the ethical authenticity of
such a denunciation. Instead, what they indicate, logically, is
that the call to resist mystification and to offer exegesis in the
face of the beautiful cannot come from the position of
accomplished *Dasein*. It can only properly appeal to us through
the performance of prophetism, the apophanisis of ethics, the
ostension of *ostention*.

NOTES

1 See, for example, Levinas 1990a: 133–41; 231–4. Some of these
ideas are also present in the three essays on aspects of Paul
Claudel: 119–32. See also Levinas 1967: 169–71.
2 It is not always obvious what exactly constitutes art or aesthetics
for Levinas. Poetry, in particular, appears not to fall within the
category whereas prose does; in this Levinas's natural inclinations
appear to be the opposite to those of Sartre. Levinas states, for
example, at the end of his essay on Blanchot, 'The Servant and her
Master': 'the word poetry does not after all name a species whose
genus is referred to by the word art. Inseparable from speech (*le
verbe*), it overflows with prophetic meanings' (1989: 159). Poetry

is here synonymous with *le dire*, a 'saying' that remains open to the other, as opposed to *le dit*, the closed 'said' of ontological language. Elsewhere he defines poetry as 'true speech' which converts mortality into infinity and exists 'as an unforgettable modality of the *otherwise than being*' (Levinas 1976: 49–56; 52, 55, 56), and the poet as someone through whom space opens up and the word God emerges (1976: 73–75; 73, 74). In other words, poetry is exempt from Levinas's negative view of art (notwithstanding Heidegger's use of it, as we shall see) because he treats it as prayer.

3 Sartre 1948a: 577–606, reprinted in Sartre 1949: 229–86. Sartre 1948b.

4 'M. Jean Giraudoux et la philosophie d'Aristote. À propos de *Choix des Élues*' in Sartre 1947: 82–98.

5 For Sartre's immediate post-war reaction to collaboration, which mentions both *Je Suis Partout* and Brasillach (which he spells Brazillach), see Sartre 1949: 43–61. Given what I say later about the sexual metaphors implicit in both Levinas and Sartre, it is interesting, if chilling, to record Sartre's view that Fascism presented 'relations between France and Germany as a form of sexual union in which France plays the role of the woman. [. . .] Insofar as we can conceive of collaboration's state of mind, we perceive it as a climate of femininity. The collaborator speaks in the name of strength, but he is not strength: he is guile, the astuteness that leans on strength, he is even charm and seduction since he pretends to play on the attraction that French culture exerts, according to him, on the Germans. It seems to me that there is here a curious mixture of masochism and homosexuality. Parisian homosexual circles, moreover, provided many dazzling recruits' (1949: 58).

6 See 'The Work of Art in the Age of Mechanical Reproduction' in Benjamin 1973: 211–35.

7 For two diverging views here see Dews, P. 1989: 1–22, and Jay, M. 1984.

8 The famous epigraph of *Otherwise than Being* (1981: v) reads: 'To the memory of those who were closest among the six million assassinated by the National Socialists, and of the millions on millions of all confessions and all nations, victims of the same hatred and of the other man, the same anti-semitism'.

9 See, for example, the description of his 1958 canvas *Le Kahéna*, in Dorival, B. 1961: 268.

10 See, for example, the interview in Valdman, E. 1991: 173–9.

11 Levinas, M., 'Jean Atlan et la tension de l'art', in Chalier, C. and

Facing the other

M. Abensour (eds) (1991) *Emmanuel Levinas*, Paris: L'Herne: 509–10. First published in 1986, *Atlan, premières périodes 1940–54*, Nantes: Musée des Beaux-Arts: 19–21.

12 The version of *Difficile liberté* (1963; 1976) published in the Albin Michel 'Présences du judaïsme' series used Atlan's *Le Kahéna* as its cover illustration.

13 Cassou, J. 1963. See also Stein, G. 1964. Stein sees Atlan's art as fundamentally an abstract conception, and convincing for very that reason.

14 Atlan, J. 1948, 'Entretien avec Aimé Patri'. Extrait de *Paru*, mai 1948, no. 42. Quoted in Cassou, 1963.

15 Atlan, J. 1953, 'Réponse à une enquête sur le Réalisme Socialiste'. Extrait de *Preuves*, juillet, no. 29. Quoted in Cassou, 1963.

16 Atlan, J. 1953, 'Réponse à une enquête sur l'art abstrait'. Extrait de *Aujourd'hui*. Quoted in Cassou, 1960: 724.

17 See also Ragon, M. 1956: 145–52.

BIBLIOGRAPHY

Adorno, T. (1984) *Aesthetic Theory*, London: Routledge and Kegan Paul.
Benjamin, W. (1973) *Illuminations*, London: HarperCollins.
Benjamin, W. (1979) *One-Way Street and Other Writings*, London: NLB.
Cassou, J. (1960) *Panorama des Arts Plastiques Contemporains*, Paris: N.R.F. Le Point du jour.
—— (1963) 'Introduction', *Jean Atlan*, Paris: Musée National d'Art Moderne.
Chalier, C. and M. Abensour (eds) (1991) *Emmanuel Levinas*, Paris: L'Herne.
Derrida, J. (1978) *Writing and Difference*, London and Henley: Routledge and Kegan Paul.
Dews, P. (1989) 'Adorno, Poststructuralism and the critique of identity', in Andrew Benjamin (ed.) *The Problems of Modernity: Adorno and Benjamin*, London: Routledge: 1–22.
Dorival, B. (1961) *L'École de Paris au Musée National d'Art moderne*, Paris: A. Somogny.
Heidegger, M. (1944) *Erläuterungen zu Hölderlins Dichtung*, Frankfurt am Main: Klostermann.
Heidegger, M. (1959) *An Introduction to Metaphysics*, New Haven and London: Yale University Press.
Heidegger, M. (1975) *Poetry, Language, Thought*, New York: Harper and Row.

—— (1981) *Nietzsche: Volume One, The Will to Power*, London: Routledge and Kegan Paul.

Jay, M. (1984) *Adorno*, London: Fontana.

Levinas, E. (1967) [1949] *En découvrant l'existence avec Husserl et Heidegger*, Paris: Vrin.

—— (1969) *Totality and Infinity*, Pittsburgh, Duquesne University Press.

—— (1976) *Noms propres*, Montpellier: Fata Morgana.

—— (1981) *Otherwise than Being or Beyond Essence*,The Hague: Martinus Nijhoff.

—— (1989) *The Levinas Reader*, Oxford: Blackwell.

—— (1990a) *Difficult Freedom*, London: Athlone.

—— (1990b) *De l'oblitération*, Paris: Éditions de la Différence.

Ragon, M. (1956) *L'Aventure de l'Art abstrait*, Paris: Laffont.

Restany, P. and M. Thévoz (1992) *Sosno*, Paris: Éditions de la différence.

Sartre, J.-P. (1947) *Situations I*, Paris: Gallimard.

—— (1948a) 'Orphée noir', in *Les Temps modernes*, 37: 577–606.

—— (1948b) *Situations II*, Paris: Gallimard.

—— (1949) *Situations III*, Paris: Gallimard.

Stein, G. (1964) 'Jean Atlan: Abstract Painting' *Yale French Studies*, 35: 118.

Thévoz, M. (1992) 'Présence – Absence', in Restany (1992): 13–37.

Valdman, E. (1991) *Le Roman de l'école de Nice*, Paris: Éditions de la Différence.

Chapter 5

'Let's Leave God Out of This'
Maurice Blanchot's Reading of
Totality and Infinity

Michael Holland
St. Hugh's College, Oxford

In the process of becoming a philosopher, Emmanuel Levinas discovered something pretty dreadful about what it is to be human. He expresses this clearly and decisively in the introduction to *Existence and Existents*:

> Is not anxiety over being – horror of Being – just as primal as anxiety over death? Is not fear of Being just as originary as the fear for Being? It is perhaps even more so, for the former may account for the latter. (1978 [1947]: 20)

This is of course the discovery of what he calls the *il y a*, the *there is*, the encounter with being as *there is*, and 'to be brushed by the *there is* is horror' (60 [translation modified]). This horror is not Heideggerian in nature: 'The pure nothingness revealed by anxiety in Heidegger's analysis does not constitute the *there is*' (62), because if there is no relief from horror *in* being, at the same time 'there are no exits from being' (64 [translation modified]). The *there is* is 'above contradiction' (64); in *Difficult Freedom* Levinas will speak of 'the horrible neutrality of the *there is*' (1990 [1963/76]: 292); and *Existence and Existents*, he says to Philippe Nemo in 1982, 'tries to describe this horrible thing, and moreover describes it as horror and panic [*affolement*]' (1985 [1982]: 49).

Maurice Blanchot's first direct reference to Levinas occurs in

91

a footnote to his long study 'Literature and the Right to Death', which was written during the year in which *Existence and Existents* was published. It consists of a paraphrased reference to precisely the passage I cited initially, followed a few pages later by a direct quotation of it (1995a: 332, 337). In this article I wish to explore how, and why, in the years following the publication of *Existence and Existents*, Blanchot seeks to hold Levinas to the latter's initial definition of existence, and in so doing oppose Levinas's attempts at extricating existence from the *there is* by finding a way out that is not an exit, but what in 1982 he calls a *deliverance* from it (1985: 52). I want, in other words, to look at some of the effects, and make some tentative suggestions as to the cause, of what throughout most of their lives has remained an absolute divergence between Levinas and Blanchot. It is a divergence which Levinas refers to pointedly in his conversations with Philippe Nemo when, describing Blanchot's then most recent book, *Writing the Disaster*, as the latest in a long chain of works arising out of the horrible experience of the *there is*, he observes: 'It would seem that for him, it is impossible to escape from this maddening, obsessive situation' (1985: 50).

Now I do not think that Levinas is right about Blanchot here. But that is neither here nor there, since what concerns me is Blanchot's reading of Levinas. At the same time, the question must arise as to what place there can be for a study of such a reading, particularly if, as I began by suggesting, Blanchot's relationship to Levinas is a *regressive* one, seeking as it does to hold Levinas to his initial version of the experience of the *there is* and so in effect hold his thinking back. What can such a retarding and retarded reading have to offer when it comes to understanding Levinas?

The answer lies in the curious form which this reading takes. In a manner which still remains to be fully documented, Blanchot's thinking about literature and the experience of literature, from about 1947 onwards, can be said gradually to *colonize* the philosophical discourse on being that Levinas begins to produce from about the same date. His 'reading' of

Levinas is thus at the same time a (re)writing of Levinas. Moreover, this is what may be termed an *absolute* colonization. For Blanchot lays claim to no originality in the domain of philosophy. Such originality, if it exists, lies in another domain entirely: that of literature. As Levinas acknowledges in *Existence and Existents*: 'Thomas l'obscur* by Maurice Blanchot opens with the description of the *there is*' (1978: 63, n. 1). In *Time and the Other* (1947/1979) he twice cites Blanchot's second novel, *Aminadab* (1942), to illustrate his argument (1987: 56, 83). And in 1982, referring implicitly to Blanchot's novel *Le Très-Haut* [*The Most High*] (1948), he says to Philippe Nemo:

> [The *there is*] is a theme I found in Maurice Blanchot. [. . .] [H]e speaks of the 'rumpus' [*remue-ménage*] of being, of its 'clamour', of its 'murmur'. A night in a hotel room where, behind the partition, 'there's endless moving about'; 'there's no way of knowing what they're doing next door'. This is something very close to the *there is*. [. . .] It is probably the true subject of his novels and his récits. (1985: 50–51 [translation modified])

This could of course mean that, following the familiar pattern of colonialism, Blanchot extends the frontiers of Literature by invading another territory: Levinas's, on another continent: Philosophy, and working its land, tilling its ground, harvesting its produce – in short, exploiting it in both senses – for the sole benefit of Literature. Indeed to some extent, this is precisely what he does. Harnessing those forces in Levinas's discourse that display the greatest affinity with his own – forces that Jacques Derrida identifies when he speaks of the *pathos* of the Levinasian use of metaphor (1978: 84, n. 7) – Blanchot's writing on literature, as it develops between about 1947 and the publication of *The Space of Literature* in 1955, can be said to expropriate Levinas's philosophical writing, appropriating its terms and putting them to work for its own purpose, to produce a hybrid discourse where they function less as signifiers of what literature might be, than as literary figures in their own right.[1]

At the same time, however, Blanchot is doing much more than that. If I have called his relation to Levinas a form of absolute colonialism, it is because its model is not to be found in the history of Western Imperialism and the hybrid societies it brings into being, but much further back, or much further forward, in situations where colonization is not an extension of Empire, but rather puts an end to a state of wandering and dispossession. That suffered by the Jews provides the model from the past, while the model from the future can be found in those space wanderers, forced to abandon a dying planet and taking with them the remnants of its civilisation in order to start up again elsewhere. Science fiction perhaps, sitting perhaps uneasily, as a model, alongside the fact of Jewish exile and its history, yet justified, I feel, in the light of the responses of both Levinas and Blanchot to the first manned space-flight in 1961, which more or less coincided with the publication of *Totality and Infinity*.[2] If it can be said that Blanchot's colonization of Levinas's writing in the years following 1947 is *absolute* in the way I have illustrated, this is because in those years, literature is becoming, for him, a dwindling and disintegrating domain. In short, it is becoming uninhabitable. Although Levinas does not perceive it, what he encounters in the language of Blanchot's fiction, under the name of the *there is*, is an experience of being which exceeds in advance the capacity of language to signify or express it. As George Bataille tellingly observed in a review of *Existence and Existents*, Levinas's claim that *Thomas the Obscure* opens with a *description* of the *there is* is less than accurate: 'Levinas describes and Maurice Blanchot cries out (decries) the *there is*' (1947: 292). By 1947, when he is simultaneously writing his last novel (*The Most High*) and his first *récit* (*Death Sentence*), the voice in which the cry has sought utterance – the voice of Literature – has begun to fail. Yet Blanchot's *experience* remains essentially literary, since literature is the original site of his encounter with being as *there is*. He is thus becoming the author of a literature without a language. His colonization of Levinas's discourse does not therefore simply annexe, appropriate or even expropriate it: it is a wholesale invasion of it. His experience inhabits Levinas's discourse, exercising its own Imperial power over it not from afar, but from within – superficially as that *imperiousness* of tone by which Blanchot had by then become recognizable (and which is as it were the echo, outside of literature, of the cry that can no longer resound within); but also (and more decisively) as a new and alien *imperative*, that of Literature and of the experience of Literature, introduced by force and as force (the desperate energy of the cry), into the domain and the civilization known as Philosophy, and causing it to mutate.

To return then to the issue of what Blanchot's reading of Levinas has to offer, the answer I gave can now I think be articulated more clearly. To utter the name Levinas, today, is to bring the name Blanchot to mind, and the opposite is equally the case. However, over and above the usual, recognizable reasons for this, which all presuppose a reversible hierarchy of naming, this bringing to mind of each by the other has a peculiar necessity of its own. Through the process I have referred to, Levinas's philosophical discourse, having encountered in Blanchot's fictional discourse another version of the encounter with the *there is* out of which it too arises, subsequently acquires a *double* in the form of Blanchot's non-fictional discourse, an almost identical twin,[3] shadowing it and repeating its gestures, while relentlessly putting pressure upon it to obey another imperative.

Because of Blanchot, in short, Levinas's discourse exists in two forms for a time: its own and that to be found in Blanchot's writing. Were this merely *parasitism* on Blanchot's part – the act of a writer with no discourse of his own – the phenomenon would be a curiosity at best. But it is because Blanchot originally *did* have his own discourse – namely fiction – and because, as Levinas recognises, it was another version of the encounter with the *there is* which he himself explores philosophically, that the doubling of Levinas's discourse by Blanchot acquires an originality which must be acknowledged and then examined.

In two stages, corresponding to the two stages of Levinas's

own response to the *there is* which he refers to in *Ethics and Infinity* (1985: 51–52), Levinas's discourse exists, under his pen and under Blanchot's, as the site of a veritable *logomachia* between two absolutely divergent imperatives or exigencies: one which Blanchot calls *literary*, one which Levinas will eventually term *ethical*. During the first stage, corresponding to the period covered for Levinas by *Existence and Existents* and *Time and the Other*, and for Blanchot by *The Space of Literature*, the struggle remains discreet: it would take a careful simultaneous reading of what each of them wrote at the time for the intensity of it to become apparent.

With the arrival of the second stage, however – the stage where Levinas seeks to 'put a stop to the anonymous and senseless rumbling [*bruissement*] of being' by deposing the sovereign Self in favour of 'the social relationship with the Other' (1985: 52) – the struggle surfaces in Blanchot's discourse, which has itself, by 1961, moved on a stage. This is thanks in no small part to his own attempts to depose the sovereign Self in favour of a social relation, but to do so *politically* not *philosophically*, through intellectual involvement in the resistance to the Algerian War. The struggle surfaces in a series of three articles, in dialogue form, published in the *Nouvelle Revue Française* and forming a response to the publication of *Totality and Infinity* in 1961.

At what is therefore, for each writer, a new stage in his development, marking and consumating, one might say, the uncoupling of their respective discourses (the colonizing intent of Blanchot's fading with his emergent anti-colonialism), the veritable *différend* that has never ceased to divide them, but which has hitherto been perceptible in its effects, emerges in Blanchot's discourse as a cause. It is a cause located in discourse itself, and its nature is, disturbingly, violence.

*

It is upon this violence that I wish to focus in the rest of my argument, for it circumscribes what for me has long remained a puzzling and troubling area in Blanchot's writing. In its minor mode, it amounts to an intensification of that imperiousness of tone characteristic of the earlier Blanchot, resulting in the brusqueness of the words which provide me with my title: 'Let's leave God out of this' (a slightly more peremptory rendering of the original 'Laissons Dieu de côté' than Susan Hanson's 'Let us leave God aside' [1993: 50]). These words occur near the beginning of the first *NRF* dialogue, 'Knowledge of the unknown', in response to the claim by what I shall call Voice I – a 'sceptical' voice – that the mystical experience, however real, is not philosophical, 'any more than a divine union could come about under the supervision of a metaphysics' (1993: 50). The reply of Voice II – an 'enquiring' voice – is: 'Why?'. It is noteworthy that this is a response to the first part of Voice I's objection only, namely that mystical experience is not philosophical. The second part, the rider which draws an analogy with the incompatibility between the relation with God and metaphysics, despite the fact that it is implied by the first part to such a degree that it appears as no more than a version of it, is simply swept aside, in what amounts to an aside: 'Let's leave God out of this – the name is too imposing'. For Voice II, in other words, mysticism may not be philosophical: it is nevertheless accessible, as such, to philosophical enquiry. The divine, on the contrary, is simply beyond the pale. Manifestly therefore, while defending freedom of enquiry against the strictures of scepticism, Voice II is imposing a peremptory restriction of its own on the course that enquiry should take.

A little further on, there comes what Jacques Derrida will subsequently criticize as a use of terms by Blanchot to define and dismiss the religious in Levinas's thought – terms which, says Derrida, Levinas 'would most likely reject' (1978: 103) – namely what Blanchot calls the *theological context* in which Levinas puts forward his philosophical claims (1993: 56). The uncharacteristic obtuseness of this choice of terms, which Blanchot will subsequently withdraw in response to Derrida's stricture,[4] marks the persistence of that bluntness with which God is initially swept aside in this opening article.

As a final reflection of this minor mode of what I find

disturbing about Blanchot's response to Levinas in 1961, there are echoes of the bluntness and brusqueness of his tone in other texts of the period. Four years earlier, writing about Simone Weil, he asserts the need for thought to maintain 'a reserve somewhere within itself [. . .], a non-thought [. . .], a lacuna' (1993: 119), before denouncing what he sees as the easy solution:

> instead of leaving the empty part empty one can name it and, in a word, fill it by obscuring it offensively [*en l'offusquant*] with the strongest, most august and most opaque name that can be found. [Translation modified]

That is, the name of God, which Blanchot again describes here as *imposing*, and also as *cumbersome*. It would appear that God is an offensive name to Blanchot in 1957, amounting to an insult to thought. And in an article entitled 'Being a Jew', written a year after his articles on Levinas, in 1962, there is a further example of what appears more clearly now as a reaction in kind to this offensive form of language. At a certain point in the argument of this article Blanchot remarks:

> Here we should bring in the great gift of Israel, its teaching of the one God. But I would rather say, *brutally*, that what we owe to Jewish monotheism is not the revelation of the one God, but the revelation of speech as the place where men hold themselves in relation with what excludes all relation: the infinitely Distant. (1993: 127 [my emphasis])

It is noteworthy that the *brutality* of tone I have been referring to is here both acknowledged and laid claim to by Blanchot, reinforcing what it is that makes me uneasy, in the minor mode, about Blanchot's reading of Levinas in 1961: namely the brutally dismissive way it responds to the religious dimension to Levinas's thinking as expressed through the name of God.

But that is, as I have said, violence in a minor mode. The major one is constituted by a decision Blanchot makes, in the third of his articles, and which I have long found difficult to comprehend. This article, published in April 1962, is entitled

'The Indestructible'. The difficulty it poses is two-fold: first, it begins by proposing no less than the withdrawal of the term *Autrui*, considered as philosophically useless, even though it is central to Levinas's thinking in *Totality and Infinity*. This move may be read in relation to the emergence in Blanchot's thinking of the category of the *neuter*, and is thus a doubly provocative one in relation to Levinas, given the latter's denunciation of the Heideggerian neuter in *Totality and Infinity*.[5] Second, and more astonishingly however, having done away with Levinas's term in this fashion, the article goes on:

> Each time the question: Who is *'Autrui'*? emerges in our words I think of the book by Robert Antelme, for it not only testifies to the society of the German camps of World War II, it also leads us to an essential reflection. (1993: 130)

This move by Blanchot is quite astonishing, not to say shocking. Antelme's book, *L'Espèce humaine* [*Humankind*] (1947/57), is an account by a non-Jew of his ordeal in a camp which was not an extermination camp. To me, this promotion of Antelme's experience in a discussion of Levinas has long appeared to display much greater brutality, to be much more offensive, than anything occurring in what I have termed the minor mode. As the culmination of what is clearly an offensive *against* Levinas's thinking in so far as it draws on Jewish religious tradition, it amounts to an absolute disregard for the history of Jewish experience in the twentieth century. As well as diverting attention away from the camps of the Holocaust, by means of its 'not only . . . but also' construction it effectively subordinates the entire question of historical experience to what it calls 'an essential reflection'.

Yet if it remains difficult not to recoil from what Blanchot appears to be doing here, I think that there is a way of responding to it differently, of accepting that the priority given by Blanchot to what he terms 'an essential reflection' may in fact have a *necessity* about it for anyone seeking to approach the question of the Other as it is raised by Levinas, but to do so from within the Western Christian tradition. Hitherto, I have always found some relief from my response to the displacement of the question onto Antelme's experience, in the fact that when the three articles on Levinas were included in *The Infinite Conversation* in 1969, only a few paragraphs of the third one were retained, and a new argument developed around them, while the main body of the article, on Antelme, was moved to a separate section of the book to become the second section of a chapter entitled 'The Indestructible', whose *first* part is formed by the article 'Being a Jew'.

Now I do not want to minimize the significance of this change: it inaugurates what will become, on Blanchot's part, an increasing acquiescence in what Levinas's thought becomes in the 1970s and 1980s, an exchange whose mode is a *Gelassenheit* rather than a confrontation, an *Auseinandersetzung* free of violence.[6] Nevertheless, I now also feel that that confrontation, as it surfaces in Blanchot's response in 1961 after years of latency, is itself rich in significance. In conclusion, I should like to indicate how that is.

*

The first article, 'Knowledge of the Unknown', opens with the question 'What is a philosopher?', to which Voice II replies:

> I will give a modern response: [. . .] today I would say, borrowing words from Georges Bataille, it is someone who is afraid. (1993: 49)

The reference to Bataille here is important, recalling as it does his critique of Levinas's reading of Blanchot. So too is the Heideggerian resonance of the question, echoing but also displacing one that Heidegger puts in 1955 at Cerisy-la Salle.[7] But what matters most is the fact that, with this answer, in advance of any consideration of *Totality and Infinity*, Blanchot is clearly siting his own argument back at that stage in Levinas's thinking which is represented by *Existence and Existents* – in the experience of *fear of Being* considered as more originary than *fear of not being*. And as a preliminary to his discussion of *Totality and Infinity* and its exploration of the face-to-face encounter with the Other, Blanchot uses the two voices in his dialogue gradually to bring out a dimension to *fear of Being* – the encounter with the *there is* – which is not present in Levinas's thinking in its first stage, nor indeed in Blanchot's own. More precisely, it is present in Levinas as the *movement* which will eventually allow what he calls *deliverance* from the *there is* in the second stage of his thinking. For Blanchot, on the contrary, this movement is a dimension which remains *confined* within fear of Being and contact with the *there is*. It thus confines thought *to* fear, *to* the *there is*. Blanchot therefore argues in effect that there is, as Levinas originally said, no exit from being, and thus implies that the *deliverance* Levinas is seeking by way of a philosophy of the Other in *Totality and Infinity* is a delusion.

Admittedly, though he is clearly still adopting that 'imperialist' stance which had previously empowered his hybridisation of Levinas's discourse, Blanchot does eventually allow that, thanks to Levinas's new book, there are certainly no grounds for despairing of philosophy. On the contrary:

> It is as though there were here a new departure in philosophy, a leap that it, and we ourselves, were urged to accomplish. (1993: 52)

At the same time, all his endeavour is directed towards deflecting this leap away from any existing plane or trajectory, from any recognisable mode of transcendence, so that it remains within the horizonless dimension of fear in which the encounter with the *there is* takes place. This endeavour can, as I have shown, be a brutal one, especially when that transcendence is given the 'offensive' name of God. Indeed this is once again acknowledged, and the brutality laid claim to, in the first of the *NRF* articles when, after an account of Levinas's category of Desire, Voice I retorts:

> Then let us say, *somewhat brutally*, that this Desire is the desire for a strict transcendence that has taken *autrui* as what it aims for, and that makes *autrui* the Transcendent. (53 [my emphasis])[8]

But what I wish to suggest is this: the unmistakable violence once again present in Blanchot's argument here is not in fact being exerted *by* Blanchot considered as the subject of the discourse (or discourses) making up his argument. On the contrary, this violence, its signifiers and its tokens, are placed there by Blanchot, I would suggest, as signs of a fundamental violence done not by one discourse against another, but to discourse itself, as it is constituted and conducted in exemplary fashion under the name of Philosophy, as soon as it seeks to approach, in its full extent, the *fear of Being* encountered in the experience of existence Levinas calls the *there is*, and which in literature cannot be described but merely cried out (de-cried).[9] 'There is in this experience', says Voice I, 'a movement that collides as though head-on with philosophy' (1993: 49). And the marks of this head-on collision that are present in Blanchot's argument (a collision which, coming *head on*, clearly pre-empts and renders impossible the *face-to-face* encounter which Levinas describes) are the sign that Blanchot, unlike Levinas, considers that *fear of Being* is, quite simply, insurmountable and inescapable by any of the means hitherto available to Philosophy, while remaining, as such, the philosophical condition *par excellence*.

This leads his argument in two directions: first, the experience of fear is explored as an encounter with the *unknown*, the *strange*, the *Other* in which I *become* other, the Other, and so coincide with my fear:

> The fearful man, in the space of his fear, participates in and unites with what makes him afraid. He is not only fearful, he is fear – that is, the irruption of what arises and is disclosed in fear. (1993: 49)

Physical contact, which is to say the experience of my own body as *abjection*, is presented as the horizonless dimension of this encounter and the shameful substance of what can no longer properly be called *my* fear. At this stage, Blanchot's relationship to Levinas is at its most 'regressive'. This is illustrated by the way in which a reference to the Most High in Levinas's thinking produces a wry allusion to Blanchot's novel of that name, written in 1948, in which the dimension of physical abjection is explored through fiction (1993: 54).

If that was all Blanchot's argument did, then it would be difficult to see it as anything other *than* regressive: a now categoric refusal to accompany Levinas beyond the experience of the *there is* as *fear of Being*. But there is a second direction to Blanchot's argument. It leads to what I shall call a *reflexivity of fear*, which corresponds, I believe, to that 'essential reflection' which he refers to at the beginning of the article on Antelme. For what is advanced early on in the first article is this: fear, to be philosophical while at the same time colliding head on with philosophy, must not simply be the fear that anyone can experience, and which inevitably leads the subject of the experience to react with violence in so far as his fear is fear at becoming other. The philosopher, says Blanchot, is 'someone who is afraid of fear', or more precisely:

> afraid of the violence that reveals itself in fear and that threatens to transform him from a frightened man into a violent man; as though he feared less the violence he suffers than the violence he might exercise. (1993: 50)

Hence, though the 'sceptical' voice persists with the simple assertion that, in fear, I am 'shamefully transformed into something other than myself', the 'enquiring' voice is equally persistent in reply:

> I see nothing shameful there – unless one should be ashamed of fearing this shame – if such a shameful movement were to permit us to relate ourselves finally to what is outside our limits. (1993: 50)

This is first of all a recognition of the inevitability of abjection in Western culture, based in Antelme's experience as well as Bataille's, but having its source in Blanchot's encounter with the *there is* through literature. But it is also an overcoming of the shamefulness of the experience through the discovery of a moment of reflexivity within it which, for Blanchot, is *more originary* than the ethical alternative offered to the West, through Levinas's philosophy, by the religion of Judaism or indeed any religion. For the subject of this reflexivity of and in fear, deliverance from fear of being comes neither as violence against the Other nor as ethical transcendence by the Other, but as the interruption of fear *by* fear: an interruption equivalent to existence itself lived, through fear, as *being Other*, and which, if it brings about a *head-on collision* with Philosophy, is itself, *in* Philosophy, a moment of absolute non-violence, a yielding in which the violence born of fear is allowed simply to flow away, be expended and go to waste.

This reflexivity in Blanchot's thinking requires much more careful examination than I can give it here. I hope to have shown, however, that by reinscribing it within Levinas's discourse, which he originally colonized, as the 'transcendence' which Levinas seeks to transcend through ethics, Blanchot is proposing a way forward for thought lying beyond the limits of both literature and philosophy. Despite the violence present in his response to *Totality and Infinity*, Blanchot is thus not seeking to *counter* Levinas's philosophy. His aim is rather to accompany it through a *detour* which will avoid the inevitable 'head-on collision' with the experience of the *there is* out of which that violence arises. Along the way, perhaps, the Christian West may at last encounter that Other which, as Michel Foucault observed in 1969, we have for so long seemed afraid to give thought to.[10]

NOTES

1 The original version of the second Appendix [*Annexe*] to *The Space of Literature*, 'The Two Versions of the Imaginary', provides one of the most striking examples of this. Written in 1951, it was revised and 'toned down' for inclusion in *The Space of Literature* in 1955. Typical of the passages left out is this one:

> image [. . .] indicates [. . .] the menacing proximity of a vague and empty outside, a neutral, nullified, limitless existence. And it is against the background of this sordid absence,

arising out of the stifling condensation where being is ceaselessly perpetuated as nothingness, that it arms things in their disappearance.

In its second version it simply reads: 'image [. . .] indicates [. . .] the menacing proximity of a vague and empty outside, the deep, the sordid basis upon which it continues to affirm things in their disappearance' (1982: 254).

2 See 'Heidegger, Gagarin and us', in Levinas (1990 [1963/1976]: 231–34). The original article appeared in *Information juive* in 1961; 'The Conquest of Space', Blanchot 1995c, originally published in Italian in *Gulliver Internazionale*, 1 (*Il Menabó*, 7 [1964]).

3 Levinas seems to anticipate this state of affairs when he writes, in *Time and the Other*:

> The relation with itself is, as in Blanchot's novel *Aminadab*, the relation with a double chained to the ego, a viscous, heavy, stupid double, but one the ego [*le moi*] is with precisely because it is me [*moi*]. (1987 [1947/1979]: 56)

4 A footnote added in 1969 to 'Knowledge of the unknown' reads:

> 'Context' here, as Jacques Derrida very aptly observes, is a word that Levinas could only deem inappropriate – just as he would the reference to theology. (1993: 56, n. 1)

5 The seventh 'Conclusion' to *Totality and Infinity* is entitled 'Against the Philosophy of the Neuter'. In it, Levinas credits Blanchot with having contributed to exposing the 'impersonal neutrality' of Being for Heidegger. (1991: 298–9 [298])

6 In '"Do not forget"' (1995b) Blanchot makes use of the term *Autrui* in a manner which is both unqualified and uncritical.

7 In *What is Philosophy?* (1963 [1955]), Heidegger approaches philosophy in terms of what touches and moves [*be-rührt*] us (27), recalling that 'Astonishment, as *pathos*, is the *archê* of philosophy' (81). Blanchot's displacement of the question away from philosophy and onto the philosopher and his fear would appear to suggest that his response to Levinas is also a response to Heidegger.

8 Significantly, 'brutally' is toned down to become 'brusquely' when the article is included in *The Infinite Conversation* in 1969.

9 In an article entitled 'Nietzsche Today', written in 1958 and included in *The Infinite Conversation*, Blanchot cites Heidegger's description of Nietzsche's philosophy as a 'written cry' [*geschriebener Schrei*] (1993: 143). See Heidegger, 1968: 48–9. I prefer 'written cry' to the translator's 'written scream'. For a discussion of

this article from a different angle, see my "'A Wound to Thought'" (1996).

10 Michel Foucault, *The Archaeology of Knowledge* (1972): 'As if we were afraid to conceive of the *Other* in the time of our own thought' (12).

BIBLIOGRAPHY

Bataille, G. (1947) 'De l'existentialisme au primat de l'économie [From Existentialism to the primacy of economics]', in *Œuvres Complètes*, vol. XI, Paris: Gallimard, 1988.

Blanchot, M. (1982) *The Space of Literature*, trans. Ann Smock, Lincoln and London: University of Nebraska Press.

—— (1993) *The Infinite Conversation*, trans. Susan Hanson, Minneapolis: University of Minnesota Press.

—— (1995a) 'Literature and the Right to Death', in *The Work of Fire*, trans. Charlotte Mandel, Stanford: Stanford University Press.

—— (1995b) "'Do Not Forget'", trans. Michael Holland, in M. Holland (ed.) *The Blanchot Reader*, Oxford: Basil Blackwell.

—— (1995c) 'The Conquest of Space', trans. Christopher C. Stevens, *ibid.*, pp. 269–71.

Derrida, J. (1978) *Writing and·Difference*, trans. A. Bass, London: Routledge.

Foucault, M. (1972) *The Archaeology of Knowledge*, trans. A. Sheridan Smith, New York: Pantheon Books.

Heidegger, M. (1963) *What is Philosophy?*, London: Vision Press.

—— (1968) *What is Called Thinking?*, trans. J. Glenn Gray, New York: Harper & Row.

Holland, M. (1996) "'A Wound to Thought'", in C. Bayley Gill (ed.) *Maurice Blanchot: Literature, Philosophy, Ethics*, London: Routledge.

Levinas, E. (1978) *Existence and Existents*, trans. A. Lingis, Dordrecht: Kluwer Academic Publishers.

—— (1985) *Ethics and Infinity. Conversations with Philippe Nemo*, trans. R. A. Cohen, Pittsburgh: Duquesne University Press.

—— (1987) *Time and the Other*, trans. R.A. Cohen, Pittsburgh: Duquesne University Press.

—— (1990) *Difficult Freedom*, trans. S. Hand, London: Athlone.

—— (1991) *Totality and Infinity*, trans. A. Lingis, Dordrecht: Kluger Academic Publishers.

Chapter 6

Infinition and Apophansis
Reverberations of Spinoza in Levinas

Benjamin Hutchens
Warwick University

In this brief commentary, I propose to demonstrate that a certain unorthodox Spinozist notion of expression serves as the missing link in explaining (or at least rendering more intelligible) the difficult but fundamental modalities of Levinas' thinking, namely 'infinition' in *Totality and Infinity* and 'apophansis' in *Otherwise than Being*. These conceptions could be regarded both as a Platonic rebellion against Hegelian totalization and its law of identity and a vaguely aesthetic and interpersonal articulation of that same law. Nevertheless, although it is very helpful (and obvious) to regard these ideas as a negative response to Hegel, it is perhaps more provocative (and more explanatory) to focus instead on the manner in which they are articulations of the notion of expression in Spinoza. In fact, the secondary literature on Levinas has not taken these aspects into account in any sophisticated (i.e. analytical) way, and this neglect leads to certain obvious deficiencies of argument. The point is to put the reverberations of Spinoza's metaphysics in Levinas' thinking to work in order to overcome the latter's rhetorical ambiguities. In order to do so, as Levinas might say, it is necessary to look beyond the letter and the 'said' of Spinoza's *Ethics* at the spirit and its 'saying'.

The Spinoza relevant for the interpretation of Levinas is the avatar of the conatus essendi/existendi, of the expression (*explicere*) of the essence and existence of man, and the modal expressions implied in these expressions as they are irreducible to the themes expressed and the one who expresses. I am thoroughly endebted to Deleuze's *Spinoza et le problème de l'expression* (Deleuze 1990) for his peculiar reading of Spinoza which rightfully and brilliantly elevates a non-terminological aspect (*explicere*) to the central notion of his thinking. Just as the conatus essendi /existendi could be read as a proleptic depiction of the meaninglessness and futility of nihilism, so could the rupturing of the law of identity in the mode of expression constitute an ethical modality of what Levinas calls 'pre-philosophical life', resonances of which are discernible ('traced') in the infinition of desire, the asymmetricality of human relationships, and the demand for justice which is, for Levinas, the birth of consciousness. Although it would be possible to show how these ideas refer (negatively or positively) to aspects of Spinoza's metaphysics, epistemology and ethics, I shall instead use 'expression' as an inroad into Levinas' thinking.

Indeed, the Spinozist undertones to Levinas' thinking are evident in the opening pages of both of his major works. It is almost startling how, in the midst of a description and critique of Heidegger, Husserl or Hegel, Levinas utilizes the Spinozist vocabulary of 'substance', 'conatus' or 'attributes', and even, as we shall see 'expression'. Indeed, Levinas most often speaks of active *l'expression* (or saying) and passive *s'exprimere* (or said) in contexts where other Spinozist terminology is manifest.

BEYOND THE CONATUS: ESSENCE AND ITS MODAL MANIFESTATION

It is well-known that Levinas is concerned with aspects of human life like responsibility, desire, justice, fecundity etc. which he thinks philosophy has not taken seriously. It is equally well known that he is a philosopher of transcendence, of infinite responsibilities. Transcendence in Levinas is normally expressed in the context of a critique of immanential thinking which excludes the ethical implications of these aspects of human life. However, what is too rarely understood is Levinas' comprehension of essence in existentialist terms. In approaching this question of essence, it is helpful to look at the presence of the Spinozist conatus essendi in Levinas' thinking. *Otherwise than Being* is introduced with the following passage:

> The essence [. . .] works as an invincible persistence in essence, filling up very interval of nothingness which would interrupt its exercise. Esse is interesse; essence is interest. This being interested does not appear to the mind surprised by the relativity of its negation, and to the man resigned to the meaninglessness of his death; it is not reducible to just this refutation of negativity. It is affirmed to be the conatus of beings. And what else could positivity mean but this conatus? Being's interest takes dramatic form in egoisms struggling with one another, each against all, in the multiplicity of allergic egoisms which are at war with one another and are thus together. (Levinas 1981: 4; Levinas 1991: 21; Levinas 1993: 79–80 and Levinas 1987: 138).

For the individual, this means that, in Heideggerian terms,

> La formule <<le Dasein est un être pour qui dans son être>> était séduisante dans *Sein und Zeit*, où elle signifiait le conatus. Mais le conatus est en réalité déduit du degré d'astriction à l'être de cet étant. Il n'y a pas d'existentialisme ici. Ici, l'homme est intéressant parce qu'il a été astreint à l'être- et son astriction à l'être est son questionnement. Le conatus mesure l'obéissance à l'être, l'intégralité de cet être-au-service-de-l'être, qui est à la charge de l'homme ('Lettre sur l'humanisme'). (Levinas 1993: 35)

Levinas' key attitude to nihilism is that it is rooted in the perseverance immanent to one's own powers He emphasizes essence as a mode rather than a state of being, a way of existing in the conatus and not the fact of existence. Although he famously insists that time is produced in the relationship with the neighbour rather than in one's own silent self-consciousness, this is so because subjectivity is patient, passive and exposed, a self that 'comes to pass' (*cela se passe*) (Levinas 1981: 53) rather than intentional, objectifying, free etc. The conatus, whether of essendi or existendi, is present throughout Levinas' work as the pure undergoing of lassitude, pain, insomnia, awaiting death. Generally speaking, it is having the time to attend to the other person, or as he puts it 'the essence of the human is not primodially conatus, but hostage, the hostage of/to the other' (*l'être humain n'est pas primordialement conatus mais otage, otage d'autrui.*) (Levinas 1993: 31 and 38). It is in the way the individual expresses itself in its exposedness, not in the way its existence actively precedes its essence, nor even in the passivity antithetical to activity (the choice not to act) that the subjectivity of man is ethically constituted (Levinas 1981: 15 and 72). Thus, the conatus essendi as hostage to the other, not the Cartesian cogito, is the opening for ethics.

The existence which is merely the essence of man is immanential. It excludes transcendence. The openness of the conatus provides the transcendental space wherein alterity can be performed. It is perhaps necessary to look briefly at Levinas' conception of infinity in order to explain this problematic description.

Essence, Levinas says, is thematizable or apophantic. That is, it can be given by the meaning it already possesses: 'the word at once proclaims and establishes an identification of this with that in the already said' (Levinas 1981: 37). However, this naming and identification do not 'reduce to definitive silence the mute resonance, the murmur of silence, in which essence is identified as an entity' (Levinas 1981: 38). Rather than simply reducing the particular entity by 'neutralizing' it in being, identification and bestowal of meaning permit the entity to be a modality (a 'way' or 'how') of essence, a *fruitio essendi*. Levinas explains that 'being's essence is the temporalization of time, the diastasis of the identical and its recapture of reminiscence, the unity of apperception'. It is the modification whereby the entity is revealed in its truth and then parts with itself, 'undoes itself into this and that', which is apophansis. The 'modification' of entities is 'multiplication of the identical' and a 'dissipating of opacity' (Levinas 1981: 29). In Spinozist terms, the essence of substance is accessible through the modifications of the entity expressing that substance, and these attributes are the empirical data whereby these modifications makes this essence discernible. With Hegel in mind, Levinas writes:

> Already the tautological predication A is A, in which an entity is both subject and predicate, does not only signify the inherence of A in itself or the fact that A possesses all the characteristics of A. A is A is to be understood also as 'the sound resounds' or 'the red reddens'- or as 'AAs'. In the 'red reddens', the verb does not signify an event, some dynamism of the red opposed to its rest as a quality, or some activity of red, for example, turning red, the passage from non-red to red or from less red to more red, an alternation. Nor in the verb to redden is there stretched some metaphor of action or alternation, founded on an analogy with the dynamism of action, which would have the preeminent right to be designated by the verb. (Levinas 1981: 38–39)

Levinas explains this by insisting that essence resounds in the verb to be. The essence of A resounds both in itself and in its opposition to B, though not in a way which merely identifies it. A's essence resounds in its relation to B. Nothing could be more Spinozist than Levinas' affirmation that '[a]ll the attributes of individual beings, of entities that are fixed in or by nouns, as predicates can be understood as modes of being; such are the qualities of which the entities make a show, the typical generalities by which they are ordered, the laws that regulate them, the logical forms that contain and deliver them'. In Levinas' reading, what matters is not an 'I' at home with itself, but an I always anxious about, enjoying, or stretching towards itself in a 'work of existing'. 'AA's' is a stretching towards the self in a non-coinciding, without completion or commensuration' (Levinas 1966: 44). The way an entity is produced in its essene will be implied within, and indeed constitutive of, its existence. 'The very individuality of an individual is a way of being. Socrates socratizes, or Socrates is socrates, is the way Socrates is' (Levinas 1981: 41). Instead of merely naming or thematizing an entity, apophansis delineates the horizon of the way it is. Generally speaking, 'the production of the infinite entity is inseparable from the idea of infinity, for it is precisely in the disproportion between the idea of infinity and the infinite of which it is the idea that this exceeding of limits is produced. The idea of infinity is the mode of being, the infinition, of infinity' (Levinas 1991: 26). Infinition is the infinite production of the infinite, or again, the way of infinity is always produced in the infinite theme. Infinition simultaneously brings the entity about (*s'évertue*) and reveals it (Levinas 1991: 26). Apophansis, or the 'life of expression', is at once what dissimulates the form of an entity in a theme, and what, in infinition, traverses this movement and undoes (*défaire*) this dissimulation.

This peculiar reading of manifestation is perhaps best clarified in the light of the Spinozist understanding of modes. In Spinoza's notion of *modus*, we find 'that which is in something else through which it is also conceived' (Spinoza 1989: section I, definition V). It is in *substantia* that modes are discernible, that is, the substance conceived in and through itself without dependence on any other conception of a thing; modes are discernible in the substance because the latter, which depends on nothing else for determination, is modified so that it also is discernible in the mode (Spinoza 1989: section I, definition III). The modal expression (Levinas' 'saying') is discernible in another expression apart from and in addition to its expression of the theme (Levinas' 'said'), and one expression which expresses another does not therefore limit it even if they are the same sort of mode. Spinoza's point is that there are infinite and immediate modes, wherein the modes of each attribute involve the conception of their attribute and not that of another attribute, so that the entity of which the mode is the attribute is a substance requiring no dependence on any other thing (Spinoza 1989: section II, proposition VI). Such modes are of a kind, that is, any finite and determinate existent must be 'determined for action and existence' by another cause which also is a finite and determinate existence, ad infinitum (Spinoza 1989: section I, proposition XXVIII). However, there are also infinite and mediate modes in which the attributes mediate the mode of the entity which 'necessarily and infinitely exists' (God) (Spinoza 1989: section I, propositions XXII and XXIII). Simply put, an entity is a *modus existendi*, a mode of being which, in its way of existing, instantiates the anonymous ground of existence: the entity expresses existence in its very way of existing. Indeed, Levinas' depiction of 'skepticism' in *Otherwise than Being* and his notion of horizons of meaning referring to other such horizons (a quasi-'Husserlian' idea) in *Totality and Infinity* demonstrate that modes express other modes in immediate form, while the hypostasis or reduction of modes to themes mediates and permits the theme to stand as a mode expressing the modality of thematization and not the designated entity. Even the saying expressing the said which refutes another said is conveyed by a saying.

Spinoza's notion of perfection or degree of reality is also evident in this quotation from Levinas' philosophy of existence. Apophansis takes the form of a quiddity standing as a modality, that is, a pass from a greater degree of perfection to a lesser degree (or vice versa). As the former suggests, 'from a given definition of anything the intellect infers certain properties, which in truth necessarily follow from the deductions (that is, the very essence of the thing), and so the more reality the definition of a thing defined involves, the more properties the intellect will infer' (Spinoza 1989: section II, propositions XVI). Spinoza also speaks of an increase or decrease in the power of the mind, by which he means 'that the mind had formed an idea of its body, or some part of it, which expressed more or less the reality than it had affirmed concerning its body. For the excellence of ideas and the actual power of thinking is estimated from the excellence of the object' (Spinoza 1989: 140). Levinas is evidently thinking according to a similar paradigm when he articulates infinition and apophansis, especially when he notes that 'it is probably [the] function of signs [to designate, like a noun, a process, thereby 'doubling up' the totality of entities and events with the system of signs of a language that is implicitly ascribed to a verb when one tries to reduce the function of the verb to the "expression' of events, actions or alternatives.' Instead, it is not by analogy with actions and processes that verbs designate, but in the very 'verbalness of the verb' that 'resounds in the predicative proposition' prior to the identification of the entity contained in the designating noun. 'AAs' does not 'double up the real' in the same way that 'A=A' does. It does not double up the totality of entities with the system of signs of a language; it is not in the 'A=A' that the essence of the nominative is discernible, but in the predication in which this nominalization takes place. 'Essence is not only conveyed in the said, is not only 'expressed' in it, but originally – though amphibologically – resounds in it qua essence' (Levinas 1981: 39). Essence just consists in thematization; it is in the theme that essence first resounds.

Levinas is elucidating the verb to be which goes beyond regarding being as a mere process or action without language, that is to say, as if language 'remains foreign to the essence of nouns, and only lets this essence be seen' (Levinas 1981: 40). 'To be' neither names being nor reduces it to an event which language reveals indifferently. Instead, language implies the disruption of substances into modalities of the expressiveness of the verb to be in the predication. Most importantly, it is language which 'exposes the silent resonance of the essence' (Levinas 1981: 46).

Modalities are infinite; they require a context, a meaning, a theme in which to be intelligibly produced. (Here the 'already said' comes into play: exegesis too permits the resonance of essence within its thematization, that is, the mode of expression of a theoretical mode is sustained by the exegetical interrogation which is itself an expression which conveys the said of the former in its own saying) (Levinas 1981: 41). Fundamentally, this means that just as modalities express and resonate in a way irreducible to themes and the qualities or attributes they name, so are themes necessary to render such expressions and resonances intelligible. This is the tension between totality and infinity, or rather, the amphibology of being and entities, the problematic of production. Logos intervenes in the tension between the way an entity exists and the theme under which that entity is designated. It (impossibly) reduces the former to the latter in an amphibology or neutralization, thereby making the logos itself ambiguous. Verbs lapse into nouns and show themselves as such; nouns implicitly resonate infinitely as verbs despite tthe reduction of the verb. Yet, since an essence is reduced to the theme rather than its way of existing, its resonances are not accounted for in the designation of essence. Its particular way of existing, a modality which determines it as a unique quiddity, is reduced as if its quiddity were like any other named entity (Levinas 1981: 42). It is precisely for this reduction that Levinas condemns the primacy of 'fundamental ontology', which accentuates the identification of Being as an entity and depreciates the metaphysical significance of a named identity continuing to resonate in its essence, in its own right. It should be noted that it is by way of Spinozist 'expressions' (though not in their name) that Levinas objects to neo-traditional (Heideggerian) ontology. It is time, he says, to 'measure the pre-ontological weight of language instead of taking it only as a code (which it is also)'. Even more importantly, it is time to 'awaken in [the themes of ontology] the [resonances of expression] which [are] absorbed in it and, thus absorbed, enter into the history that the [former] imposes'. The breathless, patient, Spinozist subject, 'on the hither side of the thematisation of the said', is not on the first occasion dependent on being as a mere entity, but resounds in its very naming of itself as 'oneself' (Levinas 1981: 43).

ETHICAL EXPRESSION

Nearly everything Levinas writes (including his understanding of manifestation and identification) refers back to the face to face relation, the immediate encounter between individual humans. Even responsibility 'despite oneself' (prior to volition and freedom) is rendered accessible as a mode expressed by other modes, and thus, there are infinite responsibilities, as Levinas frequently insists. Since expression does not 'double up the essence of man', it is not an 'act, a psychological attribute, a state of the soul, a thought among others, or a moment of being's essence', though these are modalities- originary, ontological modalities-which articulate or express expression itself (Levinas 1981: 147). Since vulnerability and exposure to the neighbour in the face to face relation is already expression (the maintenance of oneself as a sign which is itself the giving of signs) then 'openness' or 'sincerity' is not an attribute of expression; it is saying that realizes sincerity, as simple as 'Hello' (Levinas 1981: 143). An expression expresses expression(ism) itself: sincerity is an expression which is expressed by this non-active expression of saying, or mutatis mutandis, it is only in the attribute of subjectivity called 'sincerity' that the attribute called 'saying' is discernible. This should call to mind Spinoza's definition of an attribute as 'that which the intellect perceives of substance as constituting its essence' (Spinoza 1983: section I definition IV). Levinas insists that sincerity is not an attribute of saying but expresses its expression.

The modality of exposure of the face – now so famously Levinasian – is precisely the modality whereby what would negate the other exposed in the face (murder=a mode) is itself negated by what the exposed face expresses – the injunction not to murder. A mode can negate a mode, but as long as this negation is immediate (ie non-thematized, in the sense that no theme which is not also a mode can intervene) then even this negation is the affirmation of modes.

More importantly, while Levinas disparages the rational God possessing known attributes (as we have seen), claiming that theological language destroys the situation of transcendence, he does insist that in an 'ethical religion' the attributes of another person are like God's, or rather, that God's attributes of infinity (height, power, numinousness, exteriority etc.) are first of all encountered in our neighbour in the interhuman encounter (Levinas 1987: 138 and Levinas 1981: 197). These characteristics, encountered in an other person, express its existence. This understanding of God as neighbour-like is comprehensible on Spinozist terms: the neighbour is a mode of the expression of transcendence; it is in her that God is 'traced' (neither present nor absent, determinate nor indeterminate, just 'non-indeterminate' and resounding) This interlocutor is 'he to whom expression expresses, or to whom celebration celebrates, both term of an orientation and primary signification', (*celui à qui l'expression exprime, pour qui la célébration célèbre, lui à la fois, terme d'une orientation et signification première*). It is the neighbour who gives sense to my expression, for it is only by him that a phenomenon as a meaning is, of itself, introduced into being' (Levinas 1987: 95). The expressiveness of AA's is present throughout Levinas' metaphysics, especially were the apophansis of A=A is at issue. For example, expression is reflected in the 'gratitude [which is] already gratitude for this state of gratitude, which is at the same time or in turn a gift and a gratitude' (Levinas 1981: 10 and 149). There is also an 'obedience preceding the hearing of the order' (Levinas 1981: 149–150) or a 'prayer in which the worshipper asks that his prayer be heard' (Levinas 1981: 10). In order for the meaning of being to be produced, it must be conveyed or expressed in an expression: the sense of the expression expresses the meaning of being. This dialogic of encounter refuses to reduce language to the system of signs or themes conveyed by linguistic vehicles, but takes seriously the manner in which expression is the modality of essence. My expressions as attributes of my existence convey my essence to the neighbour (and vice versa) for my expressions (or hers) express themselves; they are signs made by the giving of signs, not signs of the signs given. That I persist in breathlessness, lassitude, insomnia or exposure to the other person, simply is what I am: my existence for the other, is my essence. 'Saying saying saying itself, without thematizing it, but exposing it again. Saying is thus to make signs of this very signifyingness of the exposure; it is to expose the exposure instead of remaining in it as an act of exposing' (Levinas 1981: 143). (Again in *Totality and Infinity*, in a section called

'Expression [*l'expression*] is the Principle': 'He who signals himself by a sign qua signifying that sign is not the signified of the sign – but delivers the sign and gives it') (Levinas 1991: 92). It is the possibility of giving that extirpates the gravity of the body from its conatus essendi (Levinas 1981: 142).

The expression expresses itself as a modality of expression. It is not merely the attribute or characteristic of my existence which is expressed, for this 'hypostasis' can be exhausted or extinguished by the theme (said) with which I state it. My 'saying' is a modality which expresses itself beyond its expression of what says it (an existing ego) or what is said (the theme expressed). This modality is the production of the meaning of being only because it is first the expression of infinity (or in the intersubjective relation, sincerity or responsibility). 'The absolute experience is not disclosure but revelation: a coinciding of the expressed with him who expresses . . .' (*coïncidance de l'exprimé et de celui qui exprime . . .*) (Levinas 1991: 65–66). It is in conversation that the infinition of the other, called 'face', is a mode irreducible to a 'set of qualities forming an image', overflowing all plastic images, manifesting itself *kath auto* rather than through these images.

CONCLUSION

It should be evident that the philosophy which positively motivates and illuminates Levinas' often vague and rhetorical vision is not Hegelian or Heideggerian, but fundamentally Spinozist. The fundamental point is that the Spinozist conatus essendi is the kernel of Levinas' ethical egoity, and a reading of the third part of the *Ethics* (which I have not attempted here) could bear this out given the other observations I have made about manifestation and identification. The recurrence of *l'expression* and *s'exprimere* in Levinas' work shows that he has intuitions about the role of 'expression' similar to those of Deleuze's reading of Spinoza. Whilst the Latin *exprimere* functions in Spinoza's thinking by always referring to the conatus and to the inclusivity of the attributes of substance Levinas' *l'expression* is disruptive of the said of *s'exprimere* (for example, in a section of *Otherwise than Being* called 'The Saying without the Said').

What is ultimately most Spinozist about Levinas' thinking is the relation between the act of expressing and what is expressed. In Spinoza, the attributes of God express the monistic substance of reality, and all of the entities of that manifested reality are modes which express that expression. Indeed, the expressions of human action in the endeavour to persist in being express the complicity between these attributes and these human entities. This folding of expressions is also Levinasian, though it is in dialogue that expression and manifestation occasion one another. As he writes:

A manifestation turns into an expression, a skin left desolate by an irreversible departure which immediately denies it, reverted to the status of a ridge of sand on the earth, driving out even the memory of this departure. [. . .] Expression, saying, is not added on to significations that are 'visible' in the light of phenomena, to modify them or confuse them and introduce into them 'poetic,' 'literary,' 'verbal' enigmas; the significations said offer a hold to the saying which 'disturbs' them, like writings awaiting an interpretation. But herein is the in principle irreversible antecedence of the word with respect to being, the irretrievable delay of the said after the saying. Of this antecedence, the significations which, meanwhile, suffice to themselves, bear a trace, which they forthwith contest and efface. (Levinas 1987: 69)

Hence, the distinction between expression and what it expresses is not a designating, but a resounding, activity of identification. As Levinas says in the preface of *Totality and Infinity*, it does not really matter if what is expressed also expresses, as if the signification of the said is irreducible to that said. What this means is that even hypostasis and thematization express, that is, forbid the final 'totalization' of essence in a theme. They disrupt

119

or 'disturb' the attempt to encapsulate or crystallize a designated entity within a theme; they permit its resonances in an infinite deferral of the moment of truth, in infinite horizons of meaning.

To conclude, it should be said that the complicity between the Spinozist and Levinasian understandings of personal identity and the further 'ethicization' of the former's *conatus essendi* through the latter's exposure to the face of the neighbour bolsters Levinas understanding of expression. Indeed, it is true that this constitutes a transcendental philosophy, or rather, a philosophy motivated towards transcendence: infinite expressions, significations and responsibilities. However, the significance of thematization, manifestation, apophansis, and generally *s'expremere*, points to the crucial role of 'totalization' as that which provides coherence and permits the expressiveness of themes along with the meaning of being conveyed in the sense of the expressions. The meaning of being is conveyed only in the sense of the expressions of others. It is in dialogue that the individual's way of existing is ethical.

BIBLIOGRAPHY

Deleuze, G. (1990) *Expressionism in Philosophy: Spinoza*. trans. Martin Joughin: NY: Zone.

Levinas, E. (1966) 'On the Trail of the Other' in *Philosophy Today* vol. X Spring.

—— (1981) *Otherwise than Being or Beyond Essence*. trans. A. Lingis.The Hague: Martinus Nijhof.

—— (1987) *The Collected Philosophical Papers*. A. Lingis, (ed.). The Hague: Martinus Nijhoff.

—— (1991) *Totality and Infinity: An Essay on Exteriority*. trans. A. Lingis. Dordrecht: Kluwer.

—— (1993) *Dieu, la Mort et Le Temps*. Paris: Grasset.

Spinoza. (1989) *Ethics*. trans. A. Boyle. London: James Dent and Everyman Library.

Chapter 7

A Supreme Heteronomy?
Arche and Topology in Difficult Freedom

Philip Leonard
Nottingham Trent University

John F. Taylor rose to reply . . . .
It seemed to me that I heard the voice of that Egyptian
highpriest raised in a tone of like haughtiness and like pride
. . . . Why will you jews not accept our culture, our religion
and our language? You are a tribe of nomad herdsmen, we
are a mighty people. You have no cities nor no wealth . . . .
You have but emerged from primitive conditions: we have a
literature, a priesthood, an agelong history and a polity. . . .
– But, ladies and gentlemen, had the youthful Moses
listened to and accepted that view of life, had he bowed his
head and bowed his will and bowed his spirit before that
arrogant admonition he would never have brought the
chosen people out of their house of bondage . . .
J.J. O'Molloy said not without regret:
– And yet he died without having entered the land of
promise.

James Joyce, *Ulysses*

Following Jacques Derrida's early, provocative and decisive
'Violence and Metaphysics: An Essay on the Thought of
Emmanuel Levinas' (1978) Levinas's work has been situated
as both a devastating displacement of prevailing constructions
of identity in Western thought *and* a reproductive retraversal of

121

predominant motifs in the Greek philosophical tradition. With the coterminous movements of transgression and consolidation, Levinas's response to phenomenology lays bare the spurious assumptions underpinning notions of presence, immediacy, origin and essence, yet does so while remaining firmly committed to terms and concepts that are supposedly disputed throughout his work.

The problem of this double syntax extends beyond Levinas's explicitly theoretical material. In texts which appear to renounce the main concerns of his post-phenomenological labours – most notably those texts which engage with issues in Judaic culture – Levinas simultaneously shores up conventional structures of identity while at the same time challenging the Hellenic framework within which identity is constructed. This essay will explore some ramifications of Levinas's seemingly non-theoretical writings on Judaism and will try to extrapolate from this material a cultural agenda which is, to an extent, shared with his better-known philosophical material.

THEORY AB-USED

Along with *Totality and Infinity* and *Otherwise than Being or Beyond Essence*, one of Levinas's most significant (though infrequently discussed) texts is the series of short writings anthologized in 1963 as *Difficult Freedom: Essays on Judaism*. This collection is predminantly concerned with exploring the role of Judaism in the modern world – an issue that is largely unaddressed by Levinas's philosophical writings – but does so while moving away from the incessant interrogation of language, representation and alterity that otherwise prevails in his work. In a rather anecdotal and autobiographical manner *Difficult Freedom* more or less suspends Levinas's preoccupation with identity and alterity, ethics and ontology, proximity and substitution – notions that are at the forefront of such texts as *Totality and Infinity* and *Otherwise than Being or Beyond Essence* – and instead confronts such issues as the influence of Hitlerism on Judaism and the emergence of Israel as a nation-state.

Throughout his career Levinas has maintained a fundamental scission between the dual trajectory of his work – that is, between his philosophical labour and his commentaries on Judaism. In the radio interviews conducted with Philippe Nemo, Levinas responds to the question of the degree of coexistence between the biblical and philosophical traditions and states: 'I have never aimed explicitly to "harmonize" or "reconcile" both traditions' (1985: 24). In a more recent interview, Levinas reiterates the relative autonomy of these 'two traditions' when he describes the Talmud as a source of critical stimulation:

> The essential thing was the invitation to *think* that I found in these documents. Among my publications there is a whole series of works drawn from this, but I never run together my general philosophy with what I call the more confessional writing. (Mortley 1991: 13)

This dichotomy between Levinas's philosophical and theologico-confessional writing is, however, open to question, since identifying elements of *Difficult Freedom* which connect with what Levinas calls his 'general philosophy' is a fairly straightforward exercise.[1] Two texts of 1961, 'Jewish Thought Today' (initially published in *L'Arche* and subsequently included in *Difficult Freedom*) and *Totality and Infinity* highlight the fact that intertextual relationships do exist between different aspects of Levinas's corpus. For example, the declaration in 'Jewish Thought Today' that 'Ethics is an optics of the Divine' (1990: 159) cryptically restates *Totality and Infinity*'s reformulation of ethics as countering heliocentric or scopophilic conventions of identification: 'ethics is an optics. But it is a "vision" without image, bereft of the synoptic and totalizing virtues of vision' (1969: 23). A further connection is apparent with the argument that the 'basic message' of Judaism

> consists in bringing the meaning of the ethical relation between men, in appealing to man's personal responsibility – in which he feels chosen and irreplaceable – in order to bring about a human society in which men are treated as men. (1990: 159)

Levinas here couples the notion of secular redemption in Judaic theology with his supposedly 'philosophical' claim that social structures emerge from the pre-ontological realm of ethical responsibility. Clearly, this throws into crisis any absolute distinction between Levinas's philosophical and confessional writing as it indubitably takes his post-phenomenological ethics to the terrain of Judaic commentary.

A fracture occurs in this homology between Levinas's different material, however, with the inconsistent treatments of cultural identity in 'Jewish Thought Today' and *Totality and Infinity*. *Totality and Infinity* does, of course, rail against the notion of totality in Western philosophy, particularly its attempt to conceptualize and classify otherness with essentialist, universalist and transcendental categories. But in addition to working through this familiar motif in Levinas's work, *Totality and Infinity* also contains some important – though allusive – references to imperialism. The preface, for example, contrasts ethics with the simulacrum of peace that follows imperial conflict: 'The peace of empires issued from war rests on war. It does not restore to the alienated beings their lost identity' (1969: 22). Such marginal gestures towards the non-ethical status of imperialist and colonialist practices set the agenda for interpreting the remainder of this volume as an unmistakable, though latent, critique of cultural imperialism.[2]

Difficult Freedom, in contrast, has a more complicated – and, indeed, more direct – relationship with cultural identity. Although selected essays in this volume may be construed as sympathetic with post- or anti-imperialist criticism, other essays appear to realign Levinas's position on colonialism since they display a fairly overt affinity with ideological conventions regarding the status of Eastern and Western cultural strata. This reorientation is perhaps most explicit in 'Jewish Thought Today', where Levinas claims that contemporary Judaic thought has been marked by three 'great events' (1990: 159). Two of these events are readily identifiable: the first, he explains, was the regeneration of anti-semitism in the form of German National Socialism, and the second was the establishment of an Israeli state after the second world war. But it is the third event, what Levinas calls: 'The arrival on the historical scene of those underdeveloped Afro-Asiatic masses who are strangers [*des masses sous-développées afro-asiatiques étrangères*] to the Sacred History that forms the heart of the Judaic-Christian world' (1990: 160), that seems to throw into crisis his critique of Western identity. Levinas's discussion of the first two 'great events' seems uncontroversial (it is impossible to detect Levinas's sympathies in both instances), but the final point relies on the sort of orientalist idiom and cultural narcissism so frequently problematized by recent theory. What is surprising about Levinas's (albeit unextrapolated and relatively unclear) support for Judaic national politics is that he seems to recognize the need for a geo-political reinscription of Judaism, yet fails to discuss the historical and cultural ramifications that accompanied this reinscription.

This neglect for contextual matters occurs at various points in *Difficult Freedom*, not least where Levinas argues that the creation of Israel occurred not, as might be the case with many national formations, for the accumulation of political and economic currency. Claiming that this state came into being in order to fulfil the Biblical task allotted to the chosen people, Levinas suggests that in order to understand the significance of Zionism it is necessary to step beyond recent social history and to foreground the representation of Israel in the Old Testament: 'The attempt to create a state in Palestine and to regain the creative inspiration of old whose pronouncements were of universal significance cannot be understood without the Bible' (1990: 25). This idea is further emphasized in 'Jewish Thought Today', where Levinas continues to give precedence to the ancient rather than contemporary history of Israel. He asserts that 'The State of Israel has become the place where man is uprooted from his recent past for the sake of an ancient and prophetic past, where he seeks his authenticity . . .' (1990: 164); in passages like these Levinas declares that the concerns of Israel should be given pre-eminence over those of other communities which occupy the same territorial ground. Indeed, in asking

'Surely the rise of the countless masses of Asiatic and under-developed peoples threatens this new-found authenticity?' (1990: 165), Levinas implies that subsequent (and less civilized) cultures endanger the return to an original topos by the contemporary state of Israel.

These comments regarding Judaism can be problematized on various levels. An incongruency arises, for example, between Levinas's description of dispersed and disseminated identity without value ('human autonomy rests on a supreme hetero-nomy', 1990: 11) and his later gestures towards a cultural hierarchy. Perhaps more urgent than noting theoretical discrepancies in Levinas's work is recognizing that his Manichean trope resonates with some prevailing presupposi-tions about cultural value. We could insist that Levinas's description of, on the one hand, those with an authentic right to Israeli territory and, on the other hand, his exnomination of an 'Afro-Asiatic mass' is an example of what Fredric Jameson calls a 'strategy of representational containment' (1988: 10), perpetuating what Edward Said describes as a simplistic cultural opposition between Israel and Palestine in which: '. . . Palestinians were described by . . . condemnatory and confining categories', whereas 'Israel was routinely referred to in terms indicating morality and flexibility' (1990: 271).

Other commentators on Israel testify further to the notion – unaddressed by Levinas – that the territorial dimension of the Judaic religious community has been historically inseparable from familiar imperialist practices. Stefan Goranov, for example, contends:

> Both as regards its character and its pernicious role, it [Zionism] is an inseparable component of the ideology and practice of the most reactionary and aggressive part of the international, imperialist bourgeoisie, of the forces of war, colonialism and neocolonialism. (1979: 27)

Goranov continues his polemic when, in stark contrast with Levinas's claim that Judaism is concerned with ethical relations, he further asserts that 'racist slogans' and 'immoral theses'

(1979: 28) underpin Judaism's claims to unique election by God. Commentators such as Said and Goranov therefore highlight the occlusion of recent middle-Eastern history behind Israel's appeal to an originary topology. And in so doing, they illuminate Levinas's failure to connect his Manichean idiom (differentiating an advanced people of the Book, those with a 'prophetic past' [1990: 164] from an uncivilized, homogenous orient of 'countless hordes' [1990: 165]) with the violence perpetrated against Palestinians before, during and subsequent to the transformation of Judaism from a diasporic religious community into a culture occupying a specific geographical site.

AS OLD AS THE WORLD?

In addition to questioning the legitimacy of Levinas's nomination of Judaism as *the* chosen community (a nomination that can be sanctioned only if the Judaic conception of metaphysical authority is permitted[3]), we can also contest his reliance upon an archaic classificatory framework. In spite of his apparent awareness of distortive and reconstructive temporalities (in 'Diachrony and Representation', for example, he states that 'there is a past irreducible to a presence . . . an immemorial past' [1987b: 111–12]), *Difficult Freedom* nevertheless, it would seem, relies upon an archaeological, metahistorical, transcultural positioning of Israeli and Judaic culture.

The sort of problems generated by the recourse to cultural archaeology in *Difficult Freedom* have formed the focal point for much of the recent work that has occurred in post-colonial theory[4] – not least in the anti-essentialist and anti-foundationalist undertakings of Gayatri Chakravorty Spivak's early essays. And it is Spivak's confrontation of the discursive and epistemological practices of imperialism that has most relevance for Levinas's comments on contemporary Judaism and the state of Israel. In 'A Literary Representation of the Subaltern', Spivak follows Foucault's work by declaring that: "events' are never not discursively constituted' (1988: 242) and concludes that decolonization cannot elide the effects of colonialism by attempting to represent a pre-colonial subject or national identity. Here Spivak claims that the theorization of post-coloniality must excise from its discourse all reference to an indigenous and native essence. 'If the story of the rise of nationalist resistance to imperialism is to be disclosed coherently', she states, 'it is the role of the indigenous subaltern that must be strategically excluded' (1988: 245). This position is further elaborated in 'Can the Subaltern Speak?', where Spivak professes that the search for an *arche* is, given intellectual developments in the latter part of the twentieth century, a spurious enterprise: 'This paper is committed to the notion that . . . a nostalgia for lost origins can be detrimental to the exploration of social realities within the critique of imperialism' (1993a: 87). For Spivak, then, the ideological, economic, epistemological and ontological restructuring of colonized peoples must be traversed in any critique of colonialism, and any attempt to restitute the pre-colonial character of subaltern identity is, in the wake of contemporary cultural theory, questionable.

It is precisely these elements of Spivak's work that create difficulties for Levinas's *Difficult Freedom*, since in this anthology the creation of Israel is constantly substantiated through the notions of theological primacy and divine provenance. 'Jewish Thought Today', as we have seen, attempts to interpret developments in twentieth century Jewish history with reference the 'ancient and prophetic past' of Israel. For Spivak, however, such an originary and metaphysical account of cultural identity fails to realize that historical events are irremediably reconstituted by discursive strata, and equally fails to elude the pitfalls of a vain nostalgia for an irrevocable past.

The significance of Spivak's counter-originary work for *Difficult Freedom* is compounded by the fact that Levinas repeatedly returns to the notion of Israel as *arche* culture. 'Messianic Texts', for example, is largely concerned with the particular/universal dyad in Judaic theology and attempts to articulate the privileged role of Israel in world history. But rather than simply discuss the archaic Biblical inscription of the

Judaic community (an inscription subject to innumerable cultural, epistemological and theological transformations), Levinas declares that the contemporary state of Israel rediscovers and recuperates the original properties of Judaism. Although the early character of Judaic theology has been obscured by its participation in world history, 'Messianic Texts' argues that the state of Israel constitutes a return to the primarily messianic function of Judaism:

> The messianic sensibility inseparable from the knowledge of being chosen . . . would be irremediably lost . . . if the solution of the State of Israel did not represent an attempt to reunite the irreversible acceptance of universalist history with the necessarily particularist messianism. This universalist particularism . . . can be found in the aspirations of Zionism . . . . It is in the preservation of this universalist particularism, at the heart of History in which it is henceforth to be found, that I see the importance of the Israeli solution for the History of Israel. (1990: 96)

Although hinting at the necessity to treat Israel as irretrievably distant from its initial messianism, Levinas here nostalgically claims that the founding principles of Israel are reclaimed by its recent transformation into a nation-state occupying a specific territorial topos.

Difficult Freedom, we can therefore argue, constantly constructs the contemporary cultural situation of Judaism and Israel through an appeal to its earliest creation. But it seems plausible to argue that this elision of cultural transfigurations of Judaism is deeply problematical, for just as Spivak questions empiricist attempts to identify a pre-colonial essence, so we might question Levinas's reclamation of an original Israeli culture. In these essays he displays what Spivak calls a 'nostalgia for lost origins' and (unlike such texts as *Totality and Infinity* and *Otherwise than Being or Beyond Essence*) fails to acknowledge the key developments of post-war theory (specifically in semiotics, structuralism and post-structuralism) concerning the discursive constitution of identity. Following the conclusions made by Spivak in 'Can the Subaltern Speak?' and 'A Literary Representation of the Subaltern' we could point out that between the second century and 1948 the Judaic community has occupied the unique position of being entirely diasporic, and has thus acquired the status of a subaltern culture irredeemably and irrevocably marked by various epistemological, ethical, religious, economic and social formations. It is this far-reaching transformation of Judaism that, at certain points in *Difficult Freedom*, Levinas seems reluctant to consider: he excises from his account of Israel, Zionism and Judaism the problematization of pure cultural origins, stable diasporic identity and uncompromised theological structures – a task that is at the heart of other elements of his work.

VIGILANCE AND ESSENTIALISM

Spivak's critique of foundational characterizations of nationality and identity clearly highlights some problems in Levinas's essays on Judaism and Israel. However, Spivak's concern for origins, essences and foundations need not *necessarily* result in a wholesale condemnation of Levinas's writings on Judaic culture. Interestingly, Spivak's most recent publications have moved strikingly close to Levinas by directly confronting issues that have preoccupied Levinas throughout his intellectual career. In her material of the 1990s Spivak has started to investigate, in more detail than in her previous work, the relationship between ethics and subjectivity – a relationship that is, of course, at the core of Levinas's response to Husserlian and Heideggerian phenomenology. In a recent interview, for example, she states: 'I am more interested now in imagining the other ethical subject' (Spivak *et al.*, 1993: 25) and displays an interest in an ethics beyond identity when asking: 'How is it possible to think such an (ethical) subject outside the monotheist Judeo-Christian tradition and its critique?' (1993: 25). In an essay on Echo in Ovid's *Metamorphoses* we hear a euphony with Levinas's notion of ethics as a '"relation without relation", which no-one can encompass or thematize' (1969:

295, tr. mod.) when Spivak states that 'Ethics are not a problem of knowledge but a call of relationship (without relationship, as limit case)' (1993b: 32). This turning towards ethics demonstrates a notable degree of congruence between Spivak and Levinas: by trying to 'imagine the other ethical subject' beyond comprehension, Spivak unquestionably pursues a task similar to Levinas's examination of an ethical responsibility beyond essence, identity, discourse and subjectivity.

Crucially, this movement towards ethics develops into an explicit engagement with Levinas's anti-ontological ethics of difference in Spivak's 'French Feminism Revisited: Ethics and Politics' (an essay which retraverses themes addressed in her seminal 'French Feminism in an International Frame'). Here Spivak responds to Luce Irigaray's 'The Fecundity of the Caress' (on the 'Phenomenology of Eros' section in *Totality and Infinity*) by taking Levinas to task for advancing an ethics of difference which relies too readily on prevailing ideologies of sex and gender. Thus, Spivak contends that Levinas is a 'passive-masculinist philosopher', (1992: 74–5) that 'the empirical scene of sexual congress behind Levinas's 'Phenomenology of Eros' is almost comically patriarchal' (1992: 76), and (with a virulence absent from Irigaray's essay) that she finds 'it difficult to take this prurient heterosexist, male-identified ethics seriously' (1992: 77). By adopting this position 'French Feminism Revisited' concurs with those commentators who find in Levinas's work not an 'ex-cendence', transgression or transcendence of ontologico-cultural motifs, not an unproblematic invocation of a pre-ontological, extra-discursive, dissimulated encounter with the other, but a blindness to aporia, a philosophy of difference that is profoundly invested in 'the same', in entrenched codifications of sexuality and gender, in familiar contradistinctions and binarities, and in a conventionally empirical methodology which occludes the complexities of constitutive discursivity.

However, Spivak's work is heteromorphic, auto-interruptive and internally discontinuous (in one interview she tellingly states 'my search is not a search for coherence' [1990: 11]), and because of this there are aspects of her recent work on ethics and imperialism which complicate the issues at stake in Levinas's essays on Judaism. For, in spite of her onslaught on essentialism in anti-colonial texts, Spivak does to an extent endorse essentialism by claiming that imperialist and colonial ideologies can be surmounted only by an adaptive transfiguration of those concepts, strategies and motifs that have characterized Western culture. In spite of railing against the comprehension of identity with essentialist and universalist terms in such essays as 'A Literary Representation of the Subaltern' and 'Can the Subaltern Speak?', Spivak does, in other places, endorse possible redeployments of conventionally essentialist categories. *The Post-Colonial Critic*, a collection of interviews with Spivak, at several points advocates the strategic, oppositional use of signifiers, concepts and cultural structures which have predominantly been used to marginalize specific communities. 'Criticism, Feminism and the Institution', for example, carries a telling admission:

> . . . I must say I am an essentialist from time to time . . . . I think it's absolutely on target to take a stand against the discourses of essentialism, universalism . . . . But *strategically* we cannot. Since the moment of essentializing, universalizing, saying yes to the onto-phenomenological question, is irreducible, let us at least become vigilant about our own practice and use it as much as we can rather than make the totally counter-productive gesture of repudiating it. (1990: 11)

Similarly, 'Strategy, Identity, Writing' acclaims as one of the greatest contributions made by deconstruction the notion that critique is, perforce, intimately implicated in the structure under scrutiny. The only productive response to this inescapable complicity, Spivak observes, is an 'awareness' or (to use a term favoured by Spivak) 'vigilance' of this situation: 'Since one cannot not be an essentialist, why not look at the ways in which one is essentialist, carve out a representative essentialist

132

position, and then do a politics according to the old rules whilst remembering the dangers in this?' (1990: 45).

Spivak augments this ambivalent essentialism in 'French Feminism Revisited' – a text which unequivocally attacks Levinas's work, but surprisingly reveals the possibility for other, less condemnatory readings of *Difficult Freedom*:

> . . . the generalization of a *bicameral* universal, or even two universals, to provide the impossible differed/deferred grounding of the ethics of sexual difference in the fecund caress seems to respond to the call of the larger critique of humanism with which post-coloniality must negotiate, even as it negotiates with the political and cultural legacy of the European Enlightenment. (1992: 80)

Here Spivak develops an ethics of difference by arguing that 'the critique of humanism', shared by both post-colonial and feminist criticism, is facilitated by – indeed, necessitates recourse to – universalizations that otherwise may seem problematical. Her model is therefore more complex than Benita Parry's description of it as '*against* the nostalgia for lost origins as a basis for counter-hegemonic production' (1987: 34, my emphasis), since Spivak argues that critical practices need to be vigilant towards their own participation in an irreducible cultural network, and must strive to essentialize identity only as part of counter-hegemonic resistance. In spite of various remonstrations, invectives and interdictions against reversing and reproducing the framework which violently locates identity and difference, Spivak also recognizes that, in a strategic sense, reproduction of prevailing binaries *is* necessary.

It is this equivocal position on essentialism in Spivak's work that can help us re-read with greater complexity Levinas's comments on Judaism and Israel. We have already discovered that, given the general current of post-structuralist and post-colonial theory, there are profound problems with Levinas's claim that the state of Israel reinscribes an original and divinely ordained national topology. The equivocal position on essentialism displayed by Spivak can, however, provoke a very different interpretation of Levinas's work since it becomes arguable that his archaeological approach to Judaism responds to the inescapable and overarching structures governing Hellenic hegemony by attempting an insurgent mimesis.

Various remarks in *Difficult Freedom* certainly suggest that some of Levinas's comments on the state of Israel are based upon strategic, rather than absolute, value and exemplify what Homi Bhabha describes as: 'the revaluation of the assumption of colonial identity through the repetition of discriminatory identity effects' (1986a: 173). Thus, in 'Means of Identification' he states that the preservation of Judaic culture requires certain provisional compromises:

> For many Israelis, their identity card is the full extent of their Jewish identity as it is, perhaps, for all those potential Israelis who are still in the Diaspora. But here Jewish identity runs the risk of becoming confused with national-ism, and from that point on, a loss of Jewish identity is probably the price to be paid in order to have it renewed. (1990: 51)

'The State of Israel and the Religion of Israel' similarly claims that: 'Despite being scarcely established on our own land we are happy to emulate all the "modern nations"' (1990: 216). Not simply shoring up dominant national formations, Levinas here seems to argue that the political, economic and social structures prevailing in Western metropolitan countries must be taken up and reconfigured in order to invert the dispersed and marginal positions occupied by Judaic communities in relation to the so-called advanced and civilized First World.

Reading Levinas's characterization of contemporary Judaism as simultaneously inhabiting and reworking conventional national narratives also extends to his preoccupation with the founding principles of Judaic culture. While it might seem that Levinas perpetuates a mythological, logocentric and ontological fiction when appealing to an originary Hebraic identity, it might equally be the case that his claims that Israel is 'as old as the world', (1990: 166) and that the Zionist project allows the denouement of an 'alienation that lasted a thousand years' (1990: 164), signal the fact that certain theoretical conventions (such as the notions of origin and authenticity) are prerequisites for Judaism's preservation. Similar to Spivak's equivocal and inconsistent position on essentialism, Levinas's essays on Judaism display a crucial ambivalence. But this ambivalence does not mean that these essays contain irreconcilable, disjointed or incommensurable arguments. The margins of *Difficult Freedom* do demonstrate Levinas's awareness of the problems surrounding the transformation of knowledge, subjectivity and cultural identity. But this text elides a substantial interrogation of these problems because Levinas is here principally concerned with the more urgent issue of Judaism's topographical stability and with overcoming the 'total dereliction' (1990: 11) that has marked Jewish history.

In isolation, Levinas's statements about the state of Israel are strikingly problematical, since (as Bhabha says of Fanon) they are 'too quick to name the Other' (1986b: xix) and appear to perpetuate numerous mythologies surrounding culture and difference. However, comparison with other texts by Levinas (a comparison decried by Levinas, but nonetheless crucial for understanding his work on Judaism) indicates the fallacy of attempting to treat *Difficult Freedom* as a closed and discrete text. Certainly, this anthology contains some controversial comments (not least the remarks on 'underdeveloped Afro-Asiatic masses'), but Levinas's essays on Judaism are more sophisticated than first reading suggests. Although these essays initially seem to counter a number of themes confronted by post-structuralist theory (by attempting to recuperate an originary moment), this recuperation could, in the light of Spivak's distinction between nostalgic and strategic essentialism, be interpreted as a tropology of topology, employing given structures and discourses to resist the discriminating Hellenic/Hebraic dichotomy.

To claim that there is in Levinas's work a calculated use of codes and conventions is also to question his distinction between philosophical and confessional writing. Throughout this essay it has been shown that Levinas writes in a different mode during his commentaries on the contemporary condition of Judaism. When endorsing features of Zionism, charting the emergence of Israel as a state, or reconciling contemporary Judaic thought with Old Testament theology, Levinas is less concerned with exhaustive analyses of the problems inherent in the tradition of ontology than he is in other texts. To maintain this scission between the philosophical and the theologico-confessional would, however, be disingenuous; just as the philosophical texts utilize terms and concepts drawn from Judaic theology, so the commentaries on Judaism are partly motivated by philosophical issues. While this interplay is occasionally explicit, the majority of the essays on Judaism appear to discard the theoretical rigour that is displayed in the majority of Levinas's texts. Nonetheless, it is crucial to recognize that even the seemingly untheoretical moments of his work potentially have a theoretical sur-text. Spivak's account of strategic and inverted essentialism suggests that Levinas's temporary suspension of theory is in fact motivated by a tacit hypertheoretical impulse, and that his movement away from theoretical writing highlights the cultural exigencies at stake in his work on Judaic culture.

Like *Totality and Infinity* and *Otherwise than Being or Beyond Essence*, *Difficult Freedom* is written with a double syntax, and repeatedly draws upon metaphysical conventions in order to signify a crisis in Western thought. Although *Difficult Freedom* does not engage in the detailed examination of language, epistemology, identity and alterity that preoccupies his other texts, the essays on Judaism do attempt to reconfigure the relationship between Hellenism and Hebraism and consequently share with Levinas's other work a critique of the restricted economy of identity and alterity in Western culture.

NOTES

1 In this manner, Susan Handelman argues that: 'just as his philosophical "Greek" has a strong Hebrew accent, here, too, his Hebrew is tinged with Greek' (1991: 309).
2 The argument that Levinas not only destabilizes the schematic totality of the self-same, but also critiques forms of cultural domination is taken up by Robert Young. Young claims that Levinas: 'connects the form of knowledge that is self-centred but directed outwards, philosophy as "egology", quite explicitly with the appropriating narcissism of the West' (1990: 17). Similarly, Robert Bernasconi documents Levinas's awareness of the fact that even in so-called neo-or post-colonial conditions a residual colonialism remains, and that: 'colonization does not end with the political process of decolonization' (1990: 71). Bernasconi's comments apply to the section of 'Meaning and Sense' where Levinas states that: 'the political work of decolonization is thus attached to an ontology – to a thought of being, interpreted in its multiple and multivocal cultural meaning' (1987a: 86).
3 Said, for instance, dissents, claiming that the notion of the Promised Land is 'a concept as elusive and as abstract as any that one could encounter' (1992: 95), and has become 'an anachronistic biblical argument' (1992: 137).
4 Since the emergence of post-colonial theory, the use of the prefix 'post' has been contested. Anne McClintock, for example, states that this designation is questionable because it operates with an over-arching, singular and European historical narrative, and because it naively ignores the fact that certain cultures continue to experience colonial conditions: 'Ireland may, at a pinch, be 'post-colonial,' but for the inhabitants of the Israeli Occupied Territories and the West Bank, there may be nothing "post" about colonialism at all' (1992: 3).

BIBLIOGRAPHY

Bernasconi, R. (1990) 'One Way Traffic: The Ontology of Decoloniza-tion and its Ethics', in G. A. Johnson & M. B. Smith (eds) *Ontology and Alterity in Merleau-Ponty*, Evanston: Northwestern University Press: 67–80.
Bhabha, H. K. (1986a) 'Signs Taken for Wonders: Questions of Ambivalence and Authority under a Tree Outside Delhi, May 1817', in H. L. Gates Jr. (ed.) *'Race', Writing and Difference*, Chicago: University of Chicago Press: 163–184.

—— (1986b) 'Foreword: Remembering Fanon', in Frantz Fanon, *Black Skin, White Masks*, trans. C. Lam Markmann, London: Pluto: vii–xxv.

Derrida, J. (1978) 'Violence and Metaphysics: An Essay on the Thought of Emmanuel Levinas', in *Writing and Difference*, trans. A. Bass, London: Routledge & Kegan Paul: 79–153.

Goranov, S. (1979) 'Racism: A Basic Principle of Zionism', in *Zionism and Racism*, The International Organization for the Elimination of all Forms of Racial Discrimination (ed.) New Brunswick, NJ: North American Inc.: 27–36.

Handelman, S. A. (1991) *Fragments of Redemption: Jewish Thought and Literary Theory in Benjamin, Scholem & Levinas*, Bloomington, Ill.: Indiana University Press.

Jameson, F. (1988) *Modernism and Nationalism*, Field Day Pamphlet 14, Derry: Field Day Theatre Co.

Levinas, E. (1969) *Totality and Infinity: An Essay on Exteriority*, trans. A. Lingis, Pittsburgh: Duquesne University Press.

—— (1985) *Ethics and Infinity: Conversations with Philippe Nemo*, trans. R. A. Cohen, Pittsburgh: Duquesne University Press.

—— (1987a) 'Meaning and Sense', in A. Lingis (ed.) *Collected Philosophical Papers*, The Hague, Martinus Nijhoff: 75–107.

—— (1987b) 'Diachrony and Representation' in *Time and the Other and Additional Essays*, trans. R. A. Cohen, Pittsburgh: Duquesne University Press: 97–120.

—— (1990) *Difficult Freedom: Essays on Judaism*, trans. S. Hand, London: Athlone.

McClintock, A. (1992) 'The Angel of Progress: Pitfalls of the term "Post-Colonial"', *Social Text* 1–15.

Mortley, R. (1991) *French Philosophers in Conversation*, London: Routledge.

Parry, B. (1987) 'Problems in Current Theories of Colonial Discourse', *Oxford Literary Review* 9: 27–58.

Said, E. W. (1990) '*Intifada* and Independence', in R. Radford R. & M. H. Ellis (eds) *Beyond Occupation: Jewish, Christian, and Palestinian Voices for Peace*, Boston: Beacon Press: 262–81.

—— (1992) *The Question of Palestine*, London: Vintage.

Spivak, G. C. (1988) 'A Literary Representation of the Subaltern: A Woman's Text from the Third World', in *In Other Worlds: Essays in Cultural Politics*, London: Routledge: 241–268.

—— (1990) *The Post-Colonial Critic*, London: Routledge.

—— (1992) 'French Feminism Revisited: Ethics and Politics', in J. Butler & J. W. Scott (eds) *Feminists Theorize the Political*, London: Routledge: 54–85.

—— (1993a) 'Can the Subaltern Speak?', in P. Williams & L.

Chrisman (eds) *Colonial Discourse and Post-Colonial Theory*, London: Harvester Wheatsheaf: 66–111.

—— (1993b) 'Echo', *New Literary History* 24 (1): 17–43.

Spivak, G. C., *et al.* (1993) 'An Interview with Gayatri Chakravorty Spivak', *Boundary* 2 20: 24–50.

Young, R. (1990) *White Mythologies: Writing History and the West*, London: Routledge.

Chapter 8

Levinas and the Jewish Ideal of the Sage

A. H. Lesser
University of Manchester

In his introduction to *Nine Talmudic Readings*, Levinas says:

> The Talmud is not a mere extension of the Bible. It sees
> itself as a second layer of meanings; critical and fully
> conscious, it goes back to the meanings of scripture in a
> rational spirit. The sages of the Talmud, the Rabbis, are
> called *Hakhamim* (wise men). They claim a different
> authority from that of the prophets, neither inferior nor
> superior. Does the word *Hakham* (wise) denote a sage or a
> scholar or a rational human being? We would need an exact
> philological investigation here. In any case, the Talmudists
> themselves referred to the Greek philosophers as *Hakhmei
> Yavan*, the Hakhamim of Greece. (1990: 7)

In this paper, I want to consider both the traditional Jewish
conception of the *Hakham* and Levinas's interpretation of it, in
particular his question whether a *Hakham* is a 'sage or a scholar
or a rational human being' (or all three). Not only is this
important in itself: there is the question whether Levinas has
seen himself as a *Hakham*, or as one striving to be a *Hakham*,
and whether this has affected his approach to philosophy as
well as to the study of Talmud.

We may begin with a note on authority in Judaism. It has
been pointed out (Brody, 1966) that the Judaism of the Bible

recognized four kinds of authority. There was the king, subject to the law but the supreme political authority; the priest, who maintained the sacrificial cult; the prophet, who claimed to have been spoken to by God directly (though sometimes obscurely); and the rabbi or sage, who interpreted the *Torah* (which should be translated 'teaching' rather than 'law'). Of these, only the rabbi survived the destruction of the Temple in 70 C.E.: the ending of the cult, which could only take place in the Temple, left the priests with only vestiges of their obligations and privileges, and the people as a whole under direct Roman rule, with no chance even of a non-Davidie 'king' subordinate to Rome (let alone a 'proper' king descended from David), while prophecy was considered to have ended some centuries earlier with Malachi.

This already indicates certain features of the *hakham*. He does not acquire authority through birth, like the king or priest (with the proviso that traditionally to have official authority a sage usually had to be male), nor is his authority dependent on any particular place, such as the land of Israel. Nor is he a prophet, with a 'hot line' to God: he is someone who has used the intelligence God gave him to such good effect that it is proper to recognize him as a fit person to give legal opinions and to teach – 'he may judge; he may teach' is part of the traditional formula by which rabbinical authority has been conferred.

So the authority of the *hakham* is the authority of intelligence and knowledge. But this intelligence must be appropriately used. First, the set texts on which it is exercised consist only of those, whether written or oral, recognized by tradition. Secondly – and this is the vital point – to read texts in the spirit of the *hakhamim* is at one level, despite the many different interpretative techniques used by the rabbis, to read them in a particular way – a way that contrasts both with the way of the critical academic and with the way of the dogmatic preacher.

The difference between the approach of the *hakham* and the approach of the academic is neatly summed up by Annette Aronowicz in her translator's introduction to *Nine Talmudic Readings* (xxxi), when she says that the key to Levinas' hermeneutic is 'the conviction, before one knows what the teaching amounts to, that a teaching exists in the texts to be interpreted'. She continues 'We must learn to assume *before-hand* that the other man is master, that he has something to say, that the relation to him points us in the direction of that which is true'. As she rightly points out, this does not require one to adopt the dogmatic position that truth is to be found *only* in this one tradition – one may still hold that there is good and truth in all traditions. But as regards the text one is currently studying, one has to start with the assumption that there is something true and important to be learnt from it.

Now this is not a typical academic approach. Typically, there are two kinds of academic reading of religious or philosophical texts. One is that of the historian of ideas. This is concerned with the understanding of texts in their historical context, with the influence they have had, with what earlier texts or historical events influenced them; but not with whether they are true. The same is the case with the literary approach, which asks questions about the type of literature to which a text belongs, and analyses its structure, but again 'brackets' the question of truth. The furthest one might go, with this type of approach, is to acknowledge that some emotional sympathy for the text is required simply in order to have any chance of properly understanding it: but this is still only the recognition that a sensible person, in the historical context, *could* believe it to be true, and not the assumption that it actually *is* true or contains truth.

The other academic approach, in contrast, takes truth extremely seriously, but tries to start from an entirely unbiased position, with no presuppositions as to the accuracy or value of what is being studied. Again, it may acknowledge that sympathy is required in order to understand the text, and even that if it is open to more than one possible interpretation it is appropriate to adopt the one that shows the author in the most humane and sensible light. But the starting-point is neutral: *after* investigation, one might decide that what is being said is true and important, but this cannot be presupposed. Indeed, if anything, this approach, in its methods, tends to presuppose that the text is unsatisfactory, since it commonly begins by subjecting the text to various tests – whether it is consistent, whether it is based on good evidence, etc. – and accepts it as true only if it passes these tests.

The approach of Levinas, and of Jewish tradition, is clearly very different from this. But, even though it begins with the assumption that there is something valuable to be found in the text, it is also very different from the approach of the pure preacher or the fundamentalist. This approach takes what is written as *defining* what is good and valuable, and therefore as unproblematic: our task is simply to learn from it. If it contradicts our commonsense or our ethical intuitions, this shows that 'commonsense' must be wrong: thus in his *Praeterita*, (1978: 452), Ruskin objects to the liberal Christian F.D. Maurice because he regarded the Song of Deborah (*Judges* 5) as a 'merely rhythmic storm of battle-rage', thereby 'trusting his own amiable feelings as the final interpreters of . . . all the ways of God'. If a text is inconsistent with other parts of the same tradition, this is because God requires different behaviour on different occasions, or makes occasional exceptions to his general laws: this raises no particular problems.

In contrast, the *hakhamim* look for an interpretation that is consistent both with commonsense and with the tradition as a whole. As Levinas says (*op.cit.*: 7), the Talmud 'does not have recourse to bits and pieces of what was said elsewhere, but to its concrete wholeness': the tradition, vast as it is, is regarded as being consistent in itself, and also as consistent with what we know about the world and about morality, whether by science or by commonsense or by ethical and human feeling. But any system of rules – though Torah is much more than a system of rules – however consistent in the abstract, will find in practice conflicts between its various instructions when these are applied in concrete situations, so that decisions have to be taken as to which principle takes precedence, and why. Hence, consistency with the tradition may mean *either* that when properly interpreted the text does conform to its principles, *or* that it turns out to be a 'principled exception': it is an exception to one principle because of the greater need to respect another. These considerations can apply both to interpreting a surprising legal or ethical decision and to interpreting Biblical stories in which the text appears to require us to endorse questionable behaviour. An example would be the killing of Sisera by Jael (*Judges* 4–5), already referred to. The fundamentalist, like Ruskin, will say that since the Text calls Jael 'blessed above women', God endorsed her action and it was simply right. The critical historian may regard it as a treacherous murder, approved because it was politically and militarily to Israel's advantage. Jewish tradition, in contrast to both of these, regards it as a transgression, but performed with a good intention: Jael is praised for the excellence of her motive and intention, to save Israel from their enemies – but her action is not to be imitated.

With this in mind, let us consider Levinas himself. In *Nine Talmudic Readings*, pp.25–9, he discusses 2 *Samuel*, chapter 21 and the Talmudic comment in *Yebamot* 58b–59a. The story is that there was a famine in the time of king David, and that when David 'asked the Lord' about it, he was told that it was because of the Gibeonites whom Saul put to death: the Gibeonites were slaves (later on temple slaves) of Canaanite origin, very much at the bottom of the social order. David sent for the Gibeonites and asked them how he should make atonement. They said it was 'not a matter of silver or gold' and asked for seven descendants of Saul to be handed over and put to death; and their dead bodies were left hanging or impaled on a rock (Levinas says that they were killed by being nailed to the rock: but, though this is a possible reading of the text, it is not a necessary one; and there is no need to make things more horrible than is required). Rizpah, mother of two of the seven, remained on the rock throughout the summer, covering the bodies with sacks and keeping off the birds and beasts until they were taken down and buried.

This does not bring out all the features of the story, nor even everything commented on by the Talmud and by Levinas; but it is, I hope, enough for us to consider two points. The first is the way the Talmud focuses on two difficulties in setting the text within the tradition: David's action contradicts two clear commandments of the Torah. to 'put the children to death for the fathers' is forbidden by *Deuteronomy* 24, 16, while 21, 23 says that if a man is put to death and hanged, 'his body shall not remain all night upon the tree, but you shall surely bury him the same day' – not six months later!

To these two difficulties the Talmud gives the same brief answer: 'it is better that a letter of the Torah be damaged than the name of God be profaned'. To reject the demand of the Gibeonites would be to bring the whole system of religious law, and hence God himself, into disrepute: how can God be respected if His law permits murder to be committed with impunity? And this applies to the hanging as well as the execution: if the danger of disrepute is to be avoided, it must be made absolutely clear that the sentence really has been carried out, even if this dishonours the bodies of the executed. It should also be noted that the Gibeonites' comment 'it is not a mater of silver or gold' is fully in accordance with the Torah – *Numbers* 35, 31 says 'you shall take no ransom for the life of a murderer': and this contrasts with the attitude of the Torah to physical injury and stealing property, which may be compensated. Murder is different; so different that the demand of the Gibeonites has to be met if Torah is to be taken seriously.

To this brief answer, Levinas notes, the Talmud adds a brief but very important comment, drawing attention to the fact that the murderer was king and the victims 'strangers' – non-Jews or semi-Jews from the bottom of society (27). This increases the necessity to punish the murder: it is particularly important both that kings may not oppress with impunity and that strangers are protected. 'Let passers-by know this: in Israel princes die a horrible death because strangers were injured by the sovereign. The respect for the stranger and the sanctification of the name of the Eternal are strangely equivalent' (27). This emphasis on the stranger – the Hebrew 'ger', usually so translated, is applied in particular to converts and to resident aliens – serves three purposes. It is very much in line with Jewish ethics: the command to love the stranger occurs thirty-six times in the Pentateuch. It is also – not by coincidence, probably – very much in line with Levinas' ethical philosophy. For the core of this philosophy is the unconditional taking of unlimited responsibility for other people; and it is above all in relation to strangers that the *unconditional* quality of this is displayed. It is not based on an already existing ontological relationship (as may be the case with obligations to one's family or fellow-citizens), or on a freely taken decision (such as entry into a contract), but simply required by the existence of the Other: 'a responsibility for my neighbour, for the other man, *for the stranger or sojourner*, to which nothing in the rigorously ontological order binds me' (Hand, 1989: 84). Finally, it is in line with Levinas' aim of 'translating Jewish thought into the language of modern times' (1990: ix), since it is a characteristic of the twentieth-century that its worst crimes have often taken the form of inhumanity to the resident alien, either as a result of racism or as a result of fears of a political take-over.

So in the eyes of the Talmud and of Levinas this is a story of upholding the claims of the stranger, even against the former royal family, and even at the expense of other principles of justice – that children should not be punished for their parents' crimes, and that the dead body even of a criminal must be respected. We can already distinguish this approach from both fundamentalism and critical history. The fundamentalist would presumably see no difficulty in the first place: it would be simply a story of justice, rather than a story in which one principle of justice is preferred to another and one has to understand why. The critical historian might take an entirely cynical view, that David was seizing a marvellous political opportunity to get rid of most of Saul's descendants (the man he spared, Mephi-bosheth, was lame in both legs and no threat to him) and hence of a possible challenge to his own position. Either of these approaches can be defended, and the critical one probably has its place for some purposes; but neither is as successful in deriving ethical meaning from the text as is the approach of Jewish tradition and of Levinas – the critical approach is not trying to do this, and the fundamentalist approach inevitably misses much of the subtlety. One can in addition contrast this approach with the metaphysical one. Thus Levinas says of Jewish tradition that 'the rationalism of this method . . . consists, first of all, in a mistrust of everything in the texts studied that could pass for a piece of information about God's life, for a theosophy; it consists in being preoccupied . . . with what this information can mean in and for man's life' (1990: 14) and of himself 'above all, my concern will be to keep this moral plane' (1990: 15).

This is a statement of the method: but there is also in Levinas' ethics what could be taken as a justification of it. Levinas presumably – and probably rightly – does not think one can prove that one must adopt an ethical standpoint. But he does argue, for example in 'Ethics as First Philosophy' (reprinted in Hand, 1989: 75–87), that the ethical attitude is independent of metaphysics, arises from our basic awareness of each other, and is necessarily connected with our vulnerability. For, if one goes beyond what Levinas actually says explicitly in this article, but tries to be faithful to the spirit of his words, one finds references to a triple vulnerability that is part of our basic experience. First, there is our permanent physical vulnerability: we may die any time and will certainly die sometime. Secondly, other people constitute a psychological threat: the Other is a threat simply because they are an Other. Thirdly, and most importantly, since, so to speak, I am the Other's Other, we all not only are threatened but also constitute a threat. This is something, as far as I know, dealt with rarely, if at all, by the 'classic' existentialists, such as Heidegger and Sartre, or by psychologists influenced by their brand of existentialism, such as R.D. Laing, who focus virtually exclusively on the first two kinds of vulnerability. But for Levinas it is crucial: it makes us not only psychologically and physically, but also morally vulnerable. For as a threat to others I am here in the world *with no right to exist*: if I cannot even claim to be harmless, how can I claim any right to be here? The only solution is to overcome my being a threat; and the only way to do this is to accept unconditional (and unlimited) responsibility for the Other, a responsibility that is simply taken on without having to be justified by the existence of any contract or special relationship.

It is not clear that this absolutely proves the necessity for ethics and for responsibility. What it seems to do is to argue that we have only two options – to be Hobbesian people, in a war of all against all, tempered by various mutual agreements, or to be properly ethical people, accepting responsibility whether or not there is any likelihood of a return. There is a question whether this is enough; whether someone can still ask why we are obliged to be 'ethical' rather than Hobbesian or whether such a question is logically or humanely absurd. But whether or not Levinas has proved his case, three things can be said about his approach to ethics. First, ethics is independent of metaphysics, and grounded in human experience. Secondly, it is more fundamental than metaphysics, in the sense that it deals with questions of greater importance: the question whether I have a right to exist and how that right can be acquired is more urgent than any metaphysical question. Thirdly, the basis of ethics is the acceptance of responsibility.

Suppose now that we apply these ideas to the question of how we should read philosophical or religious texts. It will follow, as Levinas says in the passage quoted above, that 'what this information can mean in and for man's life' must indeed be the central concern. It will also follow that this ethical concern is independent of, and more important than, any metaphysical concern: it does not actually entail Levinas' mistrust of 'theosophy' or theology, but it does make theology, theosophy and metaphysics all no more than optional extras, whereas ethics is essential.

The application of the basic ethical requirement, to accept responsibility for the Other, is, with regard to study, more complicated. First, it must imply not only reading the text with a special eye to its ethical content, but also reading it seriously and taking its author seriously. This does not mean that we put our critical faculties aside; but it does mean that we should approach the text as being potentially meaningful and as something from which we can learn. One might say, perhaps, that, since the text itself, even a sacred text, is written by humans, it is in itself human rather than divine (whatever its ultimate origin): 'the Torah speaks in the language of men'. But that is no reason not to take it seriously, since humans are to be taken seriously: we owe it to the author to look for what in their work is humanly and ethically valuable.

Moreover, we read the text while bearing in mind our future obligations and responsibilities. This is in line with the traditional view of the sage as one who learns both 'in order to teach and in order to practise', who learns in order to act more religiously and more humanly, and in order to pass on the teaching, not simply as he has learnt it, but with something of his own added to it or fused with it. What I am suggesting, in short, is that the adoption of Levinas' view of ethics requires us to take all texts seriously (though not uncritically), to look first and foremost (though not exclusively) at a text's human and ethical significance (in a wide sense of 'human' and 'ethical'), to be prepared to use the text to improve what we actually do and how we behave, and to pass on to others part, at least, of what is valuable in the text, in a form enriched by our own understanding and reflections. This moreover, seems to coincide with Levinas' own practice, to apply to philosophical as well as religious texts, and to be in agreement with Levinas' under-standing (correct understanding, in my view) of what it is to be a Jewish *hakham*. I suggest, therefore, that Levinas does see himself as someone at least striving to be a *hakham*, that this has indeed influenced his reading and exposition of philosophy as well as of Jewish texts, and also, very importantly, that one can argue that the approach of the *hakham* is precisely the approach that is most appropriate if one accepts Levinas' ethic of responsibility.

Two further points remain. One is the consideration of how responsibility relates to love and to justice. Responsibility for the Other does not require feelings of love, which are not under our control. But it does require going beyond strict justice, both by being prepared to help others without having entered into any contract to do so, and by being prepared to forego one's strict rights and not insist on being compensated for every wrong done: anything less than this means that one remains a threat to others, as a person whose responsibility is merely conditional and may be ended if the Other behaves inappropriately. This is not to say that self-defence, for example, or punishment are wrong: but they should not be insisted on at the expense of humanity.

In this connection, we need to return to 2 *Samuel*, 21, and to the comments by the Talmud and by Levinas. Verse 2 of this chapter says 'The Gibeonites were not part of the children of Israel'. This was presumably meant literally, but the Talmud reads it as a condemnation, understanding it to mean that, though they were fully in their *rights* in demanding the death of these seven men, 'true' Israelites, people who really practised Judaism and acted humanely, would not have insisted on their rights, but would have shown 'humility, pity and generosity' (Levinas, 1990: 28). And so Levinas ends, most appropriately, with the image of Rizpah, watching over the bodies for six months and protecting them, and through her individual sacrifice rising above the cruelty of strict justice.

When a person has understood this, is that person a sage, a scholar or a rational human being? The appropriate answer seems to be 'All three'. To read a text as a *hakham* is, as we have seen, to read neither as a fundamentalist nor as a critical academic, but as one seeking to learn, to teach and to practise ethics and humanity. To do this, one must certainly be a rational human being, or one becomes a fundamentalist; but one cannot be *only* a rational human being, or one would become a 'mere' academic, not someone learning in order to practise. One must obviously in addition be a scholar, or one will never understand the text: but to extract the ethical meaning one must be more than a scholar. This 'more' seems to be well expressed by saying that a real *hakham*, in this tradition, *is* a sage, as well as a scholar and a rational person, and that Levinas is calling us, in these passages and elsewhere, not perhaps to *be* sages (he might regard that as far too arrogant a claim even for him to make of himself!), but at least to *try* to be. Indeed, it would seem, once again, that it follows from Levinas' ethic that a rational human being must try to be a sage, but a sage, not in metaphysics, but in what is essentially human (and humane).

BIBLIOGRAPHY

Brody, B. (1966) Unpublished lectures on authority in Judaism
Hand, S. (ed.) (1989) *The Levinas Reader*, Oxford: Basil Blackwell
Levinas, E. (1990) *Nine Talmudic Readings*, trans. A. Aronowicz, Bloomington & Indianapolis, Ill.: Indiana University Press
Ruskin, J. (1978) *Praeterita*, Oxford: Oxford University Press.

Chapter 9

On Time and Salvation
The Eschatology of Emmanuel Levinas

Graham Ward
Peterhouse, Cambridge

When Derrida first drew attention to the eschatology which animates Levinas's discourse he called it messianic (1987: 130). He did this partly to distinguish it from the notion of eschatology which he found reemerging in Heidegger's work, in *Holzwege*, where Being is understood as an eschatological event. Levinas's alternative eschatology is messianic because it seems to move explicitly towards a state of non-violence, an horizon of ultimate peace. The tone of Derrida's 'messianic' epithet is derogatory, for Derrida wishes in this early essay on *Totality and Infinity* to attack radically such an ontological notion of peace. 'Peace is made only in a *certain silence*, which is determined and protected by the violence of speech', he observes (1987: 148). Speaking is always a violent tearing asunder, the assertion of an existent from the silent and anonymous origin of *il y a*. For Derrida, whose moves are always within language and for whom nothing can be said of states outside language, 'One never escapes the *economy of war*' (1987: 148). At this point in Derrida's work, because he is also attempting to show how, despite Levinas's protests, the Hegelian project is not left behind, teleology and eschatology are indissociable economies. He writes about a 'teleological or eschatological horizon', for both are restricted as distinct from his own general economy of *differance*.[1]

When Derrida returned to re-examine Levinas work in a essay written in honour of Levinas's work, he again returns to the question of Levinas's 'messianic consciousness' (1991: 31). His concern is the trace of the wholly other in the economy of discourse, as Levinas analyses it. In Levinas's appeal to transcendent interruptions of Saying within the immanence of the said, there is a privileging of 'the moment' in which there is a gift or the arrival of the wholly other. Again, Derrida compares this eschatology with Hegelian teleology, but he is more aware now that in Levinas this moment is never pure; there is only ever the trace of that which has already past. Levinas's moment is caught then between a past anterior – the description of an event which is immemorial – and a future anterior – the transcription of an event or action to the future. The present is never available, as such. The present 'moment' cannot present itself. As Derrida writes: 'The future anterior could turn out to be . . . the time of Hegelian teleology' (1991: 36), but 'the moment when it is in accord with the "he" as Pro-noun of the wholly other "always already past", it will have drawn us toward an eschatology without philosophical teleology, beyond it in any case, otherwise than it' (1991: 37). While still wishing to criticize the theological blindspots in Levinas's own philosophical discourse, the tone of Derrida's analysis is more respectful, fretted with its own self-ironization. A space is opened in the interlacing of the two voices composing this commentary on Levinas's work in which the authorial 'he' can never be precisely defined. It refers simultaneously to Levinas, to Derrida and to the operation of il-leity, God, or the Pro-noun of the wholly other. The space is opened and kept open, whereas in the earlier essay, the critique closed down Levinas's position (and Derrida's). A negotiation (an important word throughout this second essay) between Levinas and Derrida is evident. Derrida even mimics the absolute interruption of the wholly-other in this essay by inserting a female voice into a male narration – the female voice as the wholly other of Levinas's decidely masculine wholly other. Derrida interpellates a sexual difference. We will return to this difference much later in the essay. The dialogue between the male and the female moves the argument forward. The interrruption facilitates and requires further discussion.

By the time we have reached Derrida's *Specters of Marx* we find a frank espousal of messianic eschatology as an aspect of deconstruction itself. Though it is a messianism without a messiah, without content, without religion. Even so, Derrida is forced to ask whether 'one can conceive an atheological inheritance of the messianic?' (1994: 168) For in speaking about the future without which there would be neither intention, desire nor need, Derrida writes: 'Whether the promise promises this or that, whether it be fulfilled or not, or whether it be unfulfillable, there is necessarily some promise and therefore some historicity as future-to-come. It is what we are naming the messianic without messianism' (1994: 73). Another development is also discernible – a distinction is consistently drawn between teleology and eschatology. While recognizing that there is always a danger the difference will be effaced, he asks 'Is there not a messianic extremity, an *eskhaton* whose ultimate event (immediate rupture, unheard-of interruption, untimeliness of the infinite surprise, heterogeneity without accomplishment) can exceed, *at each moment*, the final term of *phusis*, such a work, the production, and the *telos* of history?' (1994: 37) Although Levinas is not named here, the language recalls his description of Levinas's project throughout that second essay. Levinas's investigation has become Derrida's own, for we will recognize in this position the contours of a Levinasian eschatology. Since the early eighties Derrida has wished to develop the ethics of deconstruction, the implications for his work in terms of justice, justice thought through on the basis of gift 'beyond right, calculation and commerce' (1994: 27). Justice is constituted in and through the excess of the other, an eschatological excess that carries the future before it, messianically. In the last pages of this work, Derrida affirms that 'the messianic appeal belongs properly to a universal structure, to that irreducible movement of the historical opening to the future, therefore to experience itself and to its language' (1994: 167). The question remaining is how this messianic eschatology can be thought alongside 'the figures of Abrahamic messianism' (1994: 167). No clear answer is given, the discussion dissolves into a plethora of possible messianisms ('quasi-atheistic', 'quasi-transcendental', 'despairing'). What is important is that what began as a critique of an important aspect of Levinas's work has become incorporated positively now into Derrida's own. Levinas has taught Derrida the importance of eschatology considered as the condition for and excess of philosophy, in general, and phenomenology in particular. Levinas's eschatology can come to the forefront of contemporary French thinking. We will discover it not only in Derrida, but also the work of Julia Kristeva, Luce Irigaray and Hélène Cixous. The pervasiveness of that influence alone (and responsibility in the sense the burden of response) demands an inquiry into the nature of eschatology in Levinas's thinking.

In this essay we will examine the nature of Levinasian eschatology – taking it as the borderline dividing the philosophical from the theological, taking it as the far edge of the philosophical and the near edge of the theological. It is Levinas's messianic eschatology that makes his work of considerable interest for the theologian. The ethics of incalculable responsibility to and for the other/Other, the exposition of love and the call to a self-emptying – all of which are common to Jewish and Christian theological discourse – are consequences of this eschatology. We will examine this theme through Levinas's early work on time (an essential criterion in eschatology), the other and the economy of desire: *Time and the Other*. We will work carefully through this text for three reasons. First, this being only a brief and preliminary essay, it hopefully can do more justice to a shorter text which nevertheless contains the central story of the *eschaton* than embarking upon either of Levinas's epics (*Totality and Infinity* and *Otherwise than Being or Beyond Essence*). Secondly, it was written before Levinas's explicitly theological preoccupations or, at least before explicit reference to the other as God, the messianic triumph, the glory of the infinite and election come to occupy important discursive space in the aforementioned epics.

God makes his entrance much later, in *Totality and Infinity*, published in 1961, fourteen years after *Time and the Other*. The earlier text then presents, more philosophically, the theological as it pertains to Levinas's project. We can appreciate more clearly how the philosophical project relates to the theological one.Thirdly, this text seems to be a miniature tableau of the much expanded and developed versions of *Totality and Infinity* and *Otherwise than Being or Beyond Essence*. Both these books recapitulate the movement of the ideas in *Time and the Other*. Therefore, this essay attempts to unmask the theological economy, the eschatology, which throbs as a groundbase through Levinas's subsequent works. This theological economy, as we will see, constitutes the other narrative, or more precisely the narrative of the other, which the philosophical narrative acts as a commentary upon. For in all three major texts there is a similar plot, variously treated, modified and philosophically examined. We begin with an exposition of the anonymity of the *il y a*, there is, from which the subject and subjectivity arise. This aloneness, the self-orientation and interiority of this subjectivity is developed and then fissured by proximity to the world and then to the face of another person. On the basis of this sociality, the ethics of substitution and responsibility issue and an investigation proceeds into the other of the Other person, the trace of the infinite in the unique and finite. We conclude with an exposition of the deduced exteriority, an outside, an otherwise to which we have arrived through participation in the unfolding of the phenomenological and analytical drama which has preceded it. We will examine in this essay the relationship between this narrative and eschatology, and then ask the question concerning the status of such narratives *vis-à-vis* both Levinas, as writer, and us, as readers. What will be suggested is that Levinas's philosophical plot is a meditation, a midrash, upon the Biblical narrative found in the Torah of Moses, the Penteteuch. His meditation is a form of textual study which, as with any study of the Torah, aims at drawing God into the play of the finite. Reading, interpreting and studying are extensions and developments of that mediation. We are drawn into a theological plot, we participate in and experience its unfolding. There is, then, a theological mimesis, a submission, a *sub-jectum* involved in the very reading of Levinas's work. We are not given an exposition of an eschatology, we are invited to participate within, and therefore continue to promote, a messianism. Paralleling Franz Rosenzweig in his volume *The Star of Redemption*, Levinas's philosophical discourse becomes a liturgical act.

Theologically, that is according to the logic of theological analysis, eschatology as a teaching cannot stand alone. It stands in systematic relation to a constellation of other doctrines: the doctrine of election, calling and vocation, on the one hand, the doctrine of revelation, history and the relationship between creature and creator in terms of the community of the chosen and the soteriological journey, on the other. From these two lines of theological teaching – the one grounded in a theological anthropology or a theological understanding of personhood and the other grounded in a theology of creation – a doctrine of God emerges. In *Time and the Other* this doctrine of God is implicit. It will only be explicitly and thoroughly developed in Levinas's later work – the essays collected in *Difficult Freedom* (1963), which followed the publication of *Totality and Infinity*, *Du sacré au saint* (1977), which followed the publication of *Otherwise than Being or Beyond Essence* and *Beyond the Verse* (1982). Nevertheless, pushing beyond the parameters of phenomenology, Levinas's notions of personhood and community, election and futurity, the temporal and the eternal, mortality and immortality in *Time and the Other* are developed through the ethical imperative beyond Being which is wholly other. This other impinges upon, through its exteriority, the orders of creation. Eschatological thinking is dynamic thinking; and the dynamic principle is the always the same – the Spirit that inspires, the desire for the absolute which can never be satisified, whose economy lies outside the economy of exchange, the market economy of need and satifisation of need. On a physiological and psychological level Levinas locates this desire 'within eroticism and the libido' (1987: 36). But like

Kierkegaard, also fascinated by Abrahamic messianism in *Fear and Trembling*, the absolute nature of desire transforms the erotic relation into a love which does not and cannot possess its object, a love stretched out towards the wholly other. It is love, as Hélène Cixous (herself concerned to map the ethics of diference) has recently described it, as 'not having' (1990: 117). Such a love operates according to a different economy of desire than desire-as-lack (which is the Hegelian and Freudian desire). This is a desire not because the wholly other presents a lack. Rather the wholly other presents an excess. In this economy of desire, it is desire as excess, as infinite that creates the tension, the separation that can never be overcome. Time, for Levinas, (therefore history, destiny, election and vocation) is created in and through this tension. Time is the labour of our love; it is a labour which makes us co-creators with the wholly other. Levinas will describe the fecundity, the paternity, the community that issues from this labour.

The question is, Where does this labour begin? If creation is the ongoing eschatological work, whence comes this creation? This is where we move outside Abrahamic messianism characterized as the journey into endless exile, the call to be nomadic, the call to move out to the wholly other. For the creation story and the narrative of election belong to the account of another exile – the first exile, that of Adam. For from the first moments of his creation he is assigned the work of multiplying and having managerial responsibility for the fish and the fowl and every living creature that moves upon the earth. And, later, on being exiled from the Garden of Eden, that call to work is only intensified, for only by the sweat of his brow will he eat bread until he returns to the dust. Levinas quotes this passage himself in the work written prior to *Time and the Other*, *Existence and Existants* (1947) and the Adamic pericope reappears throughout his later work.[2] Adam exemplifies the co-creative labour of love-in-obedience, but the whole of creation is ecstatic, living for and from beyond itself. In describing the whence and why of this condition of creation, Levinas draws upon the metaphors of the Mosaic imagination as it attempts to narrate the beginning of the world-orders in the Book of Genesis. For the existent, the eventing of what Levinas calls the hypostasis, 'is a rip in the infinite beginningless and endless fabric of existing. The present rips apart and joins together again; it begins; it is beginning itself. It has a past, but in the form of remembrance. It has a history, but not a history.' (1987: 52) This is Levinas's *midrash* (an interpretative retelling of Mose's narration) of the issuing of the existent, which is both the I and the present, from the silence, the eternal, the anonymity of existing itself, the *il y a*. 'Let us imagine all things, beings and persons, returning to nothingness. What remains after the imaginary destruction of everything is not something, but the fact that there is [*il y a*]. The absence of everything returns as a presence, as the place where the bottom has dropped out of everything, an atmospheric density, a plentitude of the void, or the murmur of silence.' (1987: 46) The existent, then, is a creation *ex nihilo*; even more profoundly *ex nihilo* than Heidegger's *es gibt* (which speaks of a gift, of a giving and, implicitly, a giver). Levinas's *il* is more impersonal. It has no name. It is unnameable, for it lies outside and yet provides the possibility for all names 'all things, beings and persons'. A number of other continental philosophers examine this heterogeneous formlessness, the origin without origin, by returning to the *chora* in Plato's *Timaeus*.[3] Later Levinas will speak of it employing the language of the Lurianic view of creation, *tzimztum*.[4]

There are times when Levinas suggests a certain aggressive self-assertion tears the existent from the anonymity of existing. The monadic obsessiveness of the existent, its solitude 'is something that comes from itself' (1987: 53), it posits 'the present as the mastery of the existent over existing' (1987: 54). And yet this assertion must also be paralleled by the command of the absolutely other to be. In a more recent essay on Rabbi Hayyim Volozhiner's meditation on the creation of Adam, Levinas makes explicit that if God withdrew from existents they would return to nothingness (1989: 230). There is a transcendent imperative to be which operates with and within the self-assertion. Here an implicit theological doctrine of emanation dialectically encounters a philosophical analysis of *Dasein*. Levinas develops his analysis of the *event of being*, the *esse*, and transcendence as the passing over to being's *other*, much later, in *Otherwise than Being or Beyond Essence*. The relation of the *il y a* to the wholly other is obscure in *Time and the Other*. (Although, even in *Otherwise than Being or Beyond Essence*, the relationship between the impersonal *il* of *il y a* and the *il* of *illeity* is no where clear). Both are described as infinite but there is no explication of the difference between the infinity of the *il y a* and 'the infinite of God' (1994: 147). Even in this earlier text, Levinas emphasizes that the existent can never forget the past that is immemorial. It can never forget the genealogy in which the existent emerges from the plurality of the *il y a*, the indifference from which difference is eventualized. It is this memory of difference, of exteriority, which enables the solitude of the hypostasis to reflect upon its own condition, to experience, its profound unhappiness, and to become preoccupied with salvation (1987: 58). This is the moment of its election, the moment of hearing the call of the other which is prior to his or her own interiority.

The election is a vocation which institutes one's uniqueness. And the verb to hear has the same root in Hebrew as the verb to obey. Election and vocation require the movement to the other which creates history as a projected future which is simultaneously scarred by the memory of a irrecoverable past. Here eschatology has its inception. Its future, like Adam's future, lies within both labouring within and being nourished by the world, and then labouring within and being nurtured by a responsibility to the Other, paradigmatically Eve or the feminine. Hence Levinas moves from Adam enjoying, in solitude, the paradise of God's new creation to Adam enjoying the feminine as Other in their mutual nakedness. The Other is the stranger and 'the relationship with the Other is the absence of the other [*autre*]; not absence pure and simple, not the absence of pure nothingness, but the absence in the horizon of the future, an absence which is time' (1987: 90). Hence, in time made continually possible only beyond time there is an eschatology rather than a teleology. Eschatology because of the responsibility for an exteriority more exterior than the neighbour or the world of nourishments. Eschatology because a transcendence ruptures and tears up the immanent orders of consciousness. Eschatology because there is no *telos* towards which time and creation is moving, no point which will finally synthesize the differences, ruptures and separations which enable an existent to be an existent. So what then is salvation as Levinas conceives it? Salvation here is not personal integration, inner healing that comes about through the reconciliation between the I and the wholly other. It is not the Protestant salvation of Luther and Calvin. Salvation here is the establishment of paternity (and hence motherhood and filiality).[5] It is the establishment of history; history as the expansion and maintenance of 'a collectivity that is not a community' (1987: 94). This ideal community is conceived in terms of the confederacy of consanguineous tribes which makes up Israel on the eve of crossing into the Promised land (the situation executed as the last act of Moses, at the end of the Penteteuch).[6] Salvation is a sociality in which justice is established and maintained; a 'pluralism that does not merge into unity' (1987: 42). Salvation is the creation and promotion of this difficult freedom [*liberté*], the freedom of obedience to the Other/other. This utopian co-existence of differences has analogues with Irigaray's notion of the age of the bride and Cixous meditations upon 'the union of two mysteries who do not try to destroy each other'.[7] All three thinkers wish to emphasize a certain kenosis before the incomprehensibility of the Other. For all three, it is a creative kenosis in which a space is opened, a difference recognized. As Irigarary describes it, it is 'God as subtending the interval, pushing the interval towards and into infinity. The irreducible. Opening up the universe and all beyond it'. In this eschatological an-economy there is both a present realization and a 'not yet'. For enjoyment of the world (*jouissance*), the pain and suffering of solitude, the unknown of death which 'indicates that we are in relation with something that is

162

absolutely other' (1987: 74) and the 'communication in eros' which is 'neither a struggle, nor a fusion, nor a knowledge' (1987: 88), all rupture the autonomy of self-presence. Hence these intimations of exteriority, that Levinas terms events, imply a collectivity because they substantiate difference. They promote the mystery of the other and the excess that defers possession and declines the future tense. 'A plurality insinuates itself into the very existing of the existent' (1987: 75). Salvation *is* the creation of history, the multiplication which the male and female made in the image of God were adverted to, the continually opening up of the revelation of the wholly other. Today's salvation promotes tomorrow's. Later Levinas, more strictly defining revelation in the Jewish tradition, will 'suggest that the totality of the true is constituted from the contributions of multiple people . . . The multiplicity of people, each one of them indispensable, is necessary to produce all the dimensions of meaning [*la multiplicité des personnes irreducibles est nécessaire aux dimensions du sens*]; the multiple meanings are multiple people' (1994: 133–4; 1982: 163 Translation modified). Salvation, the revelation of the endless meaning, the excess of the other, issues from each us living out the unappeasable responsibility for the Other.

Let us pause here. For we have now in place the main joists of Levinas's eschatology. The movement of this eschatology has been recently described as Levinas's 'drama of the education of the psyche' (Llewelyn 1995: 3).[8] Pedagogy will be a significant word henceforth. The drama enacts a pilgrimage in exile, from being and beyond into ethics, from the non-ethical to the ethical. What we have come to understand about what might be termed, theologically, Levinas's doctrine of creation, is that desire structures both its advent and perdurance. One finds this theme elsewhere in Kristeva, Cixous and Irigaray.[9] Creation arises from and continues in ruptures, separations and differences. The origin of this desire lies in the wholly other whose presence both haunts and seduces us – seduces insofar as its draws us out erotically to a salvation, a satisfaction, which is always futural because never possessed. The primordial desire for the other demands that we recognize the ethical structure of creation. Paradigmatically, eschatological desire, and the eschatological economy, operates in, through and on the condition of sexual difference, 'the absolutely original relationship of eros' (1987: 88). In this primordial difference or separation 'creation itself presupposes an opening onto a mystery' (1987: 80). The question then is what is the nature of the analogy governing the relationship of eros between self and Other [*autrui*] and the endless desire which opens us unto the mystery of the wholly other [*autre*]? Levinas will later emphasize the 'adventure of the Spirit also takes place on earth among men' (1994: 142). But what is the relationship between this Spirit issuing from the wholly other and the desire endemic to being a human being? What is the structure and economy of inspiration? This is a word Levinas increasingly employs to describe the relation. He suggests in his later work that the self in subjection is open to being inspired, open to prophecy. In which case, his depiction of the human subject, the existent, prescribes a theological anthropology – even in *Time and the Other*. The human existent is the existent made 'in the image of God' (1989: 230–1).

There is a further corollary of this analogy question and its relation both to the condition of being human and the nature of inspiration. That is: what is the relationship between the 'drama of the education of the pysche' as Levinas narrates it in all his major works and the Penteteuchal narrative upon which it seems predicated and to which it is frequently referred? For even in *Time and the Other*, there is a movement from creation *ex nihilo* to the election of Adam, the relationship with Eve and the establishment of the confederacy of Israel just prior to their entry into the Promised Land (and the tribes going their own separate ways). And throughout it is a journey into exile. What is the relationship, the nature of the analogical imagination which binds Levinas's drama, the Torah and the eschatological economy? We are no longer asking Derrida's question about how this eschatology (and Levinas's depiction of it) relates to Abraham's messianism, but the question of how it relates to

Moses'. Moses who, as traditional author of the Penteteuch, is creator or recreator of Abraham. Of course, Derrida speaks of Abraham because Levinas had outlined two economies of the same and the other – the one demonstrated by the journeying of Ulysses, who returns to the point from which he arrived. This is the Greek economy. The other the journeying of Abraham who, following a promise that is only partially fulfilled in his lifetime (it is a promise concerning the multitude of his descendants), obeys, leaves his homeland and ventures forever into exile (and fruitfulness). This is the Jewish economy.[10] In Derrida's first essay he concludes by characterizing Levinas (in terms of James Joyce) 'Jewgreek.Greekjew'. He views Levinas's project as being the synthesis of the two economies – a synthesis which would in fact only point up the Hegelian project he, Levinas, never quite shakes off. If, that is, Derrida is right and synthesis is Levinas's aim. But is Abraham's messianism as important for Levinas as Moses' messianism? Or, more precisely asked, is not Abraham's messianism interpreted in terms of a messianism evident throughout the Torah of Moses which has Moses as its author? Later, Levinas will affirm the Jewish tradition in which the five books of the Torah, 'the "Torah of Moses", as it is called – are privileged in Jewish consciousness for the relation they establish with God' (1994: 132). Abraham's messianism has to be understood in terms of the wider context of the Penteteuchal narrative (which Moses received from God who inspired him). It was not only Abraham who journeyed into ever deepening exile. There is Adam's exile, there is Jacob's and there is Moses' own. For Moses journeys also – from Egypt and back again, across the Red Sea and into the Wilderness wandering for forty years following the shekinah glory of God as a fiery pillar by night and a cloud by day, journeying towards a Promised Land which he never enters. He dies on the slopes of mount Nebo, having reached the borders of the land flowing with milk and honey, seeing the promise, without possessing it, from afar. And in his 1972 essay 'Meaning and Sense' Levinas describes this journeying in terms of the economy of being for the other, the economy of salvation: 'As an orientation toward the other, as sense, a work is possible only in patience, which, pushed to the limit, means for an agent to renounce being the contemporary of its outcome, to act without entering into the Promised Land.' (1987: 92) Each narrative of exile provides a typology for the others. Sojourning is the central preoccupation and the fundamental structure of the Penteteuchal narrative. Exile is the very movement of God in creation, that is also in time, history and human desire which creates both time and history. This continuous exile is revealed, as it is held traditionally, to Moses in the Torah. This is an eschatology in which the *eschaton* is eternally deferred. There is no messianic figure of the grand deliverer – as in Hellenistic Jewish and Christian theology. Each person is the messiah for every other. Each one bears the messianic task and its responsibility. 'Waiting for the Messiah is the actual duration of time. Or waiting for God. But now waiting no longer testifies to an absence of Godot who will never come. It testifies, rather, to the relation with something that cannot enter the present, because the present is too small for the Infinite . . . [T]he waiting for the Most-High which is a relation to Him – or, if one prefers, a deference, a deference to the beyond which creates here the very concept of a beyond or a towards-God' (1994: 143). Hence the promise of the Messianic, and the awaiting which follows it, opens up the transcendent. Levinas's eschatology then, like Derrida's, is messianic but without the Messiah and Moses is the one to whom this is revealed and who subsequently reveals and teaches it to the Jews.

In essays published in his 1982 collection *Beyond the Verse*, Levinas meditates upon studying the Torah and the sacred history chronicled there. The Bible opens what he terms a 'living space [*espace vital*]' (1994: 130). Reading and studying is an act of taking nourishment, of being drawn out towards the other. Like the other, the words of the Torah are polyvalent, they inscribe an excess, a strangeness, a mystery which propels endless hermeneutical inquiry. This is significant, for we might suspect that a philosopher who inveighs against the totalizing effected by discourses of truth and reason, might inveigh also against narratives. But the Penteteuchal narrative inscribes an excess of meaning that tears apart any single ability to close its meaning. The role of reader as auditor of the Word becomes the most important one. 'The Revelation is a constant hermeneutics of the Word, whether written or oral, discovering new landscapes', he writes (1994: 138). There is no end to such study. 'This process of liberation and universalization [of the text] must therefore be continued' (1994: 75). A fourfold obligation is laid upon those who pursue such a study – to learn it, to teach it, to observe it and to carry it out. The reason why this obligation is so important is because only through fulfilling such responsibilities is Revelation continually renewed upon the earth. To study and teach the Torah is to be involved in the process of creation, to participate in the unfolding eschatology. In his essay on Rabbi Hayyim Volozhiner, Levinas develops the Rabbi's understanding of fidelity to the Torah as that which makes God's association with the world possible. Such reading becomes a form of prayer, a form of benediction.

We return to our final question: the relationship between the Mosaic revelation, eschatology and Levinas's narrative of the education of the psyche. Despite Levinas's insistence that his philosophical work and Talmudic work were entirely distinct (a position untenable even on the premises of his philosophical work where reason, language and intelligibility are all predicated on ethical responsibility to the wholly other) – might we not see his philosophical narrative as a meditation upon the Torah?[11] Might we not see the lines of association drawn between Moses the inspired author and all subsequent authorship? In Derrida's second essay on Levinas 'At this very moment in this work here I am', the central issue concerns authorship in Levinas's work. Who is E.L., Derrida asks? Is it the *il* of the wholly other, or the Semitic name of god, or initials of Levinas, or Derrida (whose Hebrew name is Elijah which, in French, is *Elie*), or the female other of the wholly other, *elle*)? From whence comes Levinas's work and to whom must we be responsible in receiving and reading that work? Did Levinas realize the responsibilities (and agonies) of authorship more and more? Is that why his epic journeys in *Totality and Infinity* and *Otherwise than Being or Beyond Essence* are performative, requiring a language and an approach which draws the reader into the work? The prescriptive language of Levinas's earlier dramas (*Existence and Existents* and *Time and the Other*) has to go as Levinas contemplates the role of representation (even his own representation) and the other. Prescriptive language totalizes, creates objects of knowledge. The employment of metaphor militates against thematisation and theory. Performative language, like the language of the Torah of Moses and liturgy, is abrasive to reasoning. It structures an ambiguity that allows for excess of meaning and a certain haunting of the enigmatic other. Phenomenology as a philosophical method has always recognized that its descriptive powers operate upon the reader, attempting to clarify an existential position occupied by the inquiring subject. It is for this reason that phenomenological method can never extricate itself from the hermeneutical circle, as Heidegger recognized. Might we therefore understand Levinas to be writing a Jewish theology of phenomenological method? If so, then a theology of mimesis related to what he termed the ontology of Scripture emerges (1994: 137). This is distinct from a metaphysics of mimesis which would simply establish what Levinas is at pains to deny, an ontology of narrative. Mimesis, the presentation for a participation which always entails a following after,[12] the subject's necessary subjection to the authority of the author, the author over Levinas's shoulder, the other, is then itself eschatological. We return to Derrida's observation and affirm it: 'the messianic appeal belongs properly to a universal structure, to that irreducible movement of the historical opening to the future, therefore to experience itself and language'. In which case, the separation of philosophy and theology is a false one born of Enlightenment humanism, rationalism and scientific reductionism. The philosophical and the theological are two sides of the same coin. With Levinas's philosophical accounts of the genealogies of ethics, personhood and time, on the one hand, and Levinas's theological readings of the Torah, on the other, we have to recognize that each provides the conditions for the possibility, and the understanding, of the other. The philosophical is as much a necessary commentary upon the theological as the theological is a commentary upon the philosophical. It is that necessity which is significant. It announces that the economy or the structure of the movement in both discourses is eschatologically governed. Levinas returns to us a theological metaphysics where to think, to write, to read and to interpret is also to act liturgically, eschatologically.

A CODA

What about teleology? Certainly Levinas would still insist on the totalizing project of an immanent teleology, a teleology without rupture, without the in-breaking of the wholly other, teleology as the consumerism of the in-itself/for-it dialectic. He, like so many French contemporary philosophers, like also Heidegger and Karl Barth, equates such a teleology with Hegel. But Hegel, not of the *Encyclopaedia* but the *Phenomenology of Spirit* (which Hegel himself recognized could not form of a part of his system), calls attention to his own 'narrative exposition' (1977: 35). It is a narrative also in which aporia and agnosticism play fundamental roles. He writes: 'the share in the total work of the Spirit which falls to the individual can only be very small. Because of this, the individual must all the more forget himself' (1977: 45). There is no absolute knowing, nor totalizing, for this subject. Such knowing is only the horizon for his or her consciousness, like a Kantian regulative idea. The individual knows only kenosis and obedience in an ever-continuing process of actualization, ending, for him or her, with death. The economy of the Spirit is a textuality of time and (since Christianity is the absolute religion) it takes place within a messianic eschatology of sorts. So is Levinas, then, more Hegelian than he realizes? Teleologies too are textualities of time. As textualities they can constitute irreducible, polysemantic narratives, narratives of excess where what is other always remains outside the economy, perpetuating the continuation of the force, the desire, the work. The last three notions are profoundly Hegelian. As textualities of time, as narratives, in what do the differences between teleology and eschatology lie? Perhaps with Levinas's discourse on eschatology we have to reopen the question of the aporetics of Hegel's teleology.

NOTES

1 Derrida defines a 'general economy' as one which keeps the question of meaning open, whereas a 'restricted economy' limits itself to the meaning and established value of objects and their circulation. See his essay 'From Restricted to General Economy: A Hegelianism without Reserve', *Writing and Difference*, pp.251–77.

2 For a full understanding of Levinas's theological anthroplogy as it issues from a meditation on the creation of Adam see his two essays on Rabbi Hayyim's *Nefesh Hahaim*: 'In the Image of God', according to Rabbi Hayyim' in *Beyond the Verse* pp.151–167; and 'Judaism and Kenosis' in *In the Time of the Nations*, trans. Michael B. Smith, London: Athlone, 1994, pp.114–132.

3 The *chora* becomes an important notion in the later work of Derrida and the work of Kristeva and Irigaray.

4 In *Otherwise than Being or Beyond Essence*, trans. A. Lingis, The Hague: Martinus Nijhoff, pp.3-4, Levinas describes the passing over to being other as: 'Not *to be otherwise*, but *otherwise than being*. And not to not-be; passing over is not here equivalent to dying. Being and not-being illuminate one another, and unfold a speculative dialectic which is a determination of being. Or else the negativity which attempts to repel being is immediately submerged by being. The void that hollows out is immediately filled with the mute and anonymous rustling of the *there is*.' Susan A. Handelman, in her book *Fragments of Redemption: Jewish Thought and Literary Theory in Benjamin, Scholem and Levinas*, Bloomington: Indiana University Press, 1991, describes the Lurianic view of creation as the self-exile of God. '[C]reation occurs through God's "self-negation" or withdrawal, the Becoming of the world would result from the passage of Being through Nothing. The nature of this 'nothing' is the critical issue' (p.94).

5 For an examination of the male orientation of Levinas's work see Luce Irigaray 'The Fecundity of the Caress', trans. Carolyn Burke in Richard A.Cohen (ed.), *Face to Face with Levinas*, Albany: SUNY, 1985, pp.231–256; 'Questions to Emmanuel Levinas on the Divinity of Love', trans. Margaret Whitford, in Robert

Bernsconi and Simon Critchley (eds.), *Re-Reading Levinas*, London: Athlone, 1991, pp.109–118.

6 See Levinas's exposition of the Talmudic tractate *Sotah 37 a-b* as a commentary on chapter 27 of Deuteronomy and chapter 7 of Joshua in 'The Pact', *Beyond the Verse*, pp.68–85. The confederacy of tribes is viewed as a paradigm for the ideal community. He will draw out the fact that all Israel was there and positioned so that each could observe everyone else. The experience of community, the responsibility one for the Other, is 'an essential moment of revelation (p.83).

7 Cixous, *op.cit.*, p.85. See Irigaray's essay 'Divine Women', *Sexes and Genealogies*, trans. Gillian C. Gill, New York: Columbia University Press, 1993, pp.55–72 for her notion of the age of the Bride. Both Cixous' and Irigaray's utopianism depends upon the recogniton and affirmation of sexual difference. It is significant that although sexual difference is important in Levinas's work up to and including *Totality and Infinity*, following that work there is more emphasis on fraternal, paternal and filial forms of love, a 'love without eros' (*Beyond the Verse*, p.146). The Same-Other difference remains but an appreciation of the bodily, the enfleshed, disappears. Levinas's thinking becomes more concerned with conceptuality than materiality (an important emphasis in *Time and the Other*). The interpellation of the woman's voice as the other of the other in Derrida's essay 'At this very moment in this work here I am' is perhaps a reminder to Levinas of a difference he has seemingly forgotten and its consequences.

8 See also Gillian Rose (1992) *The Broken Middle* Oxford: Blackwell, p.265 for a similar suggestion.

9 Kristeva writes: 'In reality, it is the biblical God who inaugurates separation at the beginning of creation, He creates division which is also the mark of his presence.' *In the Beginning was Love*, trans. Arthur Goldhammer, New York: Columbia University Press, 1987, p.31.

10 Reference is made to Greek metaphysics and the Odyssey in *Totality and Infinity*, trans. A. Lingis, Pittsburgh: Duquesne University Press, 1969, p.102. It is one of the central themes in Levinas's essay 'Meaning and Sense', *Collected Philosophical Papers*, trans. A.Lingis Dordrecht: Martinus Nijhoff, pp.75–107.

11 In *The Broken Middle*, Gillian Rose suggests, and I think correctly, 'Levinas celebrates the end of the end of philosophy as ethics, presented philosophically as well as in Judaic form – lectures talmudiques. Yet this is a distinction with much less difference than Levinas claims.' op.cit., p.278.

12 See my discussion of this approach to the reading of Mark's Gospel in 'Mimesis: The Measure of Mark's Christology', *Literature and Theology* 8 (1), pp.1–29.

BIBLIOGRAPHY

Cixous, H. (1990) *Reading with Clarice Lispector*, trans. V. Andermatt Conley, London: Harvester Wheatsheaf.

Derrida, J. (1978) 'Violence and Metaphysics', in *Writing and Difference*, trans. A. Bass, London: Routledge.

—— (1991) 'At this very moment in this work here I am', in R. Bernasconi and S. Critchley (eds) *Re-Reading Levinas*, London: Athlone.

—— (1994) *Specters of Marx*, trans. Peggy Kamuf, London: Routledge.

Hegel, G. W. F. (1977) *Phenomenology of Spirit*, trans. A. V. Miller, Oxford: Oxford University Press.

Irigaray, L. (1993) *An Ethics of Sexual Difference, trans.* C. Burke and G. C. Gill, London: Athlone.

Levinas, E. (1982) *L'Au-Delà du Verset: Lectures et Discours Talmudiques*, Paris: Les Editions de Minuit.

—— (1987) *Time and The Other*, trans. R. Cohen, Pittsburgh: Duquesne University Press.

—— (1989) *The Levinas Reader*, S. Hand (ed.), Oxford: Blackwell.

—— (1994) *Beyond the Verse: Talmudic Readings and Lectures*, trans. Gary D. Mole, London: Athlone.

Llewelyn, J. (1995) *Emmanuel Levinas: The Genealogy of Ethics*, London: Routledge.

Bibliography

The standard bibliography of studies both by and on Levinas is Roger Burggraeve (1990) *Emmanuel Levinas. Une bibliographie primaire et secondaire (1929–1985): avec complément 1985–1989*, Leuven: Peeters.

SECTION A

Works by Levinas

Articles are not listed separately if subsequently collected by Levinas in book form. I have not included reviews, translations, correspondence or allocutions.

1930

La théorie de l'intuition dans la phénoménologie de Husserl, Paris: Alcan (Vrin, 1963), trans. A. Orianne (1973) *The Theory of Intuition in Husserl's Phenomenology*, Evanston: Northwestern University Press.

1935

'L'actualité de Maïmonide', *Paix et Droit* XV, 4: 6–7.
'L'inspiration religieuse de l'Alliance', *Paix et Droit* XV, 8: 4.

1938

'L'essence spirituelle de l'antisémitisme d'après Jacques Maritain', *Paix et Droit* XVIII, 5: 3–4.

1939

'A propos de la mort du Pope Pie XI', *Paix et Droit* XIX, 3: 3.

1946

'Tout est-il vanité?', *Les Cahiers de l'Alliance Israélite Universelle* IX: 1–2.
'Le réouverture de l'Ecole Normale Israélite Orientale', *Les Cahiers de l'Alliance Israélite Universelle* XI: 2–3.

1947

De l'existence à l'existant, Paris: Fontaine (Vrin, 1973), trans.A. Lingis (1978) *Existence and Existents*, The Hague: Martinus Nijhoff.
'Etre juif', *Confluences* VIII, 15–17: 253–64.

1949

En découvrant l'existence avec Husserl et Heidegger, Paris: Vrin (1967).
'Quand les mots reviennent de l'exil', *Les Cahiers de l'Alliance Israélite Universelle* XXXII: 4.
'En marge d'une enquête: L'érotisme ne ravale pas l'esprit', *Combat*, 30 June.

1951

'L'ontologie est-elle fondamentale?', *Revue de Métaphysique et de Morale* LVI, 1: 88–98.
'Deux promotions', *Les Cahiers de L'Alliance Israélite Universelle*, LIV-LV: 1–2.
'Préface (sur Jacob Gordin)', *Evidences* XXI: 22.

1952

'Eternité et domicile', *Evidences* XXVIII: 35–6.

1953

'L'unique apaisement', *Combat*, 2 April.

1954

'Noé Gottlieb', *Les Cahiers de l'Alliance Israélite Universelle* LXXXII: 1–3.
'Le moi et la totalité', *Revue de Métaphysique et de Morale* LIX, 4: 353–73.
'L'hébreu dans les écoles de l'Alliance', *Revue du Fonds Social Juif Unifié* X: 17–18.

1955

'Le rôle de l'Ecole Normale Israélite Orientale', *Les Cahiers de l'Alliance Israélite Universelle* XCI: 32–8.

1956

'L'Ecole Normale Israélite Orientale', *Les Cahiers de l'Alliance Israélite Universelle* C: 16–17.

Bibliography

1957

'L'Ecole Normale Israélite Orientale', *Les Cahiers de l'Alliance Israélite Universelle* CX: 15–17.

'Lévy-Bruhl et la philosophie contemporaine', *Revue Philosophique de la France et de l'Etranger* CXLVII, 4: 551–69.

'Rencontres', *Les Cahiers de l'Alliance Israélite Universelle* CXII: 13–14.

1958

'La civilisation juive (débat entre E. Berl, E. Levinas, G. Lévitte', J. Lindon, J. Neher, P. Sipriot et C. Tresmontant)', *Les Cahiers de l'Alliance Israélite Universelle* CXV: 3–12.

'Une mission à Tioumliline', *Les Cahiers de l'Alliance Israélite Universelle* CXIX: 25–7.

1960

'La laïcité dans l'état d'Israël', in A. Audibert et al. *La laïcité*, Paris: Presses Universitaires de France: 549-62.

'Le problème scolaire et nous', *L'Arche* XXXVIII: 11-15.

'Que nous apporte l'accord culturel franco-israélien? (table rond avec P.-E. Gilbert, A. Neher, E. Levinas, D. Catarivas, Ph. Rebeyrol, A. Chouraqui, M. Salomon)', *L'Arche* XXXVIII: 28–32, 61–3.

'L'accord culturel franco-israélien et les Juifs de la dispersion', *Les Cahiers de l'Alliance Israélite Universelle* CXXVIII: 1–4.

'Le permanent et l'humain chez Husserl', *L'Age Nouveau* CX: 51–6.

'L'heure de la rédemption', *Le Journal des communautés* CCLI: 4.

1961

'L'Ecole Normale Israélite Orientale: perspectives d'avenir', in *Les droits de l'homme et de l'éducation*, Paris: Presses Universitaires de France: 73–9.

Totalité et Infini. Essai sur l'extériorité, The Hague: Martinus Nijhoff.

'L'Ecole Normale Israélite Orientale', *Les Cahiers de l'Alliance Israélite Universelle* CXXXIV: 9–10.

1962

'Enseignement juif et culture contemporaine (interview)', *L'Arche* LXV: 22–5.

'L'Ecole Normale Israélite Orientale', *Les Cahiers de l'Alliance Israélite Universelle* CXXXVIII: 19–20.

1963

'Judaïsme et altruïsme', in *De l'identité juive à la communauté*, Paris: s.d.: 11–15.

'L'Ecole Normale Israélite Orientale', *Les Cahiers de l'Alliance Israélite Universelle* CXLV: 16–20.
Difficile Liberté, Paris: Albin Michel (2nd edn, 1976), trans. S. Hand (1990) *Difficult Freedom*, London: Athlone.

1964

Intervention, translated by R. Rosthal, 'Interrogation of Martin Buber conducted by Maurice S. Friedman', in S. C. Rome and B, K. Rome (eds) *Philosophical Interrogations*, New York, Chicago and San Francisco: Holt, Rinehart and Winston: 23–6.

1965

'Martin Buber', *L'Arche* CII: 10–11.
'Martin Buber prophète et philosophe', *Informations catholiques internationales* CCXVIII: 31–2.

1966

'De Sheylock à Swann', *Les Nouveaux Cahiers* VI: 47–8.

1967

'Par delà le dialogue', *Journal des communautés* CCCXCVIII: 1–3.

1968

'La renaissance culturelle juive en Europe continentale', in M. Davis et al. *Le renouveau de la culture juive*, Bruxelles: Editions de l'Institut de Sociologie de l'Université Libre de Bruxelles: 21–34.
Quatre lectures talmudiques, Paris: Editions de Minuit, trans. A. Aronowicz (1990) *Nine Talmudic Readings*, Bloomington, Ill.: Indiana University Press.
'Un Dieu homme?', *Qui est Jésus-Christ* LXII: 186–92.

1970

'Infini', *Encyclopaedia Universalis*, Paris, vol. 8: 991
'Le surlendemain des dialectiques', *Hamoré* XIII, 50: 38–40.
'Séparation des biens', *L'Arche* CLXII–CLXIII: 101–2.

1971

'Préface' to T. G. Geraets *Vers une nouvelle philosophie transcendentale. La genèse de la philosophie de Maurice Merleau-Ponty jusqu'à la Phénoménologie de la Perception*, The Hague: Martinus Nijhoff: ix–xv.

1972

'Leçon talmudique', *Jeunesse et révolution dans la conscience juive. Données et débats*, edited by J. Halpérin and G. Lévitte, Paris: Presses Universitaires de France: 59–80.
'Leçon talmudique', *Jeunesse et révolution dans la conscience juive. Données et débats*, edited by J. Halpérin and G. Lévitte, Paris: Presses Universitaires de France: 279–92.
Humanisme de l'autre homme, Montpellier: Fata Morgana.
'Centenaire de la création de l'Ecole Normale Israélite Orientale', *Bulletin intérieur du Consistoire Central Israélite de France et de l'Algérie* V, 22: 16–18.
'Evolution et fidélité', *Les Cahiers de l'Alliance Israélite Universelle* CLXXXII: 26–30.

1973

'Leçon talmudique', in J. Halpérin and G. Lévitte (eds) *L'autre dans la conscience juive. Le sacré et le couple. Données et débats*, Paris: Presses Universitaires de France: 55–74.
'Leçon talmudique', in J. Halpérin and G. Lévitte (eds) *L'autre dans la conscience juive. Le sacré et le couple. Données et débats*, Paris: Presses Universitaires de France: 173–86.
'Totalité et totalisation', *Encyclopaedia Universalis*, Paris, vol. 16: 192.

1974

Autrement qu'être ou au-delà de l'essence, The Hague: Martinue Nijhoff, trans. A. Lingis (1981) *Otherwise than Being or Beyond Essence*, The Hague: Martinus Nijhoff.
'Karl Kerényi', *Les Etudes Philosophiques* XXIX, 2: 185.
'La mort du P. Van Breda', *Les Etudes Philosophiques* XXIX, 2: 285–7.
'Leçon talmudique', *Consistoire Central Israélite*: 57–67.

1975

Sur Maurice Blanchot, Montpellier: Fata Morgana.
Noms propres, Montpellier: Fata Morgana.
'Philosophie et positivité', in *Savoir, faire, espérer: les limites de la raison*, Bruxelles: Editions Facultés Universitaires Saint-Louis, vol. 1: 194–206.
'Les dommages causés par le feu: Leçon talmudique', in J. Halpérin and G. Lévitte (eds) *La conscience juive face à la guerre*, Paris: Presses Universitaires de France: 13–26.
'Sécularisation et faim', in E. Castelli (ed.) *Herméneutique de la sécularisation*, Paris: Aubier-Montaigne: 101–9.

1977

Du sacré au saint, Paris: Editions de Minuit, trans. A. Aronowicz (1990) *Nine Talmudic Readings*, Bloomington, Ill.: Indiana University Press.

'Modèles de la permanence' in J. Halpérin and G. Lévitte (eds) *Le modèle de l'Occident. Données et débats*, Paris: Presses Universitaires de France: 199–215.

'Pensée et prédication', in Anna-Teresa Tymieniecka (ed.) *The Self and the Other. The irreducible element in man*, Dordrecht and Boston: D. Reidel: 3–6.

'Préface' to M. Buber *Utopie et socialisme*, Paris: Aubier-Montagne: 9–11.

'La lettre ouverte', *Rencontres. Chrétiens et Juifs*, LI: 118–20.

'La philosophie de l'éveil', *Les études philosophiques* III: 307–17.

1978

'Un nouvel esprit de coexistence', *Les nouveaux cahiers* LIV: 40–2.

1979

Le temps et l'autre [1947], Montpellier: Fata Morgana, (Paris: Presses Universitaires de France, 1983), trans. R. A. Cohen (1987) *Time and the Other*, Pittsburgh: Duquesne University Press.

'Les villes refuges', in J. Halpérin and G. Lévitte (eds) *Jérusalem, l'Unique et l'Universelle*, Paris: Presses Universitaires de France: 35–48.

'Un éveil qui signifie une responsibilité', in *Gabriel Marcel et la pensée allemande. Nietzsche, Heidegger, Ernst Bloch*, Paris: Aubier, *Présence de Gabriel Marcel*, cahier I: 92–5.

'Lettre à *Terriers* (à propos de Paul Celan)', *Terriers* VI: 11–12.

'De la lecture juive des Ecritures', *Lumière et Vie* XXVIII, 144: 5–23.

1980

'Exégèse et transcendance. A propos d'un texte du Makoth 23b', in G. Nahon and Ch. Touati (eds) *Hommage à Georges Vajda. Etudes d'histoire et de pensée juives*, Louvain: Peeters: 99–104.

'Le dialogue. Conscience de soi et proximité du prochain', in *Esistenza, unito, ermeneutica. Scritti per Enrico Castelli*, Padova: Cedam: 345–57.

'Exigeant Judaïsme', *Le débat* V: 11–19.

'Du langage religieux et de la "Crainte de Dieu" (sur un texte talmudique)', *Man and World* XIII, 3–4: 265–79.

Bibliography

1982

L'au-delà du verset, Paris: Editions de Minuit, trans. G. Mole (1994) *Beyond the Verse*, London: Athlone and Bloomington, Ill.: Indiana University Press.
De Dieu qui vient à l'idée, Paris: Vrin.
De l'évasion [1935], Paris: Fata Morgana.
Ethique et Infini, Paris: Fayard, trans. R. A. Cohen (1985) *Ethics and Infinity*, Pittsburgh: Duquesne University Press.

1984

Transcendance et intelligibilité, Genève: Labor et Fides.

1986

'The Trace of the Other', trans. A. Lingis, in M. Taylor (ed.) *Deconstruction in Context*, Chicago: University of Chicago Press: 345–59.

1987

Collected Philosophical Papers, trans. A. Lingis, Dordrecht: Martinus Nijhoff.
Hors sujet, Montpellier: Fata Morgana, trans. M. B. Smith (1993) *Outside the Subject*, London: Athlone.
'De l'écrit à l'oral', preface to D. Banon *La lecture infinie*, Paris: Editions du Seuil: 7–11.

1988

A l'heure des nations, Paris: Editions de Minuit, trans. M. B. Smith (1994) *In the Time of the Nations*, London: Athlone, and Bloomington, Ill.: Indiana University Press.

1989

Entretien dans J.-C. Aeschlimann (ed.) *Répondre d'autrui. Emmanuel Levinas* (Textes de P. Ricœur, S. Moses, C. Chalier, G. Petitdemange, M. Faessler autour d'un entretien avec E. Levinas), Neuchâtel (Suisse): Editions de la Bacconière.
The Levinas Reader, ed. S. Hand, Oxford: Blackwell.

1990

De l'oblitération: entretien avec Françoise Armengaud à propos de l'œuvre de Sosno, Paris: Éditions de la différence.

1991

Entre nous: essais sur le penser-à-l'autre, Paris: Grasset.

'Philosophy and Awakening', trans. M. Quaintance, in E. Cardava, P. Connor and J.-L. Nancy (eds) *Who Comes After the Subject?*, London: Routledge: 206–16.

1993

Dieu, la mort et le temps, Paris: Grasset.
La mort et le temps, Paris: L'Herne.

1994

Les Imprévus de l'histoire, St. Clément-la-Rivière: Fata Morgana.
Liberté et commandement; Transcendance et hauteur, [1953; 1962] St. Clément-la-Rivière: Fata Morgana.

SECTION B

Selected Works on Levinas

Volumes devoted to Levinas

Abensour, M. and Chalier, C. (eds) (1991) *Emmanuel Levinas*, Paris: L'Herne.

Aeschlimann, J.-Chr. (ed.) (1989) *Répondre d'autrui: Emmanuel Levinas*, Neuchâtel: La Baconnière.

Bernasconi, R. and Wood, D. (eds) (1988) *The Provocation of Levinas: Rethinking the Other*, London and New York: Routledge.

Bernasconi, R. and Critchley, S. (eds) (1991) *Re-reading Levinas*, London: Athlone Press.

Cohen, R. A. (ed.) (1986) *Face to Face with Levinas*, Albany: State University of New York Press.

Dupuis, M. (ed.) (1994) *Levinas en contrastes*, Bruxelles: De Boeck-Wesmael.

Hand, S. (ed.) (1989) *The Levinas Reader*, Oxford: Blackwell.

Laruelle, F. (ed.) (1980) *Textes pour Emmanuel Levinas*, Paris: J.-M. Place.

Petitdemange, G. and Rolland, J. (eds) (1988) *Autrement que savoir*, Paris: Osiris. (Un entretien avec Levinas et des études de G. Petitdemange et J. Rolland)

Rolland, J. (ed.) (1984) *Les Cahiers de la nuit surveillée*, no. 3, Lagrasse: Verdier.

Études Phénoménologiques (1990), vol. 6, no. 12, *Emmanuel Levinas*.
Exercices de la patience (1980), no.1, Paris: Obsidiane.

Bibliography

Books in English

Awerkamp, D. (1977) *Emmanuel Levinas: Ethics and Politics*, New York: Revisionist Press.

Burggraeve, R (1985) *From Self-Development to Solidarity: an Ethical Reading of Human Desire in its Socio-Political Relevance according to Emmanuel Levinas*, trans. C. Vanhove-Romanik, Leuven: The Centre for Metaphysics and Philosophy of God.

Chanter, T. (1995) *Ethics of Eros: Irigaray's Rewriting of the Philosophers*, London: Routledge.

Critchley, S. (1992) *The Ethics of Deconstruction: Derrida and Levinas*, Oxford: Blackwell.

Davies, P. (forthcoming) *Experience and Distance: Heidegger, Blanchot, Levinas*, Albany, N.Y.: State University of New York Press.

Gibbs, R. (1992) *Correlations in Rosenzweig and Levinas*, Princeton: Princeton University Press.

Handelman, S. A. (1991) *Fragments of Redemption: Jewish Thought and Literary Theory in Benjamin, Scholem and Levinas*, Bloomington, Ill.: Indiana University Press.

Lescourret, M.-A. (1994) *Emmanuel Levinas*, Paris: Flammarion.

Libertson, J. (1982) *Proximity, Levinas, Blanchot, Bataille and Communication*, The Hague: Martinus Nijhoff.

Lingis, A. (1985) *Libido: the French Existential Theories*, Bloomington, Ill.: Indiana University Press: 58–73, 103–20.

Llewelyn, J. (1995) *The Middle Voice of Ecological Conscience: A Chiasmic Reading of Responsibility in the Neighbourhood of Levinas, Heidegger and Others*, London: Macmillan.

—— (1995) *Emmanuel Levinas. The Genealogy of Ethics*, London: Routledge.

Manning, R. J. S. (1993) *Interpreting Otherwise than Heidegger. Emmanuel Levinas's Ethics as First Philosophy*, Pittsburgh: Duquesne University Press.

Peperzak, A. (1993) *To the Other: An Introduction to the Philosophy of Emmanuel Levinas*, West Lafayette, Ind.: Purdue University Press.

Robbins, J. (1991) *Prodigal Son/Elder Brother: Interpretation and Alterity in Augustine, Petrarch, Kafka, Levinas*, Chicago and London: University of Chicago Press.

Smith, S. G. (1983) *The Argument to the Other: Reason Beyond Reason in the Thought of Karl Barth and Emmanuel Levinas*, Chico, Cal.: Scholars Press.

Wyschogrod, E. (1974) *Emmanuel Levinas: The Problem of Ethical Metaphysics*, The Hague: Martinus Nijhoff.

Ziarek, K. (1994) *Inflected Language: Toward a Hermeneutics of Nearness*, Albany: State University of New York Press.

Facing the other

English Articles in Books

Berezdivin, R. (1991) 'Contact: Textuality, the Other, Death', in Bernasconi and Critchley: 190–200.

Bernasconi, R. (1982) 'Levinas on Time and the Instant', in D. Wood and R. Bernasconi (eds) *Time and Metaphysics*, Coventry: Parousia Press: 17–44.

—— (1985) 'The Trace of Levinas in Derrida', in D. Wood and R. Bernasconi (eds) *Derrida and Difference*, Coventry: Parousia Press: 17–44.

—— (1987) 'Deconstruction and the Possibility of Ethics', in J. Sallis (ed.) *Deconstruction and Philosophy*, Chicago, Ill.: Chicago University Press: 122–39.

—— (1988) 'Levinas: Philosophy and Beyond', in *Continental Philosophy* vol. 1, New York: Routledge & Kegan Paul.

—— (1988) 'The Silent Anarchic World of the Evil Genuis', in G. Moneta, J. Sallis, J. Taminiaux (eds) *The Collegium Phaenomenologicum: the First Ten Years*, Dordrecht: Martinus Nijhoff.

—— (1989) 'Rereading Totality and Infinity', in A. B. Dallery and C. E. Scott (eds), *The Question of the Other*, Albany, N.Y.: State University of New York Press: 23–34.

—— (1991) 'Skepticism in the Face of Philosophy', in Bernasconi and Critchley: 149–161.

Burggraeve, R. (1981) 'The Ethical Basis for a Humane Society according to Emmanuel Levinas', in C. Vanhove-Romanik (trans.) *Emmanuel Levinas*, Leuven: The Centre for Metaphysics and Philosophy of God: 5–57.

Casey, E. (1988) 'Levinas on Memory and Trace', in G. Moneta, J. Sallis, J. Taminiaux (eds) *The Collegium Phaenomenologicum: the First Ten Years*, Dordrecht: Martinus Nijhoff.

Chalier, C. (1989) 'L'utopie messianique (1989), in Aschlimann: 53–69.

—— (1991) 'Ethics and the Feminine', in Bernasconi and Critchley: 119–129.

Chanter, T. (1990) 'The Alterity and Immodesty of Time: Death as Future and Eros as Feminine in Levinas', in A. Benjamin and D. Wood (eds) *Writing the Future*, London: Warwick Studies in Philosophy and Literature, Routledge: 137–54.

—— (1991) 'Antigone's Dilemma', in Bernasconi and Critchley: 130–146.

Ciaramelli, F. (1991) 'Levinas's Ethical Discourse between Individuation and Universality', in Bernasconi and Critchley: 83–105.

Cohen, R. A. (1989) 'Absolute Positivity and Ultrapositivity: Husserl and Levinas', in A. B. Dallery and C. E. Scott (eds) *The Question of the Other*, Albany, N.Y.: State University of New York Press: 35–43.

Bibliography

Critchley, S. (1991) '"Bois" – Derrida's Final Word on Levinas', in Bernasconi and Critchley: 162–189.

Davies, P. (1990) 'A Linear Narrative? Blanchot with Heidegger in the Work of Levinas', in D. Wood (ed.) *Philosophers' Poets*, London: Routledge: 37–69.

—— (1991) 'A Fine Risk: Reading Blanchot Reading Levinas', in Bernasconi and Critchley: 201–226.

Derrida, J. (1978) 'Violence and Metaphysics', in *Writing and Difference*, trans. A. Bass, London: Routledge and Kegan Paul, Chicago: Chicago University Press: 79–153.

—— (1991) 'At This Moment In This Very Work Here I Am', in Bernasconi and Critchley: 11–48.

Durfee, H. A. (1973) 'Emmanuel Levinas' Philosophy of Language', in *Explanation: New Directions in Philosophy*, The Hague: Martinus Nijhoff: 89–120.

Faessler, M. (1989) 'Dieu envisagé', in Aeschlimann: 95–113.

Foshay, T. (1992) 'Resentment and Apophasis: The Trace of the Other in Levinas, Derrida, and Gans', in P. Berry and A. Wernick (eds) *Shadow of Spirit: Postmodernism and Religion*, London: Routledge: 81–92.

Greisch, J. (1991) 'The Face and Reading: Immediacy and Mediation', in Bernasconi and Critchley: 67–82.

Irigaray, L. 'Questions to Emmanuel Levinas: On the Divinity of Love', trans. Margaret Whitford, in Bernasconi and Critchley: 109–118.

Lingis, A. (1989) 'Face to Face', in *Deathbound Subjectivity*, Bloomington, Ill.: Indiana University Press: 135–55.

Llewelyn, J. (1985) 'Levinas, Derrida and Others vis-a-vis', in *Beyond Metaphysics? The hermeneutic circle in contemporary continental philosophy*, Atlantic Highlands, N. J.: Humanities Press: 185–198.

—— (1988) 'Jewgreek of Greekjew (J. Derrida-E. Levinas)', in G. Moneta, J. Sallis, J. Taminiaux (eds) *The Collegium Phaenomenologicum: the First Ten Years*, Dordrecht: Martinus Nijhoff.

—— (1991) 'Am I Obsessed by Bobby? (Humanism of the Other Animal)', in Bernasconi and Critchley: 234–245.

Lyotard, J.-F. (1984) 'Jewish Oedipus', in *Driftworks*, New York: Semiotext(e): 35–55.

Mosès, S. (1989) 'L'idée de l'infini en nous', in Aeschlimann: 41–51.

O'Connor (1991) 'Who Suffers?', in Bernasconi and Critchley: 229–233.

Ogletree, T. W. (1985) 'Hospitality to the Stranger: the Role of the "Other" in Moral Experience', in *Hospitality to the Stranger: Dimensions of Moral Understanding*, Philadelphia, Pa.: Fortress Press: 35–63.

Peperzak, A. (1989) 'From Intentionality to Responsibility: On

Levinas' Philosophy of Language', in A. B. Dallery and C. E. Scott (eds) *The Question of the Other*, Albany, N. Y.: State University of New York Press: 3–22.

—— (1991) 'Presentation', in Bernasconi and Critchley: 51–66.

—— (ed.) (forthcoming) *Ethics as First Philosophy: The Significance of Emmanuel Levinas for Philosophy, Literature and Religion* (Proceedings of the conference held at Loyola University of Chicago and the University of Chicago in 1993).

Petitdemange, G. (1989) 'Emmanuel Lévinas: au-dehors, sans retour', in Aeschlimann: 71–94.

Ricoeur, P. (1989) 'Emmanuel Levinas, penseur du témoignage', in Aeschlimann: 17–40.

Sallis, J. (1987) 'Deconstruction and the possibility of ethics', in J. Sallis (ed.) *Deconstruction and Philosophy*, Chicago: Chicago University Press.

Strasser, S. (1982) 'Emmanuel Levinas (Born 1906); Phenomenological Philosophy', in H. Spiegelberg *The Phenomenological Movement* (3rd revised and enlarged edition), Phaenomenologica 5/6, The Hague: Martinus Nijhoff: 612–49.

Taylor, M. (1987) 'Infinity', in *Altarity*, Chicago: University of Chicago Press: 185–216.

Watson, S. (1990) 'The Face of the Hibakusha', in D. Wood (ed.) *Writing the Future* (foreword by E. Levinas), London: Routledge: 155–173.

Wyschogrod, E. (1980) 'Doing Before Hearing: On the Primacy of Touch', in F. Laruelle: 179–203.

—— (1989) 'Derrida, Levinas and Violence', in H. J. Silverman (ed.) *Derrida and Deconstruction*, New York: Routledge.

Ziarek, E. (1993) 'Kristeva and Levinas: Mourning, Ethics and the Feminine', in O. Kelly (ed.) *Ethics, Politics, and Difference in Julia Kristeva's Writing*, New York: Routledge: 62–78.

English Articles in Journals

Bernasconi, R. (1982) 'Levinas Face to Face with Hegel', *Journal of the British Society for Phenomenology* 13, 2: 267–76.

—— (1986) 'Hegel and Levinas: the Possibility of Reconciliation and Forgiveness', *Archivio di Filosofia* 54: 325–46.

—— (1987) 'Fundamental Ontology, Meontology and the Ethics of Ethics', *Irish Philosophical Journal* 4: 76–93.

Blum, R. P. (1983) 'Emmanuel Levinas's Theory of Commitment', *Philosophy and Phenomenological Research* 44, 2: 145–68.

—— (1985) 'Deconstruction and Creation', *Philosophy and Phenomenological Research* 46, 2: 293–306.

Bouckaert, L. (1970) 'Ontology and Ethics: Reflections on Levinas' Critique of Heidegger', *International Philosophical Quarterly* 10: 402–19.

Burke, J. P. (1982) 'The Ethical Significance of the Face', *Proceedings of the American Catholic Philosophical Association* 56: 194–j206.

Cohen, R. A. (1979) 'Review of Existence and Existents', *Man and World* 12: 521–26.

—— (1981) 'Emmanuel Levinas: Happiness is a Sensational Time', *Philosophy Today* 25,3: 196–203.

—— (1983) 'The Privilege of Reason and Play: Derrida and Levinas', *Tijdschrift voor Filosofie* 45, 2: 242–55.

Davies, P. (1988) 'Difficult friendship', *Continental Philosophy and the Question of ethics. Research in Phenomenology* 18: 149–72.

De Boer, Th., (1973) 'Beyond Being: Ontology and Eschatology in the Philosophy of Emmanuel Levinas', *Philosophia Reformata* 38: 17–29.

—— (1985) 'Judaism and Hellenism in the Philosophy of Levinas and Heidegger', *Archivio di Filosofia* 53, 2–3: 197–215.

De Greef, J. (1983) 'The Irreducible Alienation of the Self', A.-T. Tymieniecka (ed.) *The Self and the Other, Analecta Husserliana* 6: 27–30.

Ehman, R. R. (1975) 'Emmanuel Levinas: the Phenomenon of the Other', *Man and World* 8, 2: 141–45.

Gans, S. (1972) 'Ethics or Ontology', *Philosophy Today* 16, 2: 117–21.

Gerber, R. J. (1967) 'Totality and Infinity: Hebraism and Hellenism – the Experiential Ontology of Emmanuel Levinas', *Review of Existential Psychology and Psychiatry* 7, 3: 177–88.

Gilkey, L. (1972) 'Comments on Emmanuel Levinas's *Totalité et infini*', *Algemeen Nederlands Tijdschrift voor Wijsbegeerte* 64: 26–38.

Kelbley, C. A. (1974) 'An Introduction to Emmnuel Levinas', *Thought* 49, 192: 81–6.

Keyes, L. D. (1972) 'An evaluation of Levinas's critique of Heidegger', *Research in Phenomenology* 2: 121–42.

Lawton, P. (1975) 'Levinas Notion of the "There Is"', *Tijdschrift voor Filosofie* 37, 3: 477–89. (Also published in (1976) *Philosophy Today* 29, 1: 67–76.

—— (1975) 'A Difficult Freedom: Levinas' Judaism', *Tijdschrift voor Filosofie* 37, 4: 681–91.

—— (1976) 'Love and Justice: Levinas' Reading of Buber', *Philosophy Today* 20, 1: 77–83.

Libertson, J. (1979) 'Levinas and Husserl, Sensation and Intentionality', *Tijdschrift voor filosofie* 41, 3: 485–502.

Lichtigfeld, A. (1983) 'On Infinity and Totality in Hegel and Levinas', *South African Journal of Philosophy* 2: 31–3.

Lingis, A. (1978) 'Emmanuel Levinas and the Intentional Analysis of the Libido', *Philosophy in Context* 8: 60–9.

—— (1979) 'Fact to Fact: a Phenomenological Meditation', *International Philosophical Quarterly* 19, 2: 151–63.

—— (1982) 'Intuition of Freedom, Intuition of Law', *Journal of Philosophy* 79, 10: 588–96.

—— (1988) 'The Elemental Imperative', *Continental Philosophy and the question of Ethics. Research in Phenomenology* 18: 3–21.

McCollester, C. (1970) 'The Philosophy of Emmanuel Levinas', *Judaism* 19: 344–54.

Masterson, P. (1983) 'Ethics and Absolutes in the Philsophy of E. Levinas', *Neue Zeitschrift für Systematische Theologie und Religionsphilosophie* 25: 211–23.

Moreno Marquez, C. A. (1987) 'The Curvature of Intersubjective Space: Sociality and Responsibility in the Thought of Emmanuel Levinas', *Analecta Husserliana* 22: 343–52.

O'Connor, N. (1977) 'The Meaning of "Religion" in the Work of Emmanuel Levinas', *Proceedings of the Irish Philosophical Society*.

—— (1978) 'Exile and Enrootedness', *Seminar*, Journal of the Philosophical Seminar, University College, Cork 2: 53–7.

—— (1980) 'Being and the Good: Heidegger and Levinas', *Philosophical Studies*, The National University of Ireland 27: 212–20.

—— (1982) 'Intentionality Analysis and the Problem of Self and Other', *Journal of the British Society for Phenomenology* 13, 2: 186–92.

Peperzak, A. (1978) 'Beyond Being', *Research in Phenomenology* 8: 239–61.

—— (1983) 'Emmanuel Levinas: Jewish Experience and Philosophy', *Philosophy Today* 27, 4: 297–306.

—— (1983) 'Phenomenology – Ontology – Metaphysics: Levinas' Perspective on Husserl and Heidegger', *Man and World* 16: 113–27.

Richard, L. (1988) 'The Possibility of the Incarnation according to Emmanuel Levinas', *Studies in Religion/Sciences Religieuses: Revue Canadienne/A Canadian Journal* 17, 4: 391–405.

Robbins, J. (1991) 'Visage, figure: Reading Levinas's Totality and Infinity, *Yale French Studies* 79: 135–49.

Smith, S. G. (1981) 'Reason as One for Another: Moral and Theoretical Argument in the Philosophy of Levinas', *Journal of the British Society for Phenomenology* 12, 3: 231–44.

Strasser, S. (1983) 'The Unique Individual and his Other', A.-T.

Tymieniecka (ed.) *The Self and the Other, Analecta Husserliana* 6: 9–26.

Tallon, A. (1978) 'Intentionality, Intersubjectivity, and the Between: Buber and Levinas on Affectivity and the Dialogical Principle', *Thought* 53, 210: 292–309.

—— (1976) 'Review of *Autrement qu'être ou au-delà de l'essence*', *Man and World* 9: 451–62.

Vasey, C. R. (1980) 'Review of *Existence and Existents*', *Thought* 44: 466–73.

—— (1981) 'Emmanuel Levinas: From Intentionality to Proximity', *Philosophy Today* 25, 3: 178–95.

Watson, S. (1986) 'Reason and the Face of the Other', *Journal of the American Academy of Religion* 54, 1: 33–57.

—— (1988) 'The Ethics of Deconstruction and the Remainder of the Sublime', *Man and the World* 21, 1: 35–64.

Webb, M. (1982) 'The Rape of Time', *Southwest Philosophical Studies* (San Marcos, Texas) 7: 147–54.

Wolosky, Shira, (1982) 'Derrida, Jabès, Levinas: Sign-Theory as Ethical Discourse', *Prooftexts: Journal of Jewish Literary History* 2: 283–302.

Wyschogrod, E. (1971) 'Review of *Totality and Infinity*', *Human Inquiries* 10: 185–92.

—— (1972) 'Emmanuel Levinas and the Problem of Religious Language', *The Thomist* 26, 1: 1–38.

—— (1980) 'The Moral Self: Emmnuel Levinas and Hermann Cohen', *Daat: a Journal of Jewish Philosophy* 4: 35–58.

—— (1982) 'God and "Being's Move" in the philosophy of Emmanuel Levinas', *The Journal of Religion* 62, 2: 145–55.

Books in French

Baeilhache, G. (1994) *Le sujet chez Emmanuel Levinas: fragilité et subjectivité*, Paris: Presses Universitaires de France.

Blanchot, M. (1969) *L'entretien infini*, Paris: Gallimard.

Chalier, C. (1982) *Figures du Féminin. Lecture d'Emmanuel Levinas*, Paris: La nuit surveillée.

—— (1987) *La persévérance du mal*, Paris: Cerf.

Ciamarelli, F. (1989) *Transcendance et éthique: essai sur Levinas*, Brussels: Ousia.

Feron, E. (1992) *De l'idée de transcendance à la question du langage: l'itinéraire philosophique de Levinas*, Grenoble: Millon.

Finkielkraut, A. (1984) *La sagesse de l'amour*, Paris: Gallimard.

Forthomme, B. (1979) *Une philosophie de la transcendance: la métaphysique d'Emmanuel Levinas*, Paris: La Pensée Universelle.

Facing the other

Greisch, J. and Rolland, J. (eds) (1993) *Emmanuel Levinas: l'éthique comme philosophie première* (proceedings of the colloquium held at Cerisy, 1992), Paris: La nuit surveillée-Cerf.

Guibal, F. (1980) *Et combien de dieux nouveaux, approches contemporaines. Vol. 2: Levinas*, Paris: Aubier-Montaigne.

Lescourret, M.-A. (1994) *Emmanuel Levinas*, Paris: Flammarion.

Malka, S. (1984) *Lire Levinas*, Paris: Cerf.

Ouaknin, M.-A. (1992) *Méditations érotiques: essai sur Emmanuel Levinas*, Paris: Balland.

Petrosino, S. and Rolland, J. (1984) *La vérité nomade. Introduction à Emmanuel Levinas*, Paris: La Découverte.

Poirié, F. (1987) *Emmanuel Levinas, Qui êtes-vous?*, Lyon: La Manufacture.

Saint-Germain, C. (1992) *Écrire sur la nuit blanche: l'éthique du livre chez Emmanuel Levinas et Edmond Jabès*, Québec: Presses de l'Université du Québec.

Articles in French

Abensour, M. (1991) 'Penser l'utopie autrement', in Chalier and Abensour: 477–493.

Armengaud, F. (1985) 'Entretien avec Emmanuel Levinas', *Revue de métaphysique et de morale* 90, 3 (juillet-septembre): 296–310.

—— (1991) 'Éthique et esthétique: De l'ombre à l'oblitération', in Chalier and Abensour: 499–508.

Aronowicz, A. (1991) 'Les commentaires talmudiques de Levinas', in Chalier and Abensour: 368–378.

Banon, D. (1991) 'Résistance du visage et renoncement au sacrifice', in Chalier and Abensour: 399–407.

Bataille, G. (1947/48) 'De l'existentialisme au primat de l'économie', *Critique* 19: 515–526, and 21: 721–741 (second part).

Bernasconi, R. (1991) 'Levinas, Hegel. La possibilité du pardon et de la réconciliation', trans. G. Petitdemange, in Chalier and Abensour: 328–342.

Bernheim, G. (1991) 'A propos des lectures talmudiques. Entretien', in Chalier and Abensour: 355–362.

Blanchot, M. (1975) 'Discours sur la patience', *Le Nouveau Commerce*, Spring: 19–44.

Cateson, J. (1953) 'Un penseur enraciné', *Critique*: 961–72.

—— (1965) 'Sur une philosophie de l'inégal', *Critique*: 629–57.

Chalier, C. (1986) 'Lectures d'Emmanuel Levinas', *Philosophie* 9 (hiver): 71–80.

—— (1991) 'L'âme de la vie. Levinas, lecteur de R. Haïm de Volozin', in Chalier and Abensour: 387–399.

Chrétien, J.-L. (1991) 'La dette et l'élection', in Chalier and Abensour: 262–275.

Ciaramelli, F. (1981) 'Défense de la subjectivité et approche de la transcendance chez Emmanuel Levinas', in J. Taminiaux and R. Brisart (eds) *Autour de l'être, du temps et de l'autre* (Cahiers du Centre d'études phénoménologiques), Louvain: Cabay/Institut supérieur de philosophie: 7–20.

—— (1982) 'De l'évasion à l'exode. Subjectivité et existence chez le jeune Emmanuel Levinas', *Revue philosophique de Louvain* 80, 4 (novembre): 553-78.

—— (1982) 'Le rôle du judaïsme dans l'œuvre de Levinas', *Revue philosophique de Louvain* 52, 4: 580-99.

—— (1990) 'De l'errance à la responsabilité', *Études Phénoménologiques* 12: 45–66.

Cohen, R. A. (1991) 'La non-in-différence dans la pensée d'Emmanuel Levinas et de Franz Rosenzweig', trans. J. Rolland, in Chalier and Abensour: 343–351.

Colette, J. (1973) 'Étranger sur terre' in *Esprit*, novembre: 694–702.

Collin, F. (1991) 'La peur. Emmanuel Levinas et Maurice Blanchot', in Chalier and Abensour: 313–328.

Cornu, M. (1984) 'Autour de Levinas', *Revue de Théologie et de philosophie* 116, 3: 241–46.

David, A. (1991) 'S'orienter dans la pensée', in Chalier and Abensour: 226–240.

De Greef, J. (1969) 'Éthique, réflexion et histoire chez Levinas', *Revue Philosophique de Louvain* 67 (3e série), 95 (août): 431–60.

—— (1970) 'Le concept de pouvoir éthique chez Levinas', *Revue Philosophique de Louvain* 68 (3e série), 100 (novembre): 507–20.

—— (1970) 'Empirisme et éthique chez Levinas', *Archives de Philosophie* 33: 223–41.

—— (1970) 'Éthique et religion chez Levinas', *Revue de Théologie et de Philosophie* 76, 4 (octobre–décembre): 36–51.

—— (1971) 'Levinas et la phénoménologie', *Revue de Métaphysique et de Morale*: 448–465.

Duval, R. (1975) 'Exode et Altérité', *Revue des Sciences Philosophiques et Théologiques* 59, 2 (avril): 217–41.

Faessler, M. (1991) 'Dieu, autrement', in Chalier and Abensour: 411–420.

Feron, E. (1977) 'Éthique, langage et ontologie chez Emmanuel Levinas', *Revue de Métaphysique et de Morale* 81, 1: 64–87.

—— (1981) 'L'horizon du langage et le temps du discours. A propos de *Totalité et Infini* d'Emmanuel Levinas', in J. Taminiaux and R. Brisart (eds) *Autour de l'être, du temps et de l'autre* (Cahiers du

Centre d'études phénoménologiques), Louvain: Cabay/Institut supérieur de philosophie: 67–92.

—— (1987) 'Respiration et action chez Levinas', *Études Phénoménologiques* 3, 5–6. 193–213.

—— (1990) 'La réponse à l'autre et la question de l'un', *Études Phénoménologiques* 12: 67–100.

Finkielkraut, A. (1991) 'Le risque du politique', in Chalier and Abensour: 468–476.

Fontenay, E. de (1991) 'L'exaspération de l'infini', in Chalier and Abensour: 212–225.

Forthomme, B. (1980) 'Structure de la métaphysique Levinassienne', *Revue philosophique de Louvain*: 385–99.

—— (1985) 'L'épreuve affective de l'autre selon Emmanuel Levinas et Michel Henry, *Revue de Métaphysique et de Moral* 91, 1 (janvier–mars): 90–114.

Gaviria, A. O. (1974) 'L'idée de création chez Levinas: une archéologie du sens', *Revue Philosophique de Louvain* 72 (août): 509–38.

Greisch, J. (1987) 'L'être, l'autre, l'étranger', *Cahiers de l'École des Sciences Philosophiques et Religieuses* 1: 127–51.

Guillamaud, P. (1989) 'L'autre et l'immanence. Étude comparée sur les ontologies de Michel Henry et Emmanuel Levinas', *Revue de Métaphysique et Morale*, 94, 2: 251–72.

Haar, M. (1991) 'L'obsession de l'autre. L'éthique comme traumatisme', in Chalier and Abensour: 444–53.

Irigaray, L. (1990) 'Questions à Levinas', *Critique*, 522 (novembre): 911–20.

Jacques, F. (1990) 'E. Levinas: Entre le primat phénomélogique du moi et l'allégeance éthique à autrui', *Études Phénoménologiques* 12: 101–40.

Kovac, E. (1986) 'Le personnalisme de Levinas ou le personnalisme de l'autre homme', *Bulletin de Littérature ecclésiatique* 87, 1 (janvier–mars): 56–70.

Krewani, W. (1981) 'Le temps comme transcendance vers l'autre. La notion du temps dans la philosophie d'Emmanuel Levinas', *Archives de Philosophie* 44: 529–60.

Lannoy, J.-L. (1990) 'D'une ambiguïté', *Études Phénoménologiques* 12: 11–44.

Lavigne, J.-F. (1987) 'L'idée de l'infini: Descartes dans la pensée d'Emmanuel Levinas', *Revue de Métaphysique et Morale* 92, 1 (janvier–mars): 54–66.

Lefevre, C. (1980) 'Autrui et Dieu. La pensée d'Emmanuel Levinas, question aux chrétiens', *Mélanges de science religieuse* 37, 4 (décembre): 255–73.

Libertson, J. (1981) 'La récurrence chez Emmanuel Levinas', *Revue Philosophique de Louvain* 79, 2 (mai): 212–52.

—— (1981) 'La séparation chez Emmanuel Levinas', *Revue de Métaphysique et Morale* 86: 433–51.

Lingis, A. (1991) 'Préface à l'édition américaine d'*Autrement qu'être ou au-delà de l'essence*', in Chalier and Abensour: 163–184.

Llewelyn, J. (1994) 'En ce moment même . . . une répétition qui n'en est pas une', in *Le passage des frontières: Autour du travail de Jacques Derrida* (proceedings of the colloquium held at Cerisy), Paris: Galilée: 245–8.

Malka, V. (1991) 'Levinas, lecteur de Rachi', in Chalier and Abensour: 366–367.

Marty, F. (1991) 'La hauteur et le sublime', in Chalier and Abensour: 304–312.

Mopsik, C. (1991) 'La pensée d'Emmanuel Levinas et la Cabale', in Chalier and Abensour: 378–387.

Olivier, P. (1983) 'L'être et le temps chez Emmanuel Levinas', *Recherches de Science religieuse* 71, 3: 337–80.

Peperzak, A. (1977) 'Emmanuel Levinas: Autrement qu'être ou Au-delà de l'essence' *Philosophische Rundschau* 24, 1–2: 91–116.

—— (1986) 'Autrui, Société, Peuple de Dieu. Quelques réflexions à partir d'Emmanuel Levinas', *Archivio di Filosofia* 54, 1–3: 309–18.

—— (1987) 'Une introduction à la lecture de Totalité et Infini. Commentaire de "La philosophie et l'idée de l'infini"', *Revue des Sciences philosophiques et théologiques* 71, 2 (avril): 191–18.

—— (1991) 'Passages', in Chalier and Abensour: 421–27.

Petitdemange, G. (1972) 'Emmanuel Levinas ou la question d'autrui', *Études* (décembre): 757–72.

—— (1976) 'Éthique et transcendance. Sur les chemins d'Emmanuel Levinas, *Recherches de Science religieuse* 64, 1(janvier–mars): 59–94.

—— (1978) 'Emmanuel Levinas et la politique', *Projet* 121 (janvier): 75–90.

—— (1991) 'Désir de l'infini, séparation de l'infini?', in Chalier and Abensour: 294–303.

Ploudre, S. and Simon, R. (1987) 'Éthique et morale chez Emmanuel Levinas', *Le supplément, Revue d'éthique et de théologie morale*, 160 (mars): 123–50.

Richir, M. (1991) 'Phénomène et infini', in Chalier and Abensour: 241–261.

Rolland, J. (1984) 'Les intrigues de la justice et du social', *Esprit*, mai: 150–61.

—— (1987) 'Décréation et Désintéressement chez Simone Weil et Emmanuel Levinas', *Les Nouveaux Cahiers* 89: 13–20.

Sartoris, G. (1983) 'La violente charité. Les *Lectures talmudiques* d'Emmanuel Levinas', *La Nouvelle Revue Française* 361: 88–9.

Schneider, M. (1991) 'La proximité chez Levinas et le *Nebenmensch* freudien', Chalier and Abensour: 431–444.

Strasser, S. (1977) 'Antiphénoménisme et phénoménologie dans la philosophie d'Emmanuel Levinas', *Revue philosophique de Louvain* 75 (4e série), 25: 101–24.

—— (1978) 'Le concept de phénomène dans la philosophie d'Emmanuel Levinas et son importance pour la philosphie religieuse', *Revue philosophique de Louvain* 76: 328–41.

Taminiaux, J. (1991) 'La première réplique à l'ontologie fondamentale', in Chalier and Abensour: 275–284.

Trotignon, P. (1991) 'Autre voie, même voix. Levinas et Bergson', in Chalier and Abensour: 287–293.

Vasey, C. R. (1980) 'Le problème de l'intentionalité dans la philosophie d'Emmanuel Levinas', *Revue de Métaphysique et de Morale* 85, 2 (avril–juin): 224–39.

Vergote, H.-B. (1987) 'Esprit, Violence et Raison', *Études* 366, 3 (mars): 363–74.

Vieillard-Baron, J.-L. (1983–84) 'Conflit et amour dans la reconnaissance d'autrui', *Philosophia* (Athène) 13–14: 79–88.

Walter, G. (1991) 'A même la philosophie', in Chalier and Abensour: 199–211.

Weber, E. (1991) 'Approche: Ritspa, Esther', in Chalier and Abensour: 454–463.

Wenzler, L. (1991) 'Postface à l'édition allemande du *Temps et l'Autre*', trans. G. Petitdemange, in Chalier and Abensour: 185–198.

Italian

Baccarini, E. (1979) 'La dimensione dell'economico nella "philosophie de l'Autre" di Emmanuel Levinas', in *La Dimensione dell'economico*, Padova: Liviana: 497–511.

Berto, G. (1985) 'La finestra rossa. Nota su Levinas e Bloch', *Aut Aut* 209–10: 254–61.

Boella, L. (1988) *Seminario: letture e discussioni intorno a Levinas, Jankelevitch, Ricœur*, Milano: Unicopli.

Bonata, B. (1985) 'Tra il desiderio e il dono. Note su Lacan e Levinas', *Aut Aut* 209–10: 237–53.

Bruno, C. G. (1987) 'Levinas: etica o giudaismo?', *Aquinas* 30: 515–23.

Burggraeve, R. (1973) 'Il contributo di Emmanuel Levinas al personalismo sociale', *Salesianum*: 569–599.

Ciaramelli, F. (1980) *Soggettività e metafisica. Emmanuel Levinas e il tema dell'altro*, Atti dell'Accademia di scienze morali e politiche, Napoli: Giannini: 1–27.

Ciglia, F. P. (1983) 'L'essere, il sacro e l'arte negli esordi filosofici di Emmanuel Levinas', *Archivio di filosofia* 34, 3 (July–September): 240–80.

—— (1983) 'Emmanuel Levinas interprete di Husserl e di Heidegger nel primo decennio della sua speculazione', *Filosofia* (Torino) 34, 3 (July–Septermber): 211–42.

—— (1988) *Un passo fuori dall'uomo: la genesi del pensiero di Levinas*, Padova: Cedam.

Comolli, G. (1985) 'Il volto delle cose. Intorno alla questione dell'arte in E. Levinas', *Aut Aut* 209–10: 219–36.

Cristin, R. (1985) 'Il Levinas di Strasser. Nuovi Stili delle fenomenologia', *Aut Aut* 209–10: 19–34.

Dal Lago, A. (1985) 'Dal luogo al desero. Levinas, la nudità, l'erranza', *Aut Aut* 209–10: 79–97.

—— (1986) 'Un etica senza mondo? Filosofia e secolarizzione', *Aut Aut* 216: 3–10.

Da Sanctis, R. (1972) 'L'estetica di due fenomenologi: Levinas e Merleau-Ponty', *Rivista di Studi crociani* IX (January–March): 26–43.

Ferraris, M. (1986) 'L'esclusione della filosofia. A proposito di ebraismo e pragmatismo', *Aut Aut* 231: 29–51.

Filoni, F. (1979) 'Dio e l'alterità nel pensioro di Emmanuel Levinas', *Aquinas* 22, 1 (January–April): 28–73.

Franck, G. (1985) 'Estetica e ontologia. Il problema dell'arte nel pensiero di E. Levinas', *Aut Aut* 901–10: 35–59.

Gevaert, J. (1970) 'Lescatologia di Emmanuel Levinas', *Salesianum* 32, 4 (October–December): 601–618.

Jedraszewski, M. (1980) *Le Relazioni intersoggetive nella filosofia di Emmanuel Levinas*, Roma: Pontifica Universitas Gregoriana.

Lissa, G. (1987) 'Critica dell'ontologia della guerra e fondazione metafisica della pace in E. Levinas', *Giornale Critico della Filosofia* 1: 119–74.

Mura, G. (1982) *Emmanuel Levinas: ermeneutica e 'separazione'*, Roma: Città Nuova.

Olivetti, M. M. (1985) 'Intersoggettività, alterità, etica. Domande filosofiche e E. Levinas', *Archivio di Filosofia* 53, 23:: 265–88.

Petrosino, S. (1985) 'Di Levinas. Passagi per una filosofia dell'altrimenti che essere', *Aut Aut* 209–10: 99–116.

Polidori, F. (1985) 'Ontologia e transcendenza. Un confronto sul tema della soggettivita in M. Heidegger e E. Levinas', *Aut Aut* 209–10: 271–85.

Prezzo, R. (1985) 'La voce chel viene dall'altro riva', *Aut Aut* 209–10: 13–34.

Ronchi, R. (1982) 'Etica e scrittura. Saggio su Emmanuel Levinas', *L'Uomo un segno* 5, 1: 143–71..

—— (1985) 'Linterpretazione come salvezza. Nota "sul" Blanchot di Levinas', *Aut Aut* 209–10: 193–205.

Rovatti, P. A. (1985) 'L'insonnia. Passività e metafora nella "fenomenologia" di Levinas', *Aut Aut* 209–10: 61–78.

Signorini, A. (1986) 'Il volto come irrapresentabile nei pensiero di Emmanuel Levinas', *Rivista Internazzionale di Filosofia Del Diritto* 63, 4: 536–75.

Tilliette, X. (1983) 'Il discorso lancinante di Emmanuel Levinas', *La Civittà cattolica* (January).

Visentin, G. (1982) 'Il guidaismo nel pensiero di Emmanuel Levinas', in *Vetera novis augere*. Studi in onore di Carlo Gianon, Roma: La Giolandica: 481–89.

German

Becker, J. (1977) *Emmanuel Levinas. Anstösse für eine Moraltheologie unserer Zeit*, Frankfurt am Main and Bern: Peter D. Lang).

—— (1981) *Begegnung–Gadamer und Levinas: der hermeneutische Zirkel und die Alteritas: ein ethisches Geschehen*, Frankfurt am Main and Bern: Peter D. Lang.

Casper, B. (1984) 'Illéité. Zu einem Schlüssel "Begriff" im Werk von Emmanuel Levinas', *Philosophisches Jahrbuch* 91, 2: 274–88.

—— (1985) 'Der Zugang zur Religion im Denken Von Emmanuel Levinas', *Philosophisches Jahrbuch* 95, 2: 268–77.

De Vries, H. (1989) *Theologie im Pianissimo & zwischen Rationalität und Dekonstruktion: die Aktualität der Denkfiguren Adornos und Levinas*, Kampen: Kok.

Gawoll, H. J. (1988) 'Die Kritik des Einen ist nicht die Epiphanie des Anderen. Bemerkungen zur Philosophie Emmanuel Levinas', *Hegel Studien* 23: 25–26.

Nosratian, K. (1992) *Trauma und Skepsis: nach Levinas*, Berlin: Akademie Verlag.

Reiter, J. (1985) 'Differenz und Entsprechung. Überlegungen zum Verhältnis von biblischem Anspruch und griechischer Denkform bei E. Levinas', *Archivio di Filosofia* 53, 2–3: 245–63.

Starobinski-Safran, E. (1987) 'Für eine jüdische Annäherung an die Philosophie', *Judaica* 43, 4: 221–37.

Strasser, S. (1978) 'Buber und Levinas. Philosophische Besinnung auf einem Gegensatz', *Revue internationale de philosophie* 32, 126: 512–25.

—— (1978) *Jenseits von Sein und Zeit. Eine Einführung in Emmanuel Levinas's Philosophie*, Den Haag: Martinus Nijhoff.

Dutch

Boehm, R. (1963) 'De kritiek van Levinas op Heidegger', *Tijdschrift voor filosofie*: 568–603.

Bouckaert, L. (1972) 'De uitganspunten van de filosofie van Emmanuel Levinas', *Tijdschrift voor filosofie* 34, 4 (December): 680–702.

—— (1976) *Emmanuel Levinas, Een filosofie van het gelaat*, Nijmegen: Uitgeverij B. Gottmer.

—— (1982) 'Een introductie in de etisch-joodsche filosofie van Emmanuel Levinas en haar kritiek op de western filosofie', *Kritiek* 3: 242–55.

Burggraeve, R. (1981) *Van zelfontplooing naar verantwoordelikjheid. Een ethische lezing van het verlangen: ontmoeting tussen psychanalyse en Levinas*, Leuven: Uitgeverij Acco.

Strasser, S. (1975) 'Erotiek en vruchtbaarheid in de filosofie van Emmanuel Levinas', *Tijdschrift voor filosofie* 37, 1 (March): 3–47.